75   70   65   60 Deg. W. from London

GINIA
MARYLAND
C. Charles
Bay of Chesapeak
Albemarle Sound
C. Hatteras
C. Look out
C. Fear
C. Cartaret
t Royal
a R.
natha R.
gustin

Barmudas III.
English

A MAP of the
WEST-INDIES &c.
MEXICO or NEW SPAIN

Also ye Trade Winds, and ye several Tr
acts made by ye Galeons and Flota from
Place to Place. By H. Moll Geographer

Note 10 of 11 Plate Flee
Ships Perished off the
coast of Florida in the
Terrible Hurricane
of 1715.

30

rallions and Flota usually
ning at the Havana ye whole
rmada Sails for Spain thro this Gulf.

ama
nck

ATLANTICK

Lucayos I.
BAHAMA
Eleuthera
ISLANDS
St. Salvador
Rum I.

OCEAN

25

Crooked I.

Maguana

Caicos R.

Tropick of Cancer

Heneago
Fortuga
N Ref
White
C. Francis

20

St. Jago
C. May
St. Anthonie
Wind
Guz.
HISPANIOLA.
Span.
St. Jago
St. ee Domingo
C. Engano
Po Real
Pte de Isab
St. Thomas P
Anegada
Sombrero
Anguilla
St. Martin
St. Bartolameo E.

Anis
Kingston
Morant
Port
Royal
Chabnin
Navaza I.
P. Vaca
C. Aßu la
P. Ermoso
Sauna
Mona
Borequen
St. Cross
D. Sabe
St. Eustatia
St. Christopher
E. Monte
out I.
Nevis

Leeward Islands
Antigo E.
Deseada E.
Guardalupa E.
Margalante
Dominica

JAMAICA
eater
Antilles Is
NORTH SEA
Caribbee I.
Martanica E.
St. Lucia E.

15

Windward
Islands
St. Vincent
Barbados E.

the Track of the Galleons from Old Spain

L. Con.
Aruba D.
Curaßow D.
Bonaire D.
Roca
Orchilla
Margarita
Tort.
Granada

C. Vel
pt. Samba
lax acha
Cong
utapori
Martha
Maracay
bo L.
Coro
G. of
Triste
Tisnao
St. Anna
Caraceo
Virina

Lit Antilles

Tabago
Trinidad I.

Cartagena
Sino Bay
St. Maria
tee
R. G. de la
Maerba

los Reyes
New Granada
Mopox
Apuerto
Truxillo
St. Christoval
Tucuyo

Caracos

New An-
dal u si a
Ariscoa
St. Thomas

oronoque R. and
Esp. Moconoto
C. Nassau

Surinam

TERRA FIRMA

GUIA
NA

R. de Carare
Pato R.

D.
m

5

75   70   65   60

Pieces of Eight

FRONTISPIECE: A gold imperial eight-escudo coin found by the treasure hunters. About the size of an American silver dollar, it is enlarged here to show its markings, which read, "Philip V, By the Grace of God, 1714." Specially struck for Spanish royalty at the Mexico City mint, it is valued today at $10,000.

Pieces of Eight

RECOVERING THE RICHES OF
A LOST SPANISH TREASURE FLEET

by Kip Wagner

AS TOLD TO

L. B. Taylor, Jr.

 LONGMANS

LONGMANS, GREEN AND CO. LTD
48 Grosvenor Street, London W.1
*Associated companies, branches and representatives
throughout the world*

Copyright © 1966 *by Real Eight Company, Inc.
and L. B. Taylor, Jr.*

This edition 1967

*Printed in Great Britain by
Jarrold & Sons Ltd, Norwich*

To my patient, understanding wife, Alice

ACKNOWLEDGMENTS

I am indebted to Carl J. Clausen, marine archeologist of the Florida State Board of Antiquities staff, for his aid during the preparation of this book in historical research pertaining to the 1715 treasure fleet, as well as for his assistance in helping to prepare the detailed listing of major finds of treasure and artifacts at the wreck sites.

I should also like to thank the National Geographic Society for its cooperation in permitting the use in the book of many of the color and black-and-white illustrations.

Among my fellow members of the Real Eight Corporation who have contributed specifically to the preparation of *Pieces of Eight*, I must especially express my gratitude to Delphine Long for his photography and to Louis J. Ullian for his work with Mr. Clausen in research and on the archeological list. To these two, together with Dan Thompson, Harry Cannon, Dr. Kip Kelso and Bob Johnson, also of the Real Eight team, go my hearty thanks also for their support in helping me to recall many significant details of the events recorded in the story of our fabulous treasure finds.

K.W.

CONTENTS

1*

ILLUSTRATIONS

MONOCHROME PHOTOGRAPHS

MAPS AND DIAGRAMS

Pieces of Eight

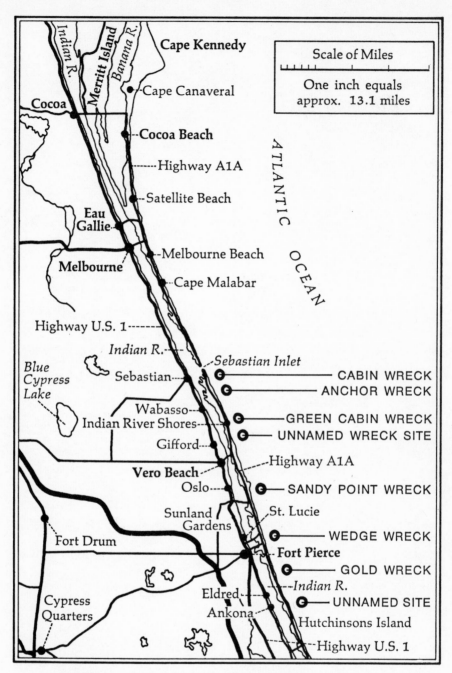

East Coast of Florida from Merritt Island to Fort Pierce, showing locations of the eight wrecks licensed to the Real Eight Corporation.

1 *Strike!*

The sea was rough and the wind brisk and bone-chilling cold on the morning of January 8, 1961. One look at the angry, frothing white caps convinced me it would be a foolish venture to nose our homely, 40-foot boat, the *Sampan*, out to sea.

But when you're sure in your heart there's a fortune in sunken gold and silver just a few hundred feet offshore, reason is often easily persuaded to give way. Treasure hunters are eternal optimists and no matter how bad conditions look, "things are always sure to clear up soon."

"Let's give it a try, Kip," Harry Cannon pleaded, as we surveyed the treacherous breakers crashing unmercifully over barely concealed, sharp-edged rocks in the narrow inlet at Sebastian, Florida, about halfway between Daytona Beach and Miami. Many a boat had run aground trying to navigate through the shallow channel in seas a lot smoother than the ones we were facing.

"Hell, the water's clear out there and once we get past the inlet we'll be all right," Harry prompted. "We can wait till high tide, then nudge her through, easylike."

I looked around at the others—Del Long, Dan Thompson, Erv Taylor and Lou Ullian—all partners with me in the quest for buried riches. I could see they were siding with Harry, but they would respect my decision.

I was against it, but I figured I owed them something. After all, they had broken their backs with me all during the long 1960 diving season, moving countless tons of ballast stones on the ocean floor by hand, and all we had to show for our efforts were a dozen or so silver wedges. They wouldn't begin to pay for the thousands of dollars we'd invested in diving and salvage equipment, and the endless, frustrating days we had spent on the search.

Despite the overall lack of success, our group of eight durable team members had stuck it out, heartened somewhat by the late season find of wedges, and hopeful this year would bring us the elusive pot of gold we knew had to be out there.

During the previous summer we had worked another wreck site, and I was sure at the time, though I dared not tell the others, that we would find little, if anything, on it. The 245-year-old bones of that ship had long been picked clean.

I also knew the wreck site we were headed for this morning would yield a far better chance of harvesting treasure, but I hadn't gone here first because I had wanted to test the men. We had formed rather hastily as a group over the winter of 1959, and I hardly knew the crew when we were ready to begin diving in the spring of 1960. I needed time to "separate the men from the boys," so I led them to the barren wreck site first to see who would stick and who would quit. To their credit, not one cracked under the strain of long hours, exhaustingly hard physical labor and one exasperating incident after another, with virtually nothing to show for it. The team made it through that miserable summer intact. Now we were ready, and I decided to lead them to this new site as soon as the water cleared up.

We spent the fall and winter months of 1960 preparing our diving gear and repairing our 40-foot converted liberty launch. Then, when the weather broke in January, everyone suggested slipping out to the new site for a look-see: a scouting run to make plans for the coming diving season.

I had agreed, and here we were. But looking at that fearsome Sebastian Inlet on this raw, windy day, I questioned my judgment. I did owe them something, however, and I must admit I was damn sure itching to explore the new site myself, so, reluctantly, I agreed to go out—but just for a short spell, and only at high tide.

Harry's face lit up like a kid's at Christmas, and the others were obviously pleased with the decision, too. We had been landlocked, chomping at the bit, since last September, and that's an eternity when you're hot on the trail of sunken treasure.

We eased the boat slowly and gently through the narrow channel, edging dangerously close past jagged layers of coral, surprisingly without incident. Once we were a few hundred feet offshore, bucking a 15-knot wind, we turned south.

I had pinpointed this wreck site some years before—after finding dozens of silver coins on the adjacent beach front—by paddling out on an old inner tube and peering down into the waters through a homemade face mask. I knew there were cannon lying on the bottom, and telltale ballast stones, but it had been some time since I'd last covered the area, and I couldn't help feeling some apprehension as we chugged through the choppy swells. I didn't want to disappoint the others—Harry, Dan, Lou, Del, Erv, and Harry Acres, a personal friend of mine who was along just for the ride. He also happened to be one of the best divers I've ever known.

It must have been 8:30 or 9 in the morning when I figured we were getting pretty close to the area I remembered as being near the wreck site. We were about two and a half miles south of the inlet, and 900 or so feet offshore. It was a particularly tricky patch of water because we were in a trough between two lengthy, hazardous reefs. As long as we stayed in this trough we were okay, but if we veered 50 to 100 feet in either direction we would be in danger of ripping a hole in the boat and sinking on the spot—just as so many treasure ships had done centuries before.

So it was with great care that we lowered about 150 feet of ¾-inch link chain holding our 50-pound anchor—all that would keep us from drifting onto the sharp-toothed edges of the reefs.

Because the water was icy-cold and Harry and Dan had the only two formfitting protective suits, made of neoprene, they volunteered to go over first and search for cannon, ballast stones or any other objects that would indicate a great ship had gone down here. They strapped on standard scuba gear, face mask, air tank and flippers, and we wished them well as they plunged into the heaving Atlantic.

One glance at their air bubbles told us there was a strong south current running, for in seconds they were drifting swiftly away from the boat in a southerly direction. I only hoped that I had led them close to the site.

The minutes seemed like hours, and I tried to busy myself topside by tidying up things on the *Sampan*, but everyone else seemed to have the same idea and we got in each other's way more than anything else.

There is a feeling about diving on a wreck site that is difficult to put into words. You become emotionally keyed up to an excited pitch even though you know the odds of finding anything, particularly on the first try, are hopelessly stacked against you.

Still, the feeling persists. It is, I'm sure, much like that of a performer who is waiting for the opening-night curtain to go up; a football player listening for the kickoff whistle; or an expectant father hearing the doctor's footsteps nearing down a hospital corridor. Whatever it is, this feeling, I know one thing. It is all-encompassing. On the *Sampan* we made small talk, and fiddled with lines, and did a number of other needless things, but the whole time our attention was concentrated on Dan and Harry, and our every other glance followed their strings of air bubbles, growing smaller in the distance with each passing minute.

It is the electric atmosphere more than anything else that inspires the treasure hunter. It is the exhilarating thrill of anticipation that fires the incentive to keep searching when things look blackest.

Such was the setting that bleak, cold day in January, 1961.

The divers hadn't been underwater more than five or six minutes when Harry abruptly surfaced, about 200 yards south of us, spit out his mouthpiece, pointed straight down, and shouted, "Cannon." A very appropriate announcement for Harry Cannon to make, I couldn't help but think.

Del and Lou literally leaped for the anchor, but in their haste had trouble securing it, and we were slow getting over to where the divers were. Meanwhile, Dan also surfaced, some yards away from Harry, and he appeared even more excited.

"Quick, bring the boat," he blurted, between the cresting waves. When we finally got to Harry we helped him aboard and threw the anchor out again. He was breathing heavily, more from excitement than exhaustion.

"There's three or four cannon down there," he eventually managed to tell us between gasps for air. "It's pretty clear, and it looks as if the sand has been cleaned off the site," he added.

"Where's Dan?" someone asked. After signaling us he had disappeared again underwater. Then we spotted his air bubbles, and from the increasing stream of them it appeared as if he were laboring down there.

No one can tell this part of the story better than the man who experienced it—Dan Thompson:

"Visibility was severely limited, but conditions weren't actually too bad. We have dived into waters where you could literally pass a hand in front of your face and not see it.

"The problem was to stay on course against the bone-breaking rollers that pounded over the second reef. If one caught us off-balance, we'd somersault head over heels in a grotesque, underwater ballet. The wave would surge on toward shore, sand torn loose from the bottom and caught in the undertow would shift back seaward, and we were somewhere in the middle of all this perpetual motion.

"Each time a comber would break, Harry and I tried to find a rock or chunk of coral—anything to hang onto until the waters subsided in the wake before the next wave.

"Still, despite the restless sea and the constant stirring on the bottom, things were fairly distinguishable. Harry and I had been down only a few minutes, working a crisscross pattern, checking every lurking shadow for any signs of a ghost galleon. We were about three fathoms down. Overhead, schools of curious grouper and snapper would eye us, and then swim along their way.

"Suddenly, in the dim distance, I could see Harry surfacing. He hadn't been down long enough to go up yet, unless he had either spotted something or was in trouble. At that time he was a novice diver, and I was half afraid, as I swam in his direction and surfaced, too, that he might need some help.

"Actually, he had come upon some long, irregular-shaped objects on the bottom that appeared too uniform to have been fashioned by nature. When he paddled over for a closer look, he damn near swam down the muzzle of a nine-foot-long, coral-encrusted cannon. He found two others lying behind it, like disarrayed spokes of a giant wheel, only partially buried in the sand.

"That's when he surfaced and I shouted for the boat to come. I was still some distance away and Harry called out, 'Come on over, Dan.'"

"We both submerged again and I began to swim upcurrent to reach him. I could see a number of objects scattered uncovered on the bottom. The entire ocean floor, in fact, looked as if it had been swept clean by some immense broom. Obviously, the severe fury of the past season's hurricanes, including one particularly destructive lady named Donna, had removed a thick layer of sand off the wreck site that had probably been several feet deep before the storms hit.

"I never made it to Harry and the cannon. About halfway I came upon two large, rocklike objects that for some strange reason instinctively aroused my curiosity. They were blackish-green on the sides, about a foot and a half across, and only lightly encrusted. When I looked at the sands around these clumps, I could barely believe my eyes, and the huge gasp I took must have sent enormous air bubbles streaming to the surface.

"Scattered on the bottom were pockets of silver pieces of eight, some lying singly, others fused together in little clusters of two or three. But these two clumps captivated me even more than the coins. Although I wasn't sure what they were, something compelled me to bring them up to the boat. I tried lifting the bulky weights, and could barely manage it. The boat was still too far away. I'd have to surface and signal them over, but I was becoming so excited I damn near blew the whole deal!

"My main fear was the very real possibility of not being able to find the area again if I surfaced, because the currents were running strong, and I didn't have a marker. In fact, several of us had even dreamed of this. Harry once told me he had a vivid nightmare in which he envisioned himself sitting on top of a pile of gold bullion, and not being able to tell anyone about it because he was afraid he would never find the spot again if he left it.

"Finally, reason outweighed anxiety, and I decided I had to chance going up. When I shouted to Kip and the others to come quick, I could see they were having some sort of trouble with the anchor, and I thought they never would get under way, even though only about 10 or 15 minutes had passed.

"I went back under, and panic froze me more than the cold water when I couldn't relocate the clumps right away. But after a few frantic seconds, I found them. This experience convinced me, however, it would be too risky to leave them again. I then got the bright idea of walking along the ocean floor, carrying the two clumps under my arms until I was directly under the boat, then surfacing. These bulky objects together weighed about 135 pounds, and even though the natural buoyancy of the salt water cut a third of their weight, I soon realized I had made another mistake. They were simply too heavy for one man to haul. I had walked no more than 50 feet when I had to stop and rest. I was, in fact, having extreme difficulty breathing.

"In desperation, I reluctantly dropped one cluster and backtracked with the other one under my arm to an iron mast strap I had found. I used this as a marker, then I immediately swam back to retrieve the second cluster and place it by the mast strap too until the boat got overhead.

"But I couldn't find the second one! I felt sick, but there was no time to brood now. When the boat neared, I scooped up a handful of the loose coins, surfaced, and called for a line. I handed the coins to Lou, on deck, and remember shouting something like, 'They're down there by the bushel. If I had a yard rake I could gather them up by the basket.' I think Lou misunderstood me and thought I said something about silver bars, but I could see he and Kip and the others were bugeyed with excitement.

"I took the nylon line and hurried back to the mast strap marker where I secured the clump, then picked it up. I had one heck of a time getting it to the surface. I must have bobbed up above the waves three or four times, paddling my flippers madly to stay surfaced, but each time I slid back underwater. Finally, with some helping hands from the boat, we got the iron-heavy object aboard.

"I followed it into the boat, physically exhausted, still not knowing what it was. It didn't take long for us to find out, for someone pushed the clump over, and on the bottom, embedded in thick clusters, were hundreds of irregular-shaped silver coins. We knew instantly they were the legendary pieces of eight, but I don't think anyone realized immediately how important a find this was.

"I was certainly glad I had submitted to my curiosity. Actually, there was no way I could have known what I had found, for no fused clusters of coins anywhere near this size had ever been recovered. It was truly a rare, if lucky, discovery."

The largest cluster of coins ever brought up before was found by famous treasure hunter Teddy Tucker, and weighed only two and a half pounds. Dan's clump weighed 77 pounds!

By conservative estimate, there were from 1,500 to 2,000 silver coins embedded in that one beautiful, blackened chunk. On the underside were visible cloth markings, which indicated the coins had originally been in sacks. We also surmised, judging from the shape of the clump, that it had also originally been in a wooden chest, the planks of which were undoubtedly eaten away by teredo worms centuries ago.

In the next few minutes, as the initial shock wore off, our pent-up emotions erupted into unabashed whoops of joy and shouts of, "We're rich, we've got it made."

How long the backslapping and hooraying lasted, I don't know, but when Dan finally managed to catch his breath and tell us about the second cluster he had dropped down there, you would have thought the boat deck had suddenly caught fire. Divers went overboard on all sides—with and without the protective rubber suits.

Within minutes Harry Acres came up with a handful of loose silver coins, as did Harry Cannon, Dan, Erv and Lou. Each trip added a few more of the greenish-black, elongated pieces of eight to our growing pile. Lou came up looking like a frozen mackerel, he was so cold. He had only been down about 15 minutes, but was shivering so uncontrollably he couldn't keep his mouthpiece in place and had to surface.

Methodically, the divers inched across the silver-littered ocean floor, searching for the missing clump. Dan said he didn't see how we could have missed it; that we must have passed within a foot or two of it several times. He and Erv, in fact, locked hands and scraped their arms across the bottom. Still no luck. At last, 45 agonizing minutes later, Acres brought it up. It too held fused clusters of coins of all shapes and sizes, around time-eaten pits and crevices.

For a short while after that it was a storybook operation. The divers would go over, swim around a little and pluck coins off the bottom as a farmer gathers eggs. Because this had just been a scouting run to get our bearings on the new wreck site, we hadn't brought any of our dredging equipment, and carried only the two formfitting protective wet suits. But this was a miraculous day for treasure recovery. We didn't need anything. What wasn't openly visible on the bottom was lying just underneath a thin surface of sand, in pockets, and the divers could easily fan this away with their hands.

It was indeed a remarkable day for unusual experiences. Harry Cannon surfaced, climbed aboard and lifted his face mask to recount a singularly fascinating incident. He had been swimming along looking for loose coins when he came upon some sort of trench, about five or six feet in width, and running ten to twelve feet long.

"It was like a slit trench," he told us. "I could see timbers in the bottom of it, and I wanted to go down and examine them closer, but I was afraid a moray eel might be hiding in the shadows down there.

"I couldn't make up my mind," Harry continued, as we sat around entranced by his adventure, "when I had it made up for me. A giant wave caught me off-balance and sent me sailing headfirst. I landed flat on my back at the bottom of the trench. I scrambled out of there in a hurry, remembering the story Del Long tells of how he once shot a moray with a spear gun, only to have the wounded monster viciously attack him, tearing at his flesh."

Just what Harry had tumbled into, we're not sure. It could well have been the wood of a nicely preserved ship's compartment that might have become buried in the sands before the worms got to it, and after hundreds of years was uncovered by the past season's hurricanes. Anyway we've never come upon that trench since, though Harry vows he'll find it again someday.

By one or two in the afternoon the wind had kicked up considerably and huge swells, six to eight feet high, crashed over the second reef, soaking everyone on board the dizzily buffeting *Sampan* with stinging sheets of salt spray. It was getting too rough for safety, and, as much as we hated to, we had to concede to the elements and wind it up. We stowed the clumps and coins in an iron box on deck and headed for shore, not even minding the precarious return trip through the inlet.

On the way in I couldn't help recall a paragraph in the book, *A Guide to Sunken Ships in American Waters,* by Adrian L. Lonsdale and H. R. Kaplan. They had said, "In today's world, pieces of eight and silver bullion aren't likely to be found outside the pages of adventure books."

If only they could have been with us today, I thought.

Ironically enough, I met these two gentlemen a few years later at a lecture I gave in Boston, during which I showed a number of slides of silver coins and wedges we had recovered. When I told them I could never forget a passage from their book, they seemed quite pleased, but when I told them which passage it was, I could see from their frowning faces that they didn't think much of my sense of humor.

Once we docked that afternoon, we went straight to a little shack behind my house north of Sebastian that I use as a retreat. We called two other members of our team, Dr. Kip Kelso and Libe Futch, and told them to come on over and see what we had found.

I cracked open a fifth of brandy, the first of many, and the party started. It was a roaring one that surely would have rivaled the bawdy celebrations pirates put on following acquisition of booty hundreds of years earlier. We began toasting our good fortune, ourselves, the coins—anything and everything.

We took the two large clumps and all the loose coins, about 500 or 600, and poured them out on the floor, and everyone just sat back smiling, staring at them as if hypnotized. Then we'd pick one or two up, rub them off searching for a date. Altogether, there must have been between 3,500 and 4,000 coins spread before us, including the ones in the large clusters.

"Look at this one," Doc Kelso would shout excitedly. Then he'd drop it in favor of another one. Lou Ullian said it was like giving a baby a handful of lollipops so it wouldn't know which one to put in its mouth and would wind up sampling them all. Del Long, who shot movies of the occasion, said we were all happier than a speckled puppy at feeding time.

I guess we were—and who could blame us. We had found treasure!

I even got caught up in the exuberance. Dan and Harry, between healthy snorts of brandy that followed more eloquent toasts, would grab double handfuls of coins and gleefully let them slip through their fingers, and I took a little coal shovel I used for the fireplace and scooped up coins till they overflowed a bucket, then I'd turn the bucket upside down, pouring the coins all over the floor in a showering cascade of silver.

Doc looked like an authentic eighteenth-century pirate—come back to life at the sound of pieces of eight clinking together. He had just had an operation on his eye and was wearing a black patch. All he needed to complete the picture was a dagger balanced between his teeth.

Actually, there are no adequate words to describe the raw emotions released at the party. It may sound silly for grown men to carry on this way, but we were cutting loose all the fears and disappointments and frustrations that had been bottled up in us for months, and, in my case, years. All the uncertainty that we might never find treasure had been forever dispelled on this one glorious, cold January day. Our months of soul-trying, back-breaking, expense-mounting searching had finally paid off.

This was the one big find, the rich strike that we needed to put us over the hill. Another season like 1960 and I'm sure the team would have broken up and gone their separate ways, our assault on the sea's boundless riches a failure.

But today had changed all that.

How lucky we had been! How thankful I was to Harry for persuading me to take the boat out through that treacherous inlet. Had we gone out a month sooner or a month later, the coins, cannon and other objects connected with the wreck would have been buried beneath an underwater mountain of sand.

Fate had ridden the waves with us that day, although how true this was, we weren't to find out until later. Nor did we have, that night before the roaring fireplace in my hut, any real idea of what this first find would lead to. Doc was dancing a jig and singing, "We're rich, we're rich, there must be at least $80,000 worth of coins here."

Hell, no one could foresee it then, particularly through our brandy-blurred vision, but within four years we'd be spending that much a year just for operational costs!

Oh, everyone, I'm sure, realized now that the treasure was there, but no one could have predicted the fabulous recoveries we would make in the years ahead. No one had any conception then that we would find, within the next four years, enough gold, silver, jewelry and rare *objets d'art* to classify the overall hoard as the greatest treasure recovery ever made in the New World.

To date, the group I head as president—Real Eight Corporation (named appropriately for the Spanish *ocho reales*, or piece of eight)—and our diving associates, Treasure Salvors, Incorporated, have found approximately $3 million in treasure on the beaches and at shallow offshore sites within a 25-mile radius of my home.

Included in our inventory are thousands of silver pieces of eight, hundreds of golden doubloons, silver bars and bullion, gold ingots, gold rings and bracelets, priceless K'ang Hsi porcelain china, and a single delicate gold necklace appraised by museums at a value of $50,000 or more.

Our collection is historically valuable also, including such archeological discoveries as silver tableware, pewter plates, candlesticks, copper pots, sounding weights, navigators' dividers, pottery shards, earthenware jars, cannon, anchors, swords and even flintlock muskets.

We are convinced that our total find now exceeds even the fabled riches Sir William Phips, commissioned by King James I of England, recovered in 1687 from the Ambrogian Reefs in the Silver Bank Passage at the southeasterly tip of the Bahamas. This has long been considered one of the greatest treasure salvages of all time. Although various history books cite vastly conflicting figures on how much Phips brought up from galleons that had sunk in 1643 carrying more than $20 million in gold and silver, a generally acceptable estimate is somewhere between $1 and $2 million.

Phips's native skin divers brought up an impressive amount of silver, but recouped only 25 pounds of gold. We have found far more than that in one day, several times!

It is a rather ironic footnote to history that Phips's first record of recovery—two silver casts, 51 pieces of eight and some broken silver plate —was entered in the ship's log on the night of January 8, 1687, precisely 274 years to the day that Dan Thompson found the two clumps of silver coins!

Our finds this day and the silver bars we had brought up from the other site the summer before were from two ships that belonged to an 11-ship Spanish Plate Fleet that sailed up the coast of Florida in the year 1715. The armada was caught off the mideast coast of the state in a fierce, early-season hurricane, and 10 of the 11 ships, carrying more than $14 million in treasure, sank after being hurled by the violent sea onto the jagged, insatiable jaws of the reefs, within a short distance from shore.

We have now located and obtained leases on eight of those 10 ships that went down, and if our luck holds, it is quite possible that over the next few years we will effect a total recovery from this ill-fated fleet that will likely never be equaled.

We know from exhaustive research that nearly $6 million of the $14 million that went down was recovered by the Spanish and by pirates and poachers, following the disaster. That left a total of $8 million on the bottom, awaiting discovery.

That night back in January, however, no one in his wildest imagination could envision such fantastic treasure finds ahead, but I don't think we could have been a happier bunch had someone told us.

The party roared on well past midnight. When we finally broke up, Doc, Harry and Dan had to be poured into their cars, and I must admit I had concern about some of the fellows driving home. But then I figured if we were lucky enough to strike it rich the way we had, nothing could happen to them.

I lay awake in bed a long time before going to sleep. Glittering, tinkling coins danced around in my head for hours. My dream—my lifelong dream—was being realized. We had found treasure, and we had found it right where I knew it had to be all these years.

2 Coins . . . What Coins?

When I was a youngster growing up in Miamisburg, Ohio, nothing was farther from my mind than the thought of becoming a professional treasure hunter. I had one burning ambition: to be a good housebuilder like my father. Oh, I suppose I let my imagination ramble a little as I thumbed through the pages of Robert Louis Stevenson's *Treasure Island*. What boy didn't? You could almost hear the screeching cry of Long John Silver's parrot, "Pieces of eight, pieces of eight!"

But had some fortune-teller told me then I would someday scoop up those very same silver pieces of eight on a beach, and dive beneath the ocean for golden doubloons, I would doubtlessly have laughed her off as a ridiculous, though amusing, crank.

Now, had she told me I would pack up my belongings one day and move to Florida with my wife, Alice, and my young son, Tom, I would surely have marveled at her perception.

I first came to the sunshine state in the winter of 1921, when I was only 15, and I have been in love with it ever since. For me there's no other place to live, and since finding treasure I've seen a pretty good portion of the world.

My older brother Ed and I drove down that winter in a Model T Ford. We had both spent long months at hard construction work to save enough dollars for that shiny vehicle, and two prouder boys couldn't be found.

I'm not sure I'm a firm believer in fate, but I have a strong feeling it rode with us on that adventurous motor trip. Halfway down the coast of

27

Florida—at a point almost directly parallel to the offshore sites where the Spanish treasure fleet went down—we broke some rivets off the Model T's differential. We coasted to a halt and pushed the car off the road into someone's front yard. The someone turned out to be a man named Earl Wellborn, who, ironically enough, was from our home town of Miamisburg. We were in the hamlet of Wabasso, which lies about 160 miles north of Miami and 200 miles south of Jacksonville.

Ed and I walked 12 miles to the nearest town that had a garage, Vero Beach, to get spare parts. We wound up spending about three or four days in Wabasso, and the tiny community and its neighborly residents made a lasting impression on me. I liked it, and I made up my mind then and there that I would come back every chance I got.

To get a better idea of how folksy this area is, even to this day, all one has to do is drive through the small town of Sebastian, where I now live, up the road a short distance from Wabasso. At each end of Sebastian's limits is a large sign welcoming travelers. The bottom line of these signs reads, "647 friendly people and six old grouches." Back in 1921, when Ed and I needed help with our car, we didn't find *any* grouches—in Sebastian or Wabasso.

Through the years, as I built up my contracting business in Ohio, I'd slip down to Florida every opportunity I got; everytime I had a few dollars saved up, or the winter got too brutal. I've been to every corner of Florida in my travels over the years, but I've never found a spot I liked as much as the Wabasso-Sebastian area.

Finally, as World War II drew to a close, the inevitable happened, and Alice, young Tom and I moved down permanently. I had contracted to build the Penn-Wood Motel in Wabasso, and we settled into a small frame house nearby.

I guess the first time I heard a word about treasure was from a building partner of mine, a colorful individual named Captain Steadman A. Parker. He had been captain on a steamship line and he could spin glorious tales of thrilling Atlantic crossings and of his adventures on the European continent. In a town the size of Wabasso, everyone knew him and of his exploits.

One afternoon when a rainstorm had given us the day off from construction work, he and I were sipping a few beers in a local tavern.

"This would be a good time to go look for some coins on the beach," Parker said.

"What coins?" I asked naïvely.

He seemed amazed at my total ignorance on the subject.

"Hasn't anyone told you about the old Spanish coins that wash up on the beach here?" he countered.

"No," I replied, "but I'm interested. Tell me about them."

The next round of beers was obviously on me. He could see in an instant he had me completely hooked. Parker then went into what sounded like a well-polished spiel about a Spanish treasure fleet that had sunk somewhere off the coast nearby, and how, over the years, he had found a number of silver coins by beachcombing the desolate sands just east of Wabasso.

"The best hunting is always after a storm or a good hard rain squall like we've got today," he pointed out. "I'm telling you, Kip, and mark my words, there's a fortune out there in the sea, and I'm going to find it one day."

I chalked it up as idle talk—good conversation for a rainy afternoon, but nothing more. Still, he had aroused my curiosity, and the first Sunday I had free, I drove across the rickety wooden bridge spanning the Indian River and parked near the ocean. I had purposely come by myself and made sure I was in a spot where no one could see me, for had they asked me what I was doing, I'm sure I would have been greatly embarrassed to tell them I was looking for buried treasure. What a silly notion!

As it turned out, I'm glad I was alone, for I didn't find anything, not even an interesting seashell. I went back to work the next day convinced that Parker must have been pulling my leg. But as time went by I began to realize he had, in fact, been telling me the truth.

In response to an innocent question here and there, other people would tell me of coins they had found. When I'd scoff, they'd stand fast and assure me there *really were* coins to be found on the beach. Some of them had silver pieces their grandfathers and great-grandfathers had uncovered years ago—all safely tucked away in old boxes or jars.

There was one particularly colorful story, which I never have heard firsthand, and wouldn't even try to substantiate, but it does seem to have a place in local folklore. It concerned a man named Larry Stokes, who supposedly had been the postmaster at Sebastian around the turn of the twentieth century. Stokes, so the tale goes, had collected a cigar box full of gold and silver coins over the years, and was mysteriously murdered one night. His stashed hoard was never found.

Another popular yarn concerned an old man named Kragle, who used to row a boat carrying mail between the mainland and a small island in the Indian River near the Sebastian Inlet. Word got around that he had spied cannon on the bottom during one of his runs. It was further said that he had found an unusually heavy "brick" in shallow waters, and when he built a fireplace in his home, he used this brick as a lintel. Allegedly, the brick melted the first time he built a fire.

Could it have been a wedge of precious metal? Was it a true story? I don't know. It was intriguing, nevertheless. There seemed, in fact, to be hundreds of legends around, and for a while I tried to collect them, but when I attempted to trace their source, I inevitably ran into a dead end. No one knew where the stories had originated.

There is one local legend that I can verify, however, because I personally interviewed the originator. I had heard that a pioneer in our area had found silver coins on the beach front for years, but he never had any around to show. The man was in his eighties when I talked to him, and he told me the story. He hadn't known what the blackened, elongated coins were, but fingering them, he found they made wonderful "skipping stones" to sail off the ocean's waves. When I asked him how many he thought he had thrown away in this manner, his answer floored me. He guessed he had tossed about 2,000 pieces of eight into the Atlantic.

One other tale concerns a local junk dealer who supposedly came upon a buried chest of gold and silver coins in the sand dunes behind the ocean front. No one knows for sure whether this is true because he has never shown anyone the contents of the chest. People have seen the chest itself, but not what is inside.

There were also a number of huge, ugly ship anchors, oxidized and coral-encrusted, in people's yards. But in Florida along the coast, cannon so encrusted were common on courthouse lawns and in city parks for years, until they were replaced successively by neater field guns of World War I, and later, World War II.

But I think the incident that first made me a believer about the coins on the beach and the treasure concerned a friend of mine whom I'll call "Tom Smith." Tom worked for me on construction jobs and was a good hand, but he had one problem. He liked to take a drink or two now and then, and it didn't matter to him if it was in the evening, over the weekend, or on a work day.

One morning he showed up on the job stone drunk. I hadn't noticed anything until he got into a scuffle with another worker. One whiff of his breath told me the story. Tom was too good a worker and too close a

Seaching for treasure in the beach sands with a mine detector. The instrument sounds a shrill whine in the operator's earphones when it passes over a metal object.

Silver pieces of eight before and after cleaning with acid to dissolve the greenish coating formed by the action of seawater on copper used in the alloy as a hardening agent.

Kip Wagner surfaces after a dive on a wreck site.

BELOW, LEFT: Colonel Dan Thompson holding a clump of clustered pieces of eight that he brought up in January, 1961. BELOW, RIGHT: Tom Wagner, the author's son, prepares to dive.

friend to let go, so I decided to take off for a while and try to sober him up. It looked like rain anyway.

I started driving over to the beach, thinking the cooling breeze off the ocean might straighten him out, or maybe he would sleep it off by the seashore. Before I was halfway there the bottom dropped out of the sky. The rain stopped when Tom and I reached the beach, and he led me to a spot I hadn't been to before.

"C'mon, follow me, Kip," he slurred, as he staggered through the palmetto fans leading down to sandy dunes hardened by the rains. I followed him not knowing where he was going and wondering at the same time how he could navigate at all. Tom swaggered all over a patch of beach-front, so drunk he could barely keep his balance. Then, he stooped down, brushed some sand aside and picked up a black, rectangular-shaped object. I asked him what it was.

"It's one of them coins," he answered, flipping it to me. Sure enough, beneath its oxide-blackened disguise, I recognized it as a piece of metal, probably silver, with a stamped design on it.

I forgot all about my plan to have Tom sleep it off and began kicking up sand and squinting at every object that didn't move. In the next half hour Tom picked up six more of the funny-looking coins. I found nothing, and I couldn't understand it. Here was a man who couldn't walk or talk straight, and I was sober, yet he was finding all the coins. It just didn't figure.

On the way back to town we stopped for a cold drink. Tom, being the generous soul he is, gave away all seven coins he had found to people who had expressed interest in them. He didn't give me one, but he did teach me a valuable lesson that day which I have never forgotten. I learned why a man whose vision was dimmed by alcohol could find coins while I couldn't. He did it, pure and simple, through experience. Tom knew what to look for and I didn't.

I had been looking for shiny silver coins just like the ones that jingled in my pockets. I hadn't reasoned that any coins that had been under the sea for centuries might not look as if they had just come from the mint. The coins bore scant resemblance to anything I'd ever seen before. They were all irregular-shaped and in different sizes, ranging from quarter size up to half dollar. They weren't round at all, but cut in a variety of shapes. In fact, of all the thousands of silver coins we have found over the years, I've never seen two with identical shapes.

And, too, there was absolutely nothing shiny or silvery about the coins

Tom found. They were sulfated black. They looked more like dirty pieces of cut metal than anything else, and I hadn't found any because I hadn't known what I was looking for. My preconceived notion of what a Spanish piece of eight looked like had quite possibly cost me any chance of finding one that day. Doubtless I had walked right past several of them lying partially uncovered by the pelting rain.

I can't help wondering how many of the hundreds of people who roam the beaches today—now that word of our treasure finds has spread—walk right over these peculiar bits of metal, just as I did years ago, completely oblivious of their value.

As the weeks went by and the summer came on, I still hadn't found any coins, but my interest had been forever piqued. I was hooked and I knew it.

It was about this time, in 1949, that Steadman Parker started talking up a recovery attempt on a wreck site he had located a short distance off the beach, in about three and a half or four feet of water. I heard about it and asked him if I could join in. I had no special skills to offer, only a strong back, a few bucks and an infectious eagerness.

Altogether, there were five of us: Parker, myself, Jimmy Russell of Orlando, Carl Wild of Fort Pierce, and George Bunnell of Miami. Russell had a little dredge, and Bunnell, a heavy-equipment operator by trade, had a dragline and a bulldozer. So, we all chipped in what resources and money we had, and, in addition to the equipment already available, we rented an air compressor with a hammer.

We had no contracts drawn up and we formed no corporation. We didn't put anything down on paper. We just mutually agreed to split whatever we found five ways. It was strictly a gentlemen's agreement. And today, now that I'm president of an incorporated treasure company and everything is done legally, by the book, I'm not convinced our earlier agreement wasn't the best method of operation after all. Seems like we didn't have any problems until the paper work started to flow.

It was June before we were ready to begin. Everyone quit his job to devote full time to an all-out assault on this wreck site. We bought jungle hammocks to sleep in, and lived on the beach, at a point about three miles south of the Sebastian Inlet, completely without shelter. When we ran out of food, someone would drive across the bridge to town and stock up. If it happened to rain during the day or at night, we just got wet. We were practically living in our bathing suits then anyway.

Thinking back on it, we must have been a peculiar-looking band—un-

Kip Wagner (*left*) and National Park Service historian Luis R. Arana, an expert on old Spanish, examine a microfilm of a document preserved in the Archive of the Indies in Seville, Spain.

Louis Ullian and Mike Hrebec, wearing Desco masks, prying loose crusted metal from a long since disintegrated wreck.

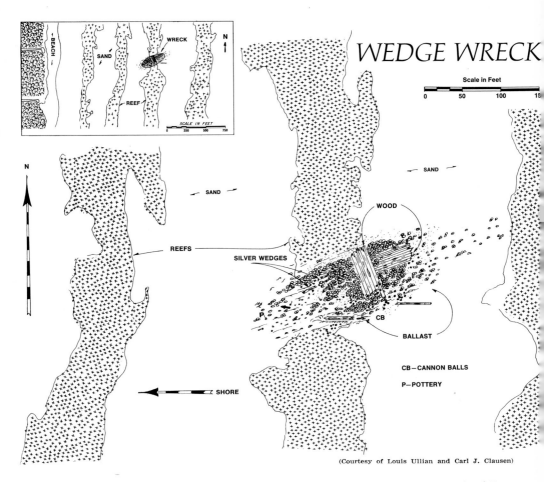

WEDGE WRECK

Scale in Feet

0   50   100   15

WOOD

SILVER WEDGES

BALLAST

CB

P

REEFS

SAND

SAND

SHORE

N

CB—CANNON BALLS

P—POTTERY

(Courtesy of Louis Ullian and Carl J. Clausen)

This diagram shows the remnants of the so-called wedge wreck, north of Fort Pierce, and the location of objects found at this site.

shaven half the time, sun-bronzed and weather-beaten. The only thing more bizarre than our physical appearance was the recovery operation itself. It was some sight.

The wreck, although only 75 to 100 feet offshore, in shallow water, was out of reach of the dragline from the beach. So we engineered a workable system of getting to it by first bulldozing huge mounds of sand into a pile on the beach adjacent to the site. We'd do this during the flood tide. Then, as the tide receded, we pushed this mountain of sand into the water and built a temporary pier into the ocean, so that, by the time the tide was low, we could run the dragline out over this hastily molded sand strip, and dip it into the wreckage. Of course, as the tide came in again it washed away our sand pier and we had to start over again.

George Bunnell operated the dragline. He would simply direct his scoop shovel into the general area and then swing it around and dump the contents onto the beach where the rest of us combed through it with metal detectors. We never did use the air hammer to pound loose fragments of the reef.

The first time the detectors acted up, we all leaped with anticipation, and trembling fingers sifted through the sand, silt and coral which George had unearthed. But all we found were ships' fasteners and metal spikes. We also found decayed wood from a ship's superstructure. These clues, proving to us that *something* was out there, kept us going that summer.

Late one afternoon I shouted excitedly to the others when Bunnell brought up a square, blackened heap. It looked like some type of container, and I let my imagination have its run. A thrilling thought pulsed through my system: was this a treasure chest? Thick metal bands were wrapped around heavy plankings. It must be. Everyone gathered close in. George damn near sprained an ankle leaping out of his cab to see what the commotion was about.

Our hopes were short-lived, however. It seemed, in fact, that fate was deliberately teasing us. On closer examination we determined our "treasure chest" to be merely a mounting for cannon. We knocked off work for the day. Our hearts just weren't in it.

Steadman Parker was a wiry, thin little man pushing 60. He had been born in Sebastian and all through his life had heard the word-of-mouth stories of treasure offshore, as they were handed down from generation to generation in this part of Florida. To make a salvage attempt as we were doing was to fulfill one of his lifelong dreams, and in the early days of the operation, when hopes were still high, he played his role to the hilt.

2

Often, when the dragline was working, he would grab an old rifle and march up and down the beach to "protect" us from any poachers. The only trespassers we saw were the formations of gulls and pelicans that passed in review overhead, and the skeptical sand crabs that peered at us from holes they had tunneled in the beach. The oceanfront in those days was just as it had been for centuries—deserted.

The waters were generally too rough and too cloudy for good fishing, and the jagged reefs, which began only a few yards out, made swimming an extra-hazardous sport. So it was a rarity to see anyone on the beach. I often wonder what Parker would have done with his rifle had anyone approached.

Not only was there no one for him to fend off, but there was no treasure—not even a single coin—to guard. As I said, it was a peculiar operation. But if Parker felt more secure patrolling the beach, who was I to argue?

At best, our work that summer was a complete washout—literally and figuratively. We had only a few hours, six at the most, to work each day. We'd pile the sand up at high tide, work the dragline as the tide went out, then bring the line back onto the beach as the relentless ocean came in again, leveling our makeshift sand road. Then, as soon as the tides changed again, we started the process all over. Because the tides switched at different times each day, we'd work almost around the clock. One day we might have high tide at eight in the morning, so by two in the afternoon, it would be low, and we'd have to knock off shortly after that. A few days later low tide might be at eight in the evening.

When the seas became too rough for us to work at all, we'd take the bulldozer and run it through the palmetto wilderness that blanketed the sand dunes in back of the beach. We would get old-timers in the area who had heard the legendary tales of sunken treasure to recount them for us, or to come over to the beach and show us areas that had yielded coins in years past.

It was on one of these days when we couldn't work in the ocean that I found my first coin. The dozer unearthed it and I eagerly picked it up. It was neither gold nor silver. It was, instead, a Spanish copper maravedi, dated 1649. Carl Wild seemed much more delighted over the discovery than I, so I gave him the coin.

It was rough going, living out in the open and toiling in the blazing hot sun all day with no protection. We must have dredged up tons of sand and coral from the ocean floor that summer. Bunnell dug a hole deep enough to sink an entire fleet in, much less one ship—but we found nothing.

By the end of August it was obvious that we had failed. The selfish sea had not yielded a single coin. After three months of backbreaking work —work you couldn't have gotten any one of us to do on a regular job for less than $4 or $5 an hour, if for that—we went broke.

Not counting our time, just the equipment and supplies and what little living costs were incurred, we had dropped $12,000. That's a helluva lot for just a few wood splinters, ships' fasteners and metal spikes—$4,000 a month to be exact. But that wasn't the worst of it. We were utterly fatigued, disillusioned, disheartened, and in total despair. Parker was heartbroken. Our wives, who had been so patient and hopeful at first, would barely speak to us, and our friends, most of whom were skeptical of such a folly from the start, would only wag their heads and say, "I told you so, but you wouldn't listen." Years later, when we did find treasure, these same friends would chortle, "I knew you'd find it all along." But such, I guess, is human nature.

All I know is by the end of that summer I was physically and emotionally drained. We dissolved our little group—there were no papers to tear up—and everyone went his separate way. The others swore off ever foraging for treasure again, but although I was at the low point in my 20-year search, the spark of hope never quite fanned out. I guess I was just too stubborn and too stupid to know when I was licked.

What we had failed to realize during this first, abortive effort was that it would have been virtually impossible for a Spanish galleon, or any other ship of considerable size, to have sunk in such shallow water. What Parker had located was not actually a wreck, then, but only part of one; some wooden superstructure that had broken loose, possibly when the ship had pounded to splinters on the reefs.

Thus, though we had wasted three months and $12,000 on mining a spot that held nothing to begin with, it was quite possible that the real wreck site was somewhere close by, in deeper waters. I made a mental note to cover the area thoroughly whenever I could get the chance.

But for the next few months, over the winter, I forgot about treasure. Broke, I worked at odd jobs, carpentry, masonry, anything I could find to get back on my feet and put some food on the family table. There wasn't time for any more searching now. But there would be—soon. I had gambled and lost this first time, and I vowed I wouldn't commit myself again without being sure.

As that long, dreary winter slowly conceded to an effervescent spring, I could feel the insatiable itch to scour the beaches come over me again. The frustrations of the past summer were behind me. What else could I lose by leisurely poking around?

So one day when my workload had slacked off, I borrowed an old metal detector from Parker and drove over to the beach. I could feel my heart pound faster as I strolled up and down the ocean front just out of reach of the lapping waves. When the detector, a war surplus SCR625 mine detector, began whining, indicating there was something metallic beneath a patch of sand, I couldn't dig fast enough. After a couple of minutes I unceremoniously uncovered a rusty tin can. Later I found more cans and some other junk, but still no coins. Had I not seen for myself pieces of eight in the homes of various friends and neighbors around Sebastian, I'm sure I would have sworn none really existed.

I began beachcombing more and more as the summer came on, and, finally, one day I found my first silver coin; a piece of eight all my own. Glory hallelujah! This legendary coin of pirate stories is about the size of a half dollar. It was worth eight reals, hence its name. British colonials called it a "cob," a word meaning lump, because of its irregular shape.

Admiring it, I knew now I would never fully be able to give up the search. I managed to spend more and more time combing the beach, and I began finding a few more coins, mostly silver cobs.

The oceanfront from Sebastian Inlet to Wabasso runs uncluttered, except for a few beach cottages, for about eight miles. Back a decade or so ago, I learned that this stretch was deserted through the week, but on weekends a few people would come over for a swim or to hot-rod beach buggies in and out of the high-sloping dunes. I made it a point to conduct my investigations during the week when I had things to myself.

At high tide the Atlantic licks near the dunes, then recedes, as the tide changes, leaving a good 100 feet or so of beach surface. I called this thin, eight-mile strip my "money beach," as I came to accumulate a considerable number of coins. Some days I would find nothing. On other days I might uncover one or two. After a lively northeaster I once found five pieces of eight. As often as not the mysterious coins would be lying partially exposed in the sand. To me it was as curious as the appearance of mushrooms in a morning meadow. I could only presume the high tides tumbled the bluff, the waves were the rocker, and the riffles on the clean beach caught the heavy silver before it could wash back out to sea.

I was conducting what must rank as the laziest, least-intensified treasure hunt in history. My finds were scanty but steady over the months, and before long I had collected about 35 or 40 coins. A few of these were gold pieces, and I would hide them in my wife's cedar box and tell no one about it. I was afraid that if someone found out I had some gold they would alert the government and Federal agents would descend upon me to reclaim it. It was years before I realized that anything found on the beach is in the province known as "treasure trove," which my lawyers tell me means, loosely, "finder's keepers."

I was much more open about my discovery of silver coins, and I was far too generous with them. I had no idea of their true value as collector's items, and I'm ashamed to admit I melted many of them down and made bracelets and necklaces for some of the neighborhood youngsters. In fact, it was a rare child in Wabasso who didn't have some silver trinket I had fashioned out of the odd-shaped pieces of eight.

I didn't always confine my searches to the beach itself. On some occasions I would take a machete and hack through the palmettos and thick underbrush in back of the high dunes that served as a natural fortress against the mighty ocean. Precisely what I was looking for I couldn't tell, but it was on such relatively high ground, in back of the beach, that I had found that 1649 copper maravedi.

As my coin collection continued to grow—a result of endless hours and days of beachcombing—I began nurturing a theory. Most of the cobs I had found were located at the very base of a high bluff on the beach, and the best yields were invariably after a heavy storm had churned the seas into a lashing fury. So I felt these coins, rather than being uncovered on the beach, were actually being washed ashore by the heavy wave action. I believed their source, then, must lie somewhere out there under the giant breakers.

To augment this theory I began swimming out offshore whenever the waters were clear enough. I would casually paddle out, looking around, and feeling on the bottom with my toes. The reefs were only a short distance off, and I could easily reach them at low tide without getting into deep water. Once on the reef I would carefully drag my toes into crevices and holes, trying to distinguish any objects that might identify a sunken ship. I can personally vouch for the razor-sharp edges of the reefs, for I still carry a number of scars on my legs—souvenirs of severe cuts and abrasions I suffered when waves slapped me into the rocks, or when I slipped while climbing about on their slippery surfaces.

With no equipment, not even a face mask, I had little success on these first few swims, but I couldn't shake my belief that the source of all the coins on the beach lay somewhere nearby in only a fathom or two of water.

The problem was to get out there and cover ground. I thought it might be solved one day as I was roaming along the water's edge. I came upon another beachcomber, a younger fellow named Gene Cheviler. Gene was from Riviera Beach, about 50 miles or so south of Sebastian, and he was an adventurer type.

With common interests at heart, it didn't take long to strike up a friendship and to pool our meager treasure-hunting knowledge. Gene showed me how to make a face mask so I could see underwater. We fashioned it out of regular window glass with inner-tube rubber tightly sealed around it. He had a small outboard, so whenever the ocean was calm enough, we would motor around from spot to spot, like a pair of impatient fishermen, looking for clues to a wreck below the surface.

We found nothing.

3   To the Books

My friend Dr. Kip Kelso disagreed with me. He thought my theory of the coins coming from the sea was all wet. Rather, he felt the pounding surf, in sweeping the beaches clean, uncovered coins that had been buried there for centuries under layers of sand.

Doc Kelso, a practicing MD, had moved to the Sebastian area only a few years after I had. And, like myself, he had become obsessed with the local tales of Spanish treasure. A man of boundless knowledge and inexhaustible energy, Doc became the new Health Department director for our area. He is a native of Atlanta, and a graduate of the University of Oklahoma's School of Medicine.

Just why so talented a man—he's a specialist in internal medicine—chose to settle in our little community, I don't know to this day. But I'm sure glad he did. Without his invaluable help—materially, through financial aid; physically, through endless research; and spiritually, through never-ceasing encouragement—I don't think I ever would have found treasure.

Doc today has a large practice that would keep two normal MD's busy. In addition, he is, or has been, president of at least half a dozen organizations, all demanding on his time. And if this weren't enough, he raised seven children by himself, while his lovely wife, Becky, recovered from an illness. You tell me how he does it.

He has the most retentive memory of any man I've ever met. Let him get a glimpse of your face and catch your name, and if he never saw you again for 20 years, you could walk through the door and he'd greet you as if you'd met just yesterday. It's amazing.

It is this fantastic memory, combined with his insatiable thirst for knowledge, that, when channeled into research on the treasure fleets, has made him a veritable walking encyclopedia of Spanish colonial history. He spews out obscure dates, long-forgotten names and little-known events with machine-gun speed and rifle accuracy. Whatever he has read about the Spanish—and it has been hundreds of volumes—he has lodged permanently somewhere in those remarkable little gray cells of his brain.

I first met Doc Kelso one night when he came over to the house to give me an insurance physical examination. Alice and I were poring over some old maps of the Florida east coast, and were trying to pinpoint what ships might have sunk where, based on the sketchy research I had done myself, and on legends I had heard from area old-timers.

Before the evening was over, Doc and I were both lying on the floor with the maps spread all over the room. He was fascinated about the prospects of treasure, and almost instantly we formed a lasting friendship based on mutual interests and respect for each other. We decided to pool our knowledge. He expressed keen interest in the few coins I had assembled, and I think this refreshing enthusiasm acted as a catalytic agent upon me, renewing my spirits.

I continued my beachcombing and my occasional swims in the surf, and little by little, added to my collection of silver cobs. And then I began to notice something peculiar about them. Not one of the coins that carried dates was minted after the year 1715. At the time this didn't ring any particular bells in my head, but, as I was soon to discover, it was to become one of the most important single clues to what lay out there under the sea.

I've read that there are supposed to be four separate types of treasure seekers. The first of these is the armchair adventurer who draws his excitement from the spoken or written word. His interest is whetted by a mere hint; his active imagination will take over from there.

The second type is the scientist or historical researcher. He cares nothing about finding gold, but derives his pleasure from proving or disproving, from identifying and cataloguing.

Active adventurers, the modern-day soldiers of fortune, make up the third group. While they look for treasure, what they are really seeking is adventure. They will run down any rumor, pursue any legend, often without even checking its authenticity.

The fourth group has the fewest members, but these are the hardened professionals who bring the vital resources of business to bear upon the glamorous world of treasure. It is this small band of pros who assemble proper supplies and equipment, gather experienced crews, research thoroughly, take the proper legal steps, and commit a major outlay of capital.

Just where I fitted in the groupings I'm not sure, but an incident soon developed during my searches that was to have a marked influence on my life, and turn me from a casual, part-time hunter to a full-time pro. It was caused by a natural phenonemon—a hurricane, just like the one that had wrecked the 1715 fleet. It was late summer when I got back from a trip to Trujillo in Honduras. A friend of mine had told me about this ancient city, and we flew down just to see it. I got back as the hurricane was ready to strike.

For two days the howling winds and driving sheets of rain pounded the Florida east coast. It was a hell of a storm. I was a member of a local Civil Air Patrol disaster unit, and toward the end of the second day I got a call from CAP headquarters to go examine the beach. The surging Atlantic had eaten far into the sand bluffs and erosion threatened to undermine several cottages.

I donned a rain slicker and climbed into my pickup truck. When I reached the ocean, I could barely believe my eyes. The familiar money beach I had combed so often over the past few years was completely re-terraced and buried a foot deep with churned flotsam from the offshore reefs. To the west, a familiar grove of stately cabbage palms looked like the wreck of a fleet of closely packed vessels, their broken masts leaning against each other in chaotic disorder. I stood on the low sand bluffs near the Sebastian Inlet, bewildered. At least 15 feet of the bluff overlooking the beach had washed away, and with it all the secret paths and patches of land I had marked at sites where I had found coins.

After checking for erosion damage, I couldn't resist the temptation to walk a ways down the beach. I knew I was the first one out since the storm. As I worked my way down by the water's edge, kicking away at clumps of purple and green seaweed and at large pieces of driftwood, I spied something far too bright to be a seashell. When I picked it up and examined it closely, I could feel the thrill of excitement throbbing through my system. It was a polygonal piece of silver, dated 1714.

I looked out at the sea as I rubbed the coin. I was certain now it must have been washed ashore by the storm after being loosened by the unrelenting thrashing of the hurricane-driven breakers. Here was practically irrefutable proof of my theory. This realization was perhaps the single

2*

most significant turning point in my life. It convinced me beyond doubt that treasure lay out there. All I had to discover was what treasure, and exactly where it lay.

When I told Doc he stubbornly stuck to his original contention that the coins had been on the beach all the time, buried under tons of sand. To help prove his point, he offered to pay for the rental of a ditchdigger, and one day we took it over to a favorite spot of mine, and turned the hungry machine loose.

For the next few hours we watched with keen interest as the digger burrowed three separate ditches 75 feet long and several feet deep, criss-crossing each other. When nothing turned up, Doc reluctantly admitted I might have a point in claiming the coins we had found were being washed ashore. I had no doubts about it.

The pieces of the giant jigsaw puzzle were slowly falling into place, but it was still way too early to get an idea of the overall picture.

By now Doc and I started getting pretty serious in our research efforts to learn just what might have gone down out there. Our strongest clue was the fact that none of the coins I'd personally found, nor any of those that I had examined in friends' collections, was dated later than 1715.

Then someone told me of a flotilla of Spanish ships carrying $14,000,-000 in treasure that had been driven onto the reefs and sunk in a great hurricane off Cape Canaveral (now Cape Kennedy) in the year 1715. Thus I first heard of one of the greatest disasters to befall the annual Plate, or Silver Fleet sent out by Spain to bring home the wealth of the New World.

But I was receiving conflicting reports. I sent the shiny 1714 silver piece I had found following the hurricane to Mendel Peterson in Washington, D.C. He was the Smithsonian Institution's curator of Armed Forces History. I asked him if it could have come from a wreck that went down in the severe storm of 1715.

Disappointingly, he wrote back that this would have been impossible, since that fleet sank off the Florida Keys, more than 150 miles south of the Sebastian Inlet. He was, in fact, writing a book on the subject. This response confused me even further, for I now had two expert opinions. One said the fleet sank off Canaveral, the other said off the Keys, yet these two points were more than 200 miles apart! Clearly, at least one authority was wrong. Could they both be? I wondered. I was to learn through the years that as we made succeeding discoveries we would upset a lot of pet theories that had been nurtured and embellished by experts for decades. Some of the authorities, in fact, didn't take it too kindly to be corrected by an ex-housebuilder, but I was gathering the proof to back my claims.

I knew one thing for certain, though: that mint-fresh 1714 silver piece was stirring up some excitement. Henry Gruenthall, the president of the American Numismatic Society, said he had never seen a coin quite like it. Bob Nesmith, curator of the Foul Anchor Archives in Rye, New York, and a man many consider America's foremost authority on early Spanish colonial coins, was interested enough to rearrange his vacation so he could come to Sebastian specifically to see that coin plus the other silver pieces I'd accumulated. I had written him for advice after talking to his daughter, who lived only 25 miles north of me in Melbourne. He was awed by my collection, but that one coin really enthralled him. It had an unusual design and a different type die he had never seen before.

This opened up a whole new vista of exploration for Nesmith, and created a long-standing friendship between us that has endured ever since. In fact, he spends many of his vacations with me in Florida now, and his counseling and guidance have proved invaluable.

With the conflicting reports on the 1715 fleet, I could be sure of only one thing: 10 ships did go down *somewhere* that year in a hurricane. I had found one wreck site under the sea after years of searching. Now it was beginning to look as if I'd have to dig just as hard and as deep to find the same wreck in the history books.

Doc Kelso and I rolled up our sleeves and began devoting every spare minute to research. We quickly devoured everything in the local libraries and then branched out to cover larger ones in Miami, Key West, at Stetson University in De Land, and the University of Florida at Gainesville. For the first few weeks it was madness—like sinking in quicksand. We found that literally hundreds, even thousands, of ships had sunk off the state's east coast. We must slowly weed them out.

I suppose no treasure hunt would be complete or even believable without some sort of map—preferably one yellowed and cracked with age, with a big X slashed across it, marking the precise location of the buried riches. Serious treasure hunting deviates from the adventure books in almost every other respect, i.e., chests brought up intact, ships lying invitingly on the bottom just as they were the day they went down, and so on.

In the case of maps, however, I found a ringing similarity between the map used in our search and the fictional ones created by Robert Louis Stevenson and others.

Rather than a frayed map cracked with age, though, ours was a clean, clear photostat. But the effect it had couldn't have generated any more excitement had it been the original copy.

How the map was discovered is a story in itself, well worth retelling. Doc had gotten so wrapped up in his research that in 1959 he bought a trailer, and, during his two-week vacation, loaded it up with his wife, Becky, his mother-in-law, and all seven of his youngsters.

He drove to Washington, set up the trailer at a scenic park overlooking the Potomac, and then left the family to sight-see while he began digging into volumes and documents at the Library of Congress. Every day, while he read, Becky took the kids to the Lincoln Memorial, the Washington Monument, the White House, and every other major point of interest in our nation's capital.

When staff members at the library saw how serious Doc was, they pitched in and helped him. They allowed him into the Congressional reading room where he worked at Harry Truman's old desk. Day after day he kept boys running with his long list of references, and he consumed volume upon volume. Perhaps the single most helpful book was Cesáreo Fernández Duro's *Armada Española,* published in 1900. From this he gleaned a more accurate story of the 1715 fleet's movements, as well as a helpful, detailed history of the Spanish in Havana and the New World.

Doc had prepared extensive lists of bibliographies he had accumulated in his readings before making the D.C. trip, and, as he methodically went down them, he came one day upon the name of Irving Rouse, a professor of anthropology at Yale, who had written a short monograph on Spanish treasure fleets in which he quoted, among his sources, a book called *A Concise Natural History of East and West Florida.* It was written by the English cartographer Bernard Romans, and published in 1775—just 60 years after the hurricane had sunk the Plate Fleet.

Sadly, Doc learned that the book was both rare and out of print. He was told original copies sold for $1,000 and more. But after some persistent detective work, librarians found a copy in their rare book section. Doc was overjoyed. He pored over the book's pages, fascinated, till his eyes ached. Halfway down page 273 he gave a little war whoop that startled other readers in the sedate surroundings. Here, in a single paragraph, was the exact information we had sought for so long. He read and reread the passages until he had committed practically every word to memory.

Here's what Romans had said nearly 200 years ago: "Directly opposite the mouth of the St. Sebastians River happened the shipwreck of the Spanish Admiral, who was the northernmost wreck of fourteen galleons, and a hired Dutch ship, all laden with specie and plate; which by [undistinguishable word] of northeast winds were drove ashore and lost on this coast, between this place and the bleach-yard, in 1715. A hired Frenchman, fortunately escaped, by having steered half a point more east than the others. The people employed in the course of our survey, while walking the strand after strong eastern gales, have repeatedly found pistareens and double pistareens, which kinds of money probably yet remaining in the wrecks, are sometimes washed up by the surf in hard winds. This Lagoon stretches parallel to the sea, until the latitude 27:20, where it has an outwatering, or mouth: directly before this mouth, in three fathom water, lie the remains of the Dutch wreck. The banks of this lagoon are not fruitful."

In one of the book's flaps was the map. This was almost too much—like having your cake and eating it too. Doc could see immediately it would be of immense value to our research. With a magnifying glass he examined every detail with exacting thoroughness. The map dedication, embraced by the traditional mythical figures, male and female, and the grotesque fishes, reads as follows:

"To all Commanders of Vessels round the Globe, this Chart is respectfully dedicated by their very humble servant B. Romans, invt. et sculpt. 1774"

Details of the coast were remarkably accurate. The San Sebastian River, with its north and south forks, was carefully delineated, and, as was proper in the eighteenth century, the Sebastian Inlet was not indicated, since it is of more recent origin. To the north, the familiar, arrow-shaped bulge of Cape Canaveral, 50 miles above Sebastian, was shown.

But what really hooked Doc's interest was a notation that read, consistently with the text of the book, "Opposite this River, perished, the Admiral, commanding the Plate Fleet 1715, the rest of the fleet 14 in number, between this & yᵉ Bleech Yard." Just below this were the words "el Palmar."

The "River" had to be the Sebastian Creek. If this were true, then the modern historians *were* wrong, and part of the fleet had gone down near Sebastian, and not off Cape Canaveral to the north, or the Florida Keys to the south, as the various reports had stated.

The "Bleech Yard" was on a peninsula at the mouth of the River St. Lucie, where it flows into the ocean. Like the Sebastian, the St. Lucie empties into the Indian River (which is actually a lagoon, an arm of the ocean), but unlike the former, the St. Lucie has sufficient force and volume for its fresh water to remain intact as a stream through a mile of salt water, and to breach the outer island, forcing a passage into the ocean.

Romans, we learned later, knew that a galleon from the fleet had attempted to gain the shelter of the Indian River through this inlet. From this point to "el Palmar," corresponding to the *Palmar de Ais*—which means palm grove of the Ais Indians—was about seven leagues.

Now the treasure fever really had us in its grip.

True, there had been but 11 ships in the 1715 armada, not 14 as Romans had listed. Yet it would have been easy to miscalculate this due to the great number of wreck sites along this part of the coast.

More importantly, since Romans had published the map in 1775, based on field trips he had made four years earlier, we reasoned that it was quite possible he had drawn some of his information firsthand, conceivably from elderly Indians who had watched their fathers aid the salvage operations following the hurricane. Such Indians, for a few trinkets, would be anxious to please their inquirers by expanding the details to satisfactory proportions. Treasure hunters do not consider such exaggerations handicaps. Nor, for that matter, did such explorers as Ponce de León, Cortez and Pizarro earnestly strive to disprove tales of a Fountain of Youth, the cities of Cibola, or a Golden Man.

Taking into consideration such probable embellishments, I was still certain we were at last on the right track to gathering the truth about this mysterious treasure fleet and what happened to it.

After Doc's success at the Library of Congress, which had, incidentally, damn near cost him a divorce in the process—and who could blame Becky after two weeks by herself in Washington with seven kids—he went on to New York. There, he walked into American Numismatic Society headquarters and met its president, Henry Gruenthall. Doc was armed with photographs of the silver coins we had found, and Gruenthall became excited when he examined them. He told Doc we were really onto something special. They had a long talk.

Later, from the Spanish-American Association in New York, Doc got the names and addresses of librarians in the archives at Havana and Mexico City. We wrote them for detailed information on the 1715 fleet, but never heard from either capital. In Mexico City, I think they were suspicious of our intentions. In Havana, a young man named Fidel Castro had just come into power and that put the quietus on our correspondence there.

While specific information seemed to be increasingly hard to track down, general facts about the ships were not too difficult to come by. They are perhaps most succinctly summed up in John S. Potter's *The Treasure Diver's Guide*. His researchers have periodically tapped, among other sources, the General Archives of the Indies at Seville, Spain, the Archives of the British Admiralty, and libraries in Peru, Mexico and Colombia. The trick—and we were to find it was an increasingly difficult one—was to assemble specific, detailed information on the 1715 fleet.

I felt we had the best chance to gather such data through the Spanish archives. I had read that the richest repository of historical Spanish-American documents in the world is housed in Seville's Archivo General de Indias.

Excitedly, I wrote the first of many letters to Dr. Don José de la Peña, curator of the archives. I had a young friend studying languages at New Mexico State University at the time, and he offered to translate my English into Spanish, and vice versa on the return mail. For this he would receive credit in one of his courses, and I would have the services of an eager and competent translator, free of charge.

As can be imagined, the correspondence took considerable time. After a couple of weeks I began to look in the mailbox every day, with as much anticipation as a retiree expecting an overdue pension check. But I had to resign myself to the fact there was nothing to do but wait. I might add here, if this treasure-hunting business has taught me one thing, it has been an appreciation of those who are able to master the fine art of patience.

Finally, the return letter from Dr. Peña arrived, and Doc Kelso and I could hardly wait to read it. We received a severe jolt. Rather than being helpful, Dr. Peña's information was vague and sketchy. What he did say about the 1715 fleet we already knew. Doc and I were depressed beyond description. We had felt all along that the answers to our questions lay buried in the archives. This was quite a letdown.

But the fate and fortunes of treasure seekers rise and fall like a tossing surf, and it wasn't long before our hopes were once again buoyed. A close friend of mine, Mrs. Libby Walker of Vero Beach, was planning a vacation trip to Spain. She called me one day to ask if there was anything she could do for me while she was overseas. Indeed there was.

She had an eventful trip, and we didn't learn what had happened until she returned several weeks later. The Archives of the Indies are a complicated maze of records, documents, statistics—the whole works—and it is impossible for an amateur to find anything of value there, regardless of the time spent, without professional help. It thus becomes necessary to hire experienced researchers with years of training, who know the intricate ins and outs of the complex archives. I felt that in having Libby see Dr. Peña personally for us, we had gone the usual system one better.

To interview a Spanish official, such as a curator of archives, one generally must have a letter of introduction from a ranking dignitary of his own country. To get around this, I had given Libby a handful of dated silver pieces of eight, to prove our intentions were serious. This had done the trick, and without too much red tape, she was shown into Dr. Peña's office. Through an interpreter, she explained precisely what detailed information we needed to verify our beliefs about the Plate Fleet.

Dr. Peña understood, but unexplainedly began crying. The interpreter finally managed to extract from him the fact that political pressures from his superiors had forced him to send us the sketchy data. He had what we wanted and he was willing to give it to us, but his hands were tied. Someone, apparently, was suspicious of the American treasure hunters. Before the interview ended, Libby was weeping too. Dr. Peña told her that although he could not give her the information we so desperately needed directly, he would try to mail it to her after she returned to the States.

"I'm sorry I don't have anything now to show you, Kip," she said one night in her living room, freshly adorned with Spanish goatskins and other souvenirs. "But Dr. Peña has promised to mail me some microfilm on the documents pertaining to the 1715 fleet."

I nodded, but deep in my stomach I had a gnawing feeling that we would never hear from him again. Yet it was only a few days later that Libby called me.

"It's here," she screamed into the telephone, jarring my eardrums. "The microfilm is here. It just arrived."

I'm glad there were no highway patrolmen on the road that day, for my pickup truck practically flew the few miles to Vero Beach. When I stepped into her living room, gasping for breath, I felt like giving Libby a bear hug. In the package, postmarked with a number of multicolored, interesting-looking stamps, were 3,000 beautiful feet of microfilm. It cost us $25. I felt as if I had just scooped up a double handful of golden doubloons from a sunken galleon. The film, as I was to appreciate later, was worth far more.

My enthusiasm was quickly tempered that night, however, when Dr. Kelso and I projected the film onto a screen. Oh, I was still certain it contained all the vital facts and clues we had been searching for, but it might as well have been sent to us in code form. The microfilmed documents were all written in archaic Spanish.

Now I have a workable, speaking, listening, reading knowledge of Spanish, and Doc is fluent in the language, but after looking at those words traced in fine script, we stared blankly at each other in total dismay. Now we, too, felt like crying.

But as the days went by, the initial shock wore off and Doc and I went to work. It was an agonizingly slow process. We projected each document onto the screen and tried to fit modern Spanish words that looked applicable beneath the archaic ones. These we would, in turn, translate into English. We'd get as much in a sentence or a paragraph as we could, leaving blank the spaces we weren't sure of. Often we could fill out enough of a line to make an educated guess at what was missing.

An added obstacle, we soon learned, was that the eighteenth-century scribes who recorded these pages of history often wrote words as they sounded phonetically, and not as they should have been spelled. Illiteracy was so widespread in those days they probably thought no one would ever notice the difference. We sure did. Also, they used a lot of cryptic abbreviations.

As the winter months passed, Doc and I worked at the difficult documents every chance we got. Often, I'd call him at his office during the day and ask him what he thought this or that word could mean. If he was working on it at night, he'd call me when he got stuck.

I made a trip to St. Augustine to consult with Louis Arana of the National Park Service there—an acknowledged expert in archaic Spanish. He was helpful, but he couldn't spare the time really to delve into the voluminous reports we had. It was grueling, unglamorous work, but slowly, surely, the puzzle pieces began falling into place. The undecipherable words became fewer and fewer as we plodded on, and the more we learned, the more encouraged we became.

We worked hard on those microfilmed documents for about a year (and, in fact, we still go over them occasionally), but our industrious efforts were worth it. We pieced together the history of an era in Spanish colonization. We learned the background of late seventeenth-century and early eighteenth-century plate fleets: where they sailed, what manifests they carried, who their captains were and how many men were aboard. We read in awe of the magnificent hoards of treasure many of them carried.

With keen interest we traced the specific history of the 1715 fleet; of its multimillion-dollar cargo of gold, silver and jewelry. We followed the path of the ships from Havana up the east coast of Florida as if we were sailing with them. And when we read of the disaster that befell them as a vicious hurricane battered the ships to splinters on treacherous reefs, I could almost feel and hear the fierce wind howling and taste the salt spray on my lips.

But what really captured our interest were the explicit details of the recovery operations following the sinkings. Wreck locations were pinpointed—all in the Sebastian–Fort Pierce area—and a campsite, or base of operations for the salvagers, was described at length. Our hearts skipped a beat as we read that less than half of the fleet's $14 million worth of treasure was recovered.

4 Disaster
on the High Seas

In 1715, Philip V, grandson of Louis XIV, was King of Spain. Two hundred and twenty-three years earlier, Christopher Columbus had landed on the tiny island of San Salvador, laying open the unsuspecting New World for Spanish conquest by the middle of the sixteenth century. Colonies ran thousands of miles down the coasts from Veracruz, Mexico, to Concepción, Chile.

The plundering of vast riches—gold, platinum and silver, pearls, emeralds and other jewels—began immediately. Tens of millions of dollars worth were exported from Mexico, Panama, Colombia, Cuba, Puerto Rico, Hispaniola, Santo Domingo and the Lesser Antilles. Fabulous hoards poured out of Peru from the Inca King's ransom. Still, the insatiably greedy, corrupt administrations of the Spanish government demanded more.

Great treasure fleets brought $10 million annually to the Mother Country, then $20 million, then $30 million, until the stored wealth of the New World was completely exhausted. Then, natives of entire Indian empires were cruelly forced into slave labor to mine the ore. When existing sites petered out, new ones were sought. Indians were tortured and beaten to death for not revealing hidden locations. Others, by the thousands, died from the relentless, inhuman treatment at the hands of merciless slave drivers.

Despite the deaths, the flow of gold and silver continued unabated as the land was raped and its natural riches looted. Ore was processed and sent to New World royal mints at Mexico City, Santa Fe de Bogotá, Lima and Potosí. The earliest silver and copper coins of America, in fact, were struck at Mexico City, where the first mint was established in the spring of 1536.

With Philip V on the throne, $30 to $40 million was harvested annually and sent to Spain. From the beginning of the sixteenth century until well into the nineteenth, the total exportation of precious metals and jewels reached high into the billions, and though historians disagree widely on what the precise figures were, it was probably somewhere between $8 and $12 billion.

How much more was en route and got high-jacked on the open seas by flourishing bands of pirates, or how much sank during the fierce tropical storms, are figures that can only be speculated upon. Some authors have said as much as one-eighth of all gold and silver shipped during this period now lies on or under the ocean floor. It is likely that a higher percentage made its way into the hands of cutthroat buccaneers who roamed the Caribbean freely for decades, and flashed their spoils openly at Port Royal, near Kingston, in Jamaica—home base for Henry Morgan and hundreds of others.

Many of them were initially sent to the New World by enemies of Spain to prey upon the legendary treasure fleets. The privateers, in fact, were commissioned to act as men-of-war and to seize and plunder Spanish ships, which was tantamount to having a license to steal and kill.

Spain countered the unabashed larceny on the high seas by building larger, stronger armadas. The Bureau of Trade and the Council of the Indies laid down strict rules for fleet admirals to follow. Treasure-bearing cargo ships were to cross the Atlantic in convoys of six to 10, each escorted by heavier galleons and lighter, utility vessels, which served as scouts for the fleets.

By the middle of the sixteenth century, after much internal wrangling by the corrupt Spanish bureaucracies, it was decided to send annually two armadas to the Indies. They were the New Spain, or Nueva España, and the Tierra Firme fleets, and on the western run they carried rich, if perishable, cargoes of expensive clothing and material, fine cheeses, rare wines, glass and ironware and the all-important mining equipment. The fleets consisted of merchant vessels escorted by heavily armed warships to discourage attacks of belligerents and pirates.

The New Spain armada sailed for Veracruz, via Puerto Rico, Hispaniola and Cuba. Cartagena, in present-day Colombia, was the destination of the Tierra Firme ships, by way of Venezuela. They later sailed on to the Isthmus of Panama. For the return journey across the Atlantic, the New Spain armada carried gold and silver from Mexico and Honduras, as well as silks, spices and china from the Orient, brought by Manila galleons to Acapulco and then by mule across the mountains to Veracruz. Meanwhile, the Tierra Firme stocked valuable cargo arriving from practically every settlement on the western coast of South America, including silver from Colombia and Peru. South Pacific goods were off-loaded at Panama and also carried across land by muleback.

From Cartagena, the fleet sailed northward, up the Yucatan Channel, to rejoin the New Spain armada in Havana—the "Key to the New World." Then, after taking on food, water and supplies at Spain's largest port in the Americas, the combined armadas crossed the tricky Florida Straits and hugged the southeastern coastline, following the New Bahamas Channel. Between St. Augustine and Cape Hatteras they swung eastward and rode the prevailing westerlies home. An earlier, alternate route—up the Old Bahamas Channel north of Cuba, and then northeast by the Mayaguana, Caicos, Mouchoir or Silver Banks passages—was largely abandoned when increasing numbers of ships sank on hazardous shoals.

But the route past Florida was little better, and the fleets were ever at the mercy of the driving winds of northeasters and hurricanes. For this reason, sailings were scheduled as early as possible—usually in June, ahead of the peak storm season.

Leading each armada was a large fighting galleon, called the *capitana*. It was heavily armed and carried no bulky cargo, only treasure. A second, sturdy, armed galleon, designated the *almiranta*, brought up the rear of the fleet. These ships were about 150 to 175 feet long, and their weight varied from 700 to 2,000 tons. Decks were lined with tiers of iron cannon.

The commanding officer of the entire armada, a general, was aboard each *capitana*, and had overall responsibility for seeing that all ships made the round trip from Spain safely. Journeys lasted several months. An admiral sailed on the *almiranta*, and if pirates attacked, he assumed command of the armada.

A variety of ships were escorted by the fighting galleons. The nao, of virtually the same construction and class as the galleon, with a cargo capacity of several hundred tons, was used as a general freighter or transport. These were the merchant vessels. *Urcas* were also employed as freighters, and closely resembled the naos, although their cargo capacity was a little less. Swift, light *galleoncetes* were used as scouts. Awesome, gun-carrying *navíos* were heavy warships that often escorted treasure fleets. These floating forts averaged about 1,500 tons and had more than 100 guns, mounted on several decks. All-purpose pataches accompanied most armadas and often carried rich consignments of gold and silver. Occasionally, sleek pirogues would serve as escorts. These swift, slim ships were specially designed to combat pirates.

Enterprising statisticians have calculated that if all the ships that carried New World riches to Spain were divided into the total amount that reached the Continent—a figure well into the billions, even by conservative estimate—it would work out, on paper at least, that each ship carried more than half a million dollars worth of cargo. Of course, in reality, this rule of thumb could not be accurately applied. Treasure fleets guarded their manifests and their movements as closely as possible and cargoes varied in value, depending upon a number of factors, from a few thousand dollars (or pesos) to $20 million or more.

Philip V and his predecessors claimed a large percentage, usually 20 percent, of all incoming treasure as taxes. It was called, appropriately, the Royal Fifth. To avert this heavy slice from their profits, merchants bribed shipping officials to undervalue the cargoes. Bribes were costly, too, but still not as much as was the "official" tax bite. Thus, it was rather common for a ship carrying, say, $10 million worth of registered treasure, to have perhaps $12 or $15 million or even more in actual value. Occasionally, ships carried cargoes listed at less than half their real worth. Such crookedness was so commonplace, in fact, it was generally accepted as a way of life with the Spaniards.

The series of incidents that led to the sinking of the 1715 Plate Fleet began 13 years before, when the War of Spanish Succession began, in 1702: about the same time period, ironically, that an alleged $50 million was lost by an armada sunk off Vigo Bay. For nearly a dozen bloody years the war raged, first in Italy, Flanders and the Americas, but finally on Spanish soil. It embroiled half the powers of Europe before peace was signed at Utrecht in 1713. The fighting delayed the sailing of the silver fleets for two years.

Such was the setting when the "Combined Armada of 1715" gathered in Havana, carrying an unusually heavy load of treasure for the long return trip to an embattled Spain.

The New Spain Armada, under the command of General Don Juan Esteban de Ubilla, had arrived in Veracruz in December, 1713, after making the long Atlantic crossing from Seville. The voyage from Spain to the New World took several months—for the ships didn't have the added natural advantage of a three-knot Gulf Stream current which they had pushing them on their return to the Mother Country.

The Tierra Firme Armada, commanded by General Don Antonio de Echeverz y Zubiza, sailed for Cartagena. Each fleet had cargoes of farming implements, pipes, buttons, needles, fabrics, grain, arms, ammunition, horses, cattle, clothing, glass, paper, cutlery, textiles, watches, clocks, quicksilver, shoes, books, pictures, wines, fruits—whatever was needed to maintain a colony where the native Indians were still somewhat hostile.

In Veracruz, General Ubilla grew progressively impatient, then angry. Finally, he was steaming. His ships had been in port for months and still they were not ready for the return home. After arriving, the vessels were careened and natives began the slow, grimy job of scorching the persistent teredo worms, which, if left unattended, would literally eat a ship from under its captain. The vessels' bottoms were first burned and scraped. Then pitch sulfur and cowhair were evenly applied and the whole thing was covered with wood sheathing. Sails were repaired and riggings and anchor ropes were renewed with hemp from Manila. Fresh coats of paint were liberally applied.

In those days, the disease-ridden Indian stevedores, forced into slave labor, only went through the motions of working. Every time the general looked, they were having a siesta, or were eating lunch. They seemed to move in perpetual slow motion. There were sacks of coins and heavy bars of silver from the mines and mints of Mexico to be loaded, but no one was in a hurry. It was always *"mañana,* tomorrow, *amigo.* There is always tomorrow."

When Ubilla's ulcers would take no more, he went to the Viceroy of Mexico and suggested executing a few Indians in a sacrificial demonstration to shake the others up. He was told, politely, that it wouldn't work, simply because it had been tried before with no appreciable effect. Such delays had gotten progressively worse through the years and were now accepted matter-of-factly.

In Cartagena, De Echeverz was faring little better. Consignments of gold, silver and precious stones were slow in arriving from the rich reservoirs of Potosí, Lima, and other points on the western side of South America. Part of Ubilla's cargo was also late coming, for it had a long way to go for the rendezvous—more than halfway around the world. K'ang Hsi Chinese porcelain came by traders' caravan and Chinese junk to a Philippine bazaar, then, on the annual cruise of the Manila galleons, across the mighty Pacific to Acapulco. Here, at a colorful and impressive fair, merchants dickered for the china, spices, rich silks and brocades, tea, gold, carved wood, ivory, jade and other art objects, pearls, cochineal, indigo, cocoa, tobacco and hides. The cases of porcelain destined for Seville merchants then crossed Mexico by muleback to arrive at Veracruz. That such delicate porcelain could survive that long, arduous journey attests to the skilled work of those who packed it so securely in cartons sealed with a special, protective mud.

At last, after Ubilla's impatience had reached the point of desperation, for it was now well into the spring of 1715, the fleet was ready to sail for Havana. He had been docked in Veracruz for well over a year. He arrived in Havana some time later and was met by De Echeverz and his ships. Even when Ubilla had been finally ready to sail for Havana, it was not merely a short hop across the Yucatán Channel, as one might imagine today. Instead, he sailed to what is now Corpus Christi, and Houston, Texas, then stayed close to the present southeastern United States coastline to Appalachicola and down to Tampa, Florida, and *then* crossed over to Havana. Such a roundabout route was followed to ease navigation problems by sticking within sight of known land masses. But, again, there was a penalty time-wise, for the duration of the journey was much longer, and now every day was beginning to count.

In Havana, there was more waiting to be done. Merchants there had bought cargo space on this "freight-train of the seas," and their wares had to be loaded. The New World Spaniards stopped at no extreme in trying to disguise their riches to evade King Philip's 20-percent cut. Some had their silver molded into plates and consigned to chapels in their provinces in Spain. The fact that they owned the chapels would likely never be uncovered; thus they would retain the full value of their properties. Full value, that is, excepting the slice they must pay to grease the palms of those in the know.

As if the dickering with such dealers and the loading of their cargo wasn't taking enough time, Ubilla and De Echeverz had to play diplomat for Casa Torres, the Governor of Havana. He was 90 years old, and he loved to throw parties when the plate fleets were in port. It was always a festive occasion.

The weeks slipped by—into June, and then July and then late July. Then came another delay. Captain Don Antonio Daré was desperate. His ship was laden with a cargo worth far more than the $50,000 listed in the official manifest. His problem was that he had gone to General Ubilla requesting that his ship, *El Grifón*, be allowed to accompany the Plate Fleet on its voyage back to Spain. He had good basic reasons for this request. With an armed armada, his ship and all its stored riches were reasonably safe from anything but the natural elements. Without the protection of a convoy, he knew *El Grifón* was open prey for the pirates of Jamaica. If he sailed alone, he might as well run a flag up the main mast advertising treasure aboard. The ruthless cutthroats at Port Royal had spies watching every move his ship and others in the fleet made. They would know the exact moment of his departure, and undoubtedly would ambush him before *El Grifón* could get across the Florida Straits.

But Ubilla had enough on his mind without having to bother with a maverick French vessel tagging along. He wouldn't budge. Daré then went to the highest Spanish officials in Havana whom he could bribe his way in to see. He had a valid argument. His ship was carrying cargo for merchants who would raise hell with the administration if he were highjacked on the seas simply because the fleet's commander wouldn't accept him. Visualizing the inevitable reprimands that would follow, should *El Grifón* not get through, the officials applied sufficient pressure on Ubilla, forcing him to accept Captain Daré, his ship, crew and cargo. The combined fleet was now at full strength, consisting of 11 vessels.

The delays had been costly. Expenses mounted. Repairs had to be made, salaries paid, crews fed. Even more important, the good weather of the spring and early summer was now past.

Finally, on Wednesday morning, July 24—a full 20 months after the ships had arrived from Spain—the combined armada was ready to set sail. They had waited long past the normal time to begin the return voyage, but still it was early in the season for hurricanes. Most of the tropical disturbances didn't arise until August or September, or, as a popular West Indies jingle goes: "June, too soon; July, stand by; August, come they must; September, remember; October, all over."

The Havana sun was hot on the backs of laborers as they hauled the last few loads of supplies aboard. Seamen kissed their girls, promising to see them next year. Ships' officers checked their navigational charts and what scanty weather reports were available at that time.

In today's world of reconnaissance aircraft, radar screens and orbiting meteorological satellites, a tropical storm is spotted almost the instant it is born, no matter how remote the spawning grounds. Its movements are then followed closely for the duration of its northerly run. Had such facilities been available to the Spanish 250 years ago, the 1715 fleet would have calculated the probable path of the hurricane that was already stirring up the sweltering seas to the southeast, and the voyage surely would have been delayed until the storm passed, with the ships riding it out in the relatively sheltered safety of the huge harbor of Havana.

But at that time there was no way for anyone to foresee trouble. The young storm was too far away to cause even a ripple in the Cuban area. The sun was bright, the skies clear and the seas calm. The rough weather was still several hundred miles down in the tropics. But it was coming. . . .

The New Spain Armada, under Ubilla, and the Tierra Firme Armada, commanded by De Echeverz, together made a handsome fleet of 11 ships as they hoisted great iron anchors, and sailed past the fortress El Morro's walls, out of the harbor and onto the open sea, heeling to the wind in the Gulf Stream's steady pull.

There was a rare beauty about these classic galleons. They made an impressive sight with their deep, square sails unfurled from the heavy yards on foremasts and mainmasts. Lateen sails and square topsails caught the breezes from their mizzen masts. The long, raised quarterdeck ran from the mainmast toward the stern, where a still higher level, the poop deck, was located. The sides of the fighting galleons were pierced for batteries of large guns, with smaller ones mounted above on the upper decks.

They were more eye-catching, however, than practical. The Spanish ships were much less manageable and more difficult to maneuver than the sleeker English models. At best, they were heavy, slow, unwieldy vessels that could make an average of only seven knots or so per hour on the ocean. But when a fleet sailed, it was, nevertheless, a colorful show.

Onward they went, with some 2,000 men aboard, across the Florida Straits. Soon, they were astride the Florida Keys, which stretch out into the blue-green-aqua waters like so many scattered fingers.

By Monday, the 29th of July, the first ominous warnings of trouble ahead were noted, but even then only to the more experienced sailors, who had ridden out hundreds of howlers in a lifetime on the seas. They looked with apprehension at the slight haze that was beginning to pale the still-bright sunshine. The ships were rolling in the long swells of a comparatively smooth sea, but telltale "weather bones and joints were aching." There was something in the wind.

Moving parallel to the fleet, several hundred miles to the east and a little north, a great hurricane, belting out fierce winds of more than 100 miles an hour, was charting directions of its own that would soon run collision course into the Spanish galleons. Nurturing strength from the open waters, the storm had reached full fury. Then, in a characteristic, unpredictable move, it suddenly changed direction and headed due west.

Monday night the wind was easterly as usual, but less than half its normal strength of 15 to 18 knots. As dawn breaks Tuesday, there is an increasingly uneasy feeling aboard the ships. The weather is unusually oppressive and sultry, even for late July. The winds are fickle. Occasionally there are periods of dead calm. Fine wisps of cirrus clouds appear to the east. By noon Tuesday, even the youngest apprentice seaman is aware of the oncoming danger. Had there been modern barometers aboard the vessels, the seamen might have panicked at the rapidly plunging pressure. Slowly, from the northeast, the wind picks up and is steady and gusty, from about 10 to 20 knots. The great ships begin rolling on the heave of enlarging swells.

Heavy altostratus clouds blot out the sun, and by midafternoon, it is dark and the large ships' lanterns are lighted and put in place. Seamen begin battening the hatches for the inevitable blow they know is coming. The roar of drumming raindrops is heard from far off across the seas. It closes in fast, drenching the foremast hands as they scramble through their storm preparations. The rain passes, but the wind, now coming from the north-northeast, begins gusting to 30 knots and higher, kicking the seas to frightening heights. A young galley steward, on his first crossing, eyes the rampaging surf with stark fear. More experienced hands have seen the seas much wilder, but they know the worst is yet to come and they try to busy themselves and not think about it.

It is now too late to seek shelter in a cove or inland harbor. The fleet is still somewhere south of Cape Canaveral, and Generals Ubilla and de Echeverz know that until they pass the Cape the coastline is heavily fortified with natural ship-wrecking hazards—the camouflaged shoals and the threatening reefs. They must now meet the storm head on—on its own terms and at a location favoring the winds and rains.

By 10 P.M. another pounding squall hits, sending stinging, wind-whipped rain pelting into the grim faces of crewmen standing watch. This time the rain is hard and lasts longer. Even though it eventually slacks off, a persistent drizzle sets in, soaking sailors to the bone. The squalls are more frequent now, hitting every few minutes, and the wind seems to grow more gusty with each passing rain squall. But it is difficult to distinguish which is rain and which is salt spray, whipped into lashing sheets by an angrily mounting sea.

There is a steady howling, which increases over the next hour into a head-raking, earsplitting scream. Frantically shouted orders are lost in the deafening roar. There are no swells now, only mad, frothing, towering waves. One after another they clap relentlessly across the bows of the ships—which suddenly seem like toy vessels being playfully tossed about by some irate giant.

Sometime past midnight the wind reaches hurricane force—75 miles per hour; but even yet, the full battering impact of the storm has not hit. Mountainous waves—40 to 50 feet high—descend upon the helpless galleons, lifting them up and then smashing them down into valley-like troughs separating the giant combers. Rain is coming down in a near-horizontal line.

By 2 A.M. the full wrath of the hurricane is unleashed, and winds of 100 miles per hour crack masts and tear loose secured sails and rip them into ribbons. Surging waves continue their battering, and, without prejudice, sweep seamen off the slippery decks into the heaving, tormented ocean. For them there is no hope. They are lost forever in a swirling black chasm. Each captain tries desperately to maneuver his ship, but there is little that can be done. Man's ingenuity is no match for nature's overpowering might.

Slowly, the galleons are driven shoreward. The men, numbed with fear, can feel what is happening. They know there is no hope now, and it's only a matter of time until the ships' great timbers smash onto the reefs and shoals. They cross themselves and pray. There is no letup from the mountainous sea, and one by one, the once-proud ships are dashed onto the reefs. Thunderous crashes roll out as the huge hulls are ripped open, then shattered into splinters. Men are violently hurled into the boiling caldron. Some are swallowed immediately, never to be seen again. Others paddle furiously trying to stay above water. Even the strongest swimmers are helpless. Heavy beams, sent flying as the ships break up, add to the hazard, braining the luckless. Desperately, the men claw for a piece of wood, a crate—anything to hang onto.

General Ubilla's *capitana* is gutted by a huge reef and sinks in about thirty feet of water. The general and 225 of his men are either smashed upon the rocks or are drowned. The *Nuestra Señora del Carmen y San Antonio,* General de Echeverz' *capitana,* hopelessly demolished by the storm, sinks directly off a point of land. Despite the nearness of the beach, the general and 113 others perish.

De Echeverz' *urca* and his nao San Miguel vanish at sea, with no survivors to tell of their last minutes. The *Nuestra Señora del Rosario y San Francisco Xavier*, the *almiranta* of De Echeverz' fleet, disintegrates completely after being crushed under tons of water. Two of Ubilla's pataches, the *Nuestra Señora de las Nieves y las Ánimas* and the *Santa Cristo del Valle y Nuestra Señora de la Concepción*, are shattered by 50-foot waves, killing three dozen or more seamen. Miraculously, a large segment of deck breaks loose from one of the pataches, and 100 or more men hang onto it for a wildly buffeting ride that carries them ashore.

The second *almiranta*, Ubilla's, is wrecked in shallow waters, but raging breakers batter the hull to splinters, and thrash 123 men to death before they can swim or wade to shore. Ubilla's *urca* (or hooker) *Nuestra Señora de la Regla* runs aground at the mouth of a river with 35 crewmen, and the Dutch nao is blown in so close it also becomes grounded, and is helplessly torn apart, although the crew members get out in time to reach land.

Several hundred yards out at sea, Captain Don Antonio Daré masterfully heads his French ship *El Grifón* into the teeth of the wind and somehow manages to stay clear of the reefs. His is the only ship to survive the catastrophe, and he saves it, ironically, by disobeying fleet orders and sailing one-half point farther northeast.

In all, 10 ships, more than 1,000 men and over $14,000,000 in registered treasure are lost. It is one of the greatest sea disasters of all time.

As the winds slam the sea hard onto the beaches, the waters bite deeply into the high sand dunes, eroding acres of beachfront. Straggling, dazed survivors, spitting out spume that has filled their lungs, drag themselves weakly across the sands, and claw their way up the dunes. They are more dead than alive. In the blackness there are no shore lights to guide them, no shelters to ride out the storm, no one to help them.

By dawn the winds subside to gale force, and the sea retreats. The beach looks like a battlefield strewn with bodies and littered with ships' timbers. Slowly, life stirs. Weakened, half-drowned, bloodied seamen, bewildered and beaten by the brute force of nature, stagger to their feet.

Doc Kelso was rummaging through the files of the Florida Historical Society in St. Augustine one day in 1959 when he stumbled onto some information pertaining to the 1715 fleet's disaster. It was of first-rank importance. With the help of librarian Doris Wilds, Doc found some microfilm of eyewitness accounts by survivors of the hurricane that had been taken down at St. Augustine just a few days after the sinkings. Some of the sworn statements were by sailors who had scrambled up the coast for nearly 150 miles to recount the disaster and plead for food, weapons and clothing for those who remained on the beaches. Other microfilm contained confessions to priests by condemned sailors who had been caught stealing gold and silver from the sunken wrecks. We paid the Historical Society $100 for the loan of that film, and then set to work translating it from the original Spanish.

According to the best information we can assemble, there were hundreds of survivors, perhaps a thousand or more, who staggered to the beaches during the predawn hours on the morning of July 31, 1715. Many men died within a few hours from exhaustion, exposure, heart attacks and a number of other causes. Food, drinking water and other provisions went down with the gold and silver. Virtually nothing was saved.

The survivors had little time to rest. As the storm passed inland across the state, the scorching Florida sun beat unmercifully down on naked and near-naked bodies. The Spaniards, without proper leadership, were completely disorganized and bewildered by their cruel fate. They didn't venture inland for fear of Indian attacks. Most of them huddled in groups on the dunes overlooking the beach. For some, however, the sequence of events presented a golden opportunity to get rich quick. Many of these renegades stuffed their pockets with coins and jewels and deserted into the thick underbrush.

A small party of survivors was selected to take the one or two long boats that had been beached in reasonably good shape, and head north to St. Augustine to bring help. The others were to stick together on the beach for mutual protection, and were also to safeguard the sunken treasure as best they could.

It took several days for the hardy band to reach St. Augustine. They traveled part of the way by boat and walked a good portion of the distance, arriving late in the first week of August. News of the disaster spread rapidly through the Spanish stronghold in Florida, and a board was quickly set up by the governor to take down testimony. Havana and Seville would want some answers—and soon. For days the men recounted their horrifying story. Some broke down and wept; others were angry; but most were in a hurry—to get help for those they had left back at Sebastian.

"From my heart I tell you, the fatality was the biggest in this century you have ever seen," one sailor related. "Not a single ship of the fleet was left afloat," he added, not knowing that Don Antonio Daré had skillfully guided his ship, *El Grifón*, to safety. This wasn't known, in fact, until he reached Havana, several days after the storm.

"The men are all lost without food and clothing," another survivor said. "I beg you to send us help with whatever you can, or we will all die. We need clothing, 20 guns with bullets and powder, and all you can possibly send. Also half a dozen axes, and other half dozens of shovels and some tools to help dig out the sand under which the silver is." He further explained the necessity to crack open the part of the ship's hull where Philip's treasure had been stored, in the hold.

One survivor was more graphic in describing the dire need of the sailors, stranded to the south: "Please, we need supplies. The men are eating horses, dogs, cats, grapes from the palms and other types of animals." He added that even these sources of sustenance were quickly being depleted, and if help weren't soon forthcoming, all the men would die—from thirst, from hunger, from exposure or from the Indians.

Rescue parties were quickly assembled and boats full of supplies dispatched to the area. Meanwhile, a detachment of soldiers was sent to the watchtower at the Matanzas Inlet, a short distance south of St. Augustine, to be on the lookout for the deserters. They were making their way northward to the city on foot, and hoped to sneak in undetected, and then capitalize on their ill-gotten spoils.

But to reach St. Augustine, they would have to cross the wide-mouthed inlet at Matanzas. Sure enough, over the next week or so, they came, and one by one they were captured, their pockets so filled with coins they could barely swim across the channel. Each deserter was sentenced to execution, and many of them added to the overall picture of the fleet's disaster in final confessions to their priests.

Letters containing the eyewitness accounts were forwarded to the King, and a request was sent to Havana to have the survivors picked up. Seven rescue ships arrived at Sebastian in September, ending six weeks of nightmarish existence for those who lived to tell the tale.

5 Spanish
Campsite

When word reached Havana of the disaster, the city's sergeant major, Don Juan del Hoyo Solórzano, an important man in the New World, was placed in charge of salvage operations. In March, 1716, he sailed across the Straits of Florida with several sloops (historians vary on the exact number), retracing the fleet's route. He was led to the wreck sites by survivors, and set up a base camp about two and a half miles south of the Sebastian Inlet, opposite one of the sunken galleons.

The recovery of treasure, even from ships that had only recently been sunk and had not yet deteriorated, was, nevertheless, a slow, painstaking process. The severity of the hurricane had not just wrecked the ships. It had splintered them, scattering cargoes over acres of ocean floor. So it was not a simple matter of diving into a ship's hold and tying lines around locked chests. It was first a matter of locating the treasure—and then bringing it up. Already, in the few months that had elapsed since the storm, a light coating of sand had been swept over bits and pieces of the wreckage. There would be only a limited number of days through the summer when the water would be clear.

Good visibility was vital to Hoyo Solórzano, for his native Indian divers had no face masks, no flippers or air tanks, not even a spear gun to frighten sharks and moray eels. They dived naked, carrying with them a heavy stone so they could sink quickly to the bottom. There, they would release the stone and search for valuables until their breath gave out and they had to surface. The best could stay down for only three or four minutes at a time, although some were taught to dive with a weighted

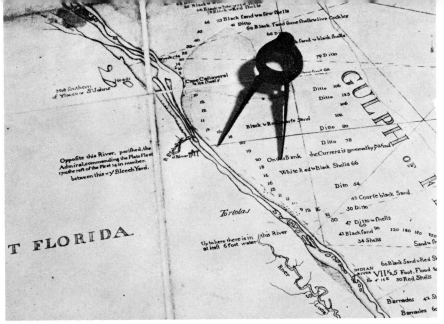

ABOVE: This 1774 chart of east Florida by Bernard Romans, found by Dr. Kelso in the Library of Congress, yielded valuable facts about the Spanish treasure ships wrecked in the waters near the author's home. Beside the Sebastian River and "el Palmar," it reads: "Opposite this River, perished, the Admiral, commanding the Plate Fleet 1715. . . ." The eighteenth-century dividers, recovered from one of those same ships by Kip Wagner's team, still work. BELOW: An *almiranta*, or Spanish admiral's flagship of the period of the 1715 fleet. Measuring 155 feet in length, and with mainmast 150 feet tall, its poop rose 27 feet above the sea. Such fighting ships, armed with from 50 to 60 guns, convoyed the merchant galleons but carried little cargo themselves other than treasure.

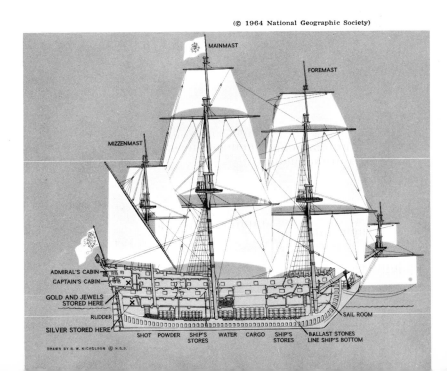

Spanish doubloons, golden ingots and graceful Chinese porcelain recovered by the author and his associates from the treasure fleet wrecked in 1715 in the waters seen in the background.

bucket, which they carried down inverted so it could hold trapped air. Then, when their initial air was used, they'd duck under the bucket for a fresh supply. This allowed them to stay down longer, but it was a dangerous way to do it, particularly in deeper waters. That more than a third of the 280 Indian divers drowned while on the bottom didn't matter a particle to the Spanish. The treasure did matter.

When the Indians did sight something to be recovered, they took down lines and, in teams, secured the object for crewmen in the sloops to haul to the surface. Hoyo Solórzano set up a small fort at the campsite, and posted armed sentries around it as the recovered treasure began to mount. The Spanish kept elaborate daily records, and each item was meticulously listed on large parchment sheets.

But Spanish officials were not the only ones to receive the news of the fleet's sinking. Just below Cuba, at Port Royal on the Island of Jamaica, the story spread with speed and increasing embellishment upon each recounting. And it fell upon eager ears, for here, in the heyday of the Spanish Main, was the stronghold of such legendary characters as Captain Edward Teach—the notorious Blackbeard. Piracy in these days embodied the romance of the oceans. In the lore of the sea the buccaneer is far and away the most picturesque figure, and at Port Royal and throughout the Caribbean, he was king.

As recovery operations continued, the Spanish had their hands full battling off recurring attacks from pirates. They chased away small sloops "fishing" over one wreck site, only to have other invaders attack campsites. It was a constant battle. It seemed, in fact, as though every seamy character within a thousand-mile range had been attracted, like sharks to blood, by the strong scent of treasure. Despite the Spanish efforts, thousands of pesos, possibly hundreds of thousands, were sacked from the open wrecks. Even the Indian divers and workers smuggled coins out—at the risk of their lives. This undoubtedly accounts for a number of cobs and other artifacts that have turned up in Indian burial mounds inland from the ocean.

English governors in the Americas, while officially going through the motions of suppressing claim-jumping attacks by their countrymen, unofficially endorsed such acts, and took great delight in the Spaniards' predicament. Governor Spotswood at Williamsburg, Virginia, in fact, encouraged a daring English privateer to "see what was about."

The man Governor Spotswood chose was Captain Henry Jennings. He was, at the time, a British privateer in reasonably good standing. He com-

3

manded a ship commissioned by Lord Hamilton for the suppression of piracies, but Jennings had other ideas. He sailed for Florida with two brigantines and three luggers. By Spanish accounts he raided their main base camp in July, 1716, with 300 well-armed men (other accounts vary from 300 to 600), running off the guards. Historians are in general agreement that Jennings made off with about 350,000 pesos.

The story of his raid is perhaps best told in *A General History of the Robberies and Murders of the Most Notorious Pyrates*, which was published in 1724. It reads:

"Several vessels from the Havana were at work, with diving engines [diving bells], to fish up the silver that was on board the galleons.

"The Spaniards had recovered some millions of pieces of eight and had carried it all to the Havana, but they had at present about 350,000 pieces of eight in silver, then upon the spot, and were daily taking up more. In the meantime, two ships and three sloops, fitted out from Jamaica, Barbadoes, etc., under Captain Henry Jennings, found the Spaniards there, upon the wreck. The money before spoken of was left on shore, in a storehouse under the government of two commissaries and a guard of about 60 soldiers.

"The rovers came directly upon the place, bringing their little fleet to an anchor, and landing 300 men, they attacked the guard who immediately ran away; and thus they seized the treasure which they carried off, making the best of their way to Jamaica."

Jennings had been shrewd and fiendishly clever in his attack. He had lain offshore, watching the movements of the salvagers and guards through a powerful eyeglass. When the Indians had carefully stacked their pesos in neat piles, he made his move and grabbed the treasure as if it had been a payroll shipment waiting to be picked up.

Once back in Port Royal, however, Jennings couldn't openly gloat—on two counts. First, his pillaging of the campsite was conducted at a time of supposed peace between England and Spain, even if the peace existed only on paper (the Treaty of Utrecht, signed three years before). Second, although Jennings had made a major coup of 350,000 silver pieces, he had missed a cache 10 times that size by only a few weeks. Hoyo Solórzano had managed to load a ship with nearly four million pesos and send it back to Havana. It was a remarkable accomplishment in those pirate-infested waters. Still, the recovery of between a fourth and a third of the registered treasure could not keep a host of merchants in Seville and other cities from going bankrupt.

After his arrogantly bold attack on the main campsite, Jennings could no longer hide behind the semirespectable cloak of "privateer." He was now, pure and simple, a pirate. His taste for freebooting had become so whetted, in fact, that he later sailed around the tip of Florida into the Gulf of Mexico and stripped a Spanish brigantine of more than $100,000 in gold.

It is an interesting footnote to add that Captain Henry Jennings managed to escape the grisly fate of so many other corsairs who were hung, beheaded or otherwise executed. Three years after his raid he turned up at Nassau when the King's pardon was offered there to all pirates willing to surrender and quit the cutthroat business. Jennings returned to Bermuda, where he settled down to a life of respectability with his fellow countrymen, and undoubtedly lived well, drawing on a tall stack of Spanish pieces of eight.

To discourage any future attacks upon their sites, the Spanish sent reinforcements to Florida and regained control of the salvage operations, though pirates continued to harass them. This area became their unofficial "fishing grounds." That is, they'd hover over the area and steal from the sunken galleons whenever there were no ships around to sack. It was their rendezvous point for years.

Although Hoyo Solórzano recovered most of the treasure that was easily accessible in the immediate months following the disaster, work continued through 1717. The following year Manuel Miralles, a "diving contractor," who had struck a deal with the Spanish government for a percentage of what he could bring up, arrived. His appearance upon the scene was a complete surprise to eight assorted vessels, who were caught "fishing" over a wreck site. Miralles probably recovered more that day—nearly 200,000 pesos along with 300 prisoners, mostly English—than he made from salvage work in the next few months.

Finally, in 1719, almost four years after the galleons had gone down, recovery work was halted. The best "educated guess," based on our research, indicates that treasure worth at somewhere around $6 million was salvaged—less than half of the estimated registered $14 million worth that was lost.

Inspired by the hopeful clues Doc and I had ferreted out of the microfilm, I decided to search the beaches as I had never done before. We figured, logically, that if we could ever find the main Spanish campsite, set up by Hoyo Solórzano, we'd be in business. Surely, it must be somewhere close by, a short distance south of the Sebastian Inlet. But where? I had covered that stretch of beach a hundred times or more in the past without a trace of a camp, fort or anything else. But now I was armed with a new weapon, and a damn valuable one at that—knowledge. From our studies I had learned to look for mounds or depressions in the landscape that might appear unnatural and thus could possibly have been man-made.

One of the first things I did was spend $15 for a war surplus military mine detector. By today's standards it was an antique, but I really thought I was something, parading up and down the oceanfront, pushing the round metal lid, with earphones strapped across my head. When the detector sensed metal under the sands it made a high-pitched whine. The first time it sang out as I walked along, I dug into the loose sand like a dog for a long-lost bone. Disappointingly, I uncovered the rear springs of a Model T Ford. I looked around quickly to see if anyone was watching. There was no one, thank goodness, otherwise I'm sure I would have shriveled in embarrassment. You old fool, I couldn't help but think.

But I wasn't one to give up easily, and I continued my stroll down the beach, pushing the odd-looking, saucer-shaped instrument. Ping . . . the earphones vibrated again. I dug once more, this time with a little less gusto. My reward: a rusty bedspring. In the next hour or two I managed to turn up dozens of beer cans, bottle caps, more bedsprings and the corroded remains of a coffee grinder, 1920 vintage. "Some treasure," I said aloud. I could do better than this without the detector. My back was tired and my fingers aching when I got home that night, but worst of all was the hurt deeper inside.

I had to reconcile myself once again to the fact that this treasure business is a soul-testing operation. One doesn't stumble onto a heap of gold on the first try—even if he has read every cussed document on two sides of the Atlantic telling him where it must be. I wished I could have had the authors of those papers and books walking with me that day. I would have taken great delight in grilling them.

"You say the treasure's right here? The campsite is here? Okay, wise guys, show me. C'mon, quit stalling, show me!" I would have shoved their aristocratic noses into the sands.

But as time passed, so did my useless hostilities. Each time I beach-combed I started with high hopes, but it began to look as if I were in the wrong business. Had I been a junk dealer I would have been wallowing in prosperity. I must have unearthed hundreds of tin cans, bobby pins, springs, old chains, metal rods and pipes—even half a pair of patented divining rods. You name it, I found it.

Then one day as I was walking high on a bluff, looking to the west, across a sandy wasteland covered with palmetto scrub, something special caught my eye. It looked like a large depression. A reminder bell rang in the back of my head—"depression or mound, possibly unnatural and man-made."

I credit an old hound dog that accompanied me on a number of those early-day wanderings with being the real finder of the Spanish campsite. When I got down to the depression, after half tearing my clothes off on the jagged edges of the palmetto spikes, I was about to write it off as being anything but a natural low spot. I had noticed an old hole that had long since been partially filled in, though there was still water there. But salt-water springs and holes were common all along the oceanfront. I poked around and found nothing of interest and was about to leave when I saw something singularly curious. The dog was drinking water from that old well. It must be fresh water! If it was, this could have been a man-made well, and I might have stumbled onto the campsite after all. I scooped out double armfuls of sand until I had cleared enough away to reach down and bring up a cupped handful of water. I tasted it. Sure enough, it was fresh. That damnable, recurring bug—treasure fever—hit me hard again.

But wouldn't you know it? I had today of all days left my metal finding machine at home. I carefully logged the well's location in my mind and drove home to get the detector. Within the hour I was back, listening for the familiar whining. It didn't take long. This time I had better luck. Instead of a rusted can, I turned up a ship's spike, and, minutes later, a cannonball. Now I was onto something for sure. The periodic pings in my headset fast became a steady, high-pitched scream. The metal detector was going crazy. Instead of digging at each strike, I decided to chalk off the area of highest metal content. It covered a half acre. I retreated at sunset and regrouped my thoughts to formulate an organized plan for search.

But before I invested any great amount of time on what could prove to be another frustrating boondoggle, I wanted to make sure I was on the right track. I wrote to a Mr. True (his first name escapes me now) who was then secretary of the South Florida Historical Society. I told him what I had found and asked his opinion if this could possibly be the campsite. He did better than venture an opinion. He came up to see it for himself, and brought along a geologist to boot. After tromping around for a half hour or so, and examining what I had found, they told me they were sure this was it. Bingo!

I could almost feel the grinning ghost of Henry Jennings peering over my shoulder.

The mode of search I decided to follow was simple, yet it proved effective. After posting off my half acre, I rented a bulldozer to clear the thick scrub. Then I took a shovel and screen, and inch by inch began to sift through the sands. The work was painfully slow, but I always managed to turn up something of enough interest to keep me going. There were chips of Peruvian or Mexican potsherds of coarse brown ware; a few broken pieces of Chinese porcelain, which might have come from an admiral's mess; a hopper and the shaft of a small iron coffee mill; olive jar fragments; bricks; musket balls; a bullet mold; and irregular sheets of lead.

These weren't found in any one day, or even within a period of several days. I worked the area every chance I got between jobs on the mainland, and occasionally I'd hire a Negro helper to dig beside me. Under the blazing hot sun I got such a tan I was damn near the shade of brown he was. Over the weeks and months that I sifted through sands—I was digging to a depth of two feet—I began uncovering some more interesting artifacts. One day it was a pair of cutlasses that lay side by side a few inches down in the sand, just as if they had been in a leather case which time and the elements had long ago eaten away. The blades themselves were half gone from rust.

It wasn't long after this that my trusty detector—and what a bargain it proved to be for just $15—whined in my ears again. Filtering through the soft sand I discovered three blackened, rectangle-shaped pieces of metal. Later, at home, after scraping them and running a few tests, they turned out to be fragments of silver. Since I had found them near some buried bricks, it didn't take much imagination to picture a small kiln that had been set up either by corrupt Spanish salvagers or by pirates to melt down silver coins into bars for easier transporting, or smuggling, whatever the case may have been.

Now luck was really running my way. The next day I dug enthusiastically and was quickly rewarded beyond all expectation. I had barely broken ground with my shovel when a bright-yellow gleam, reflecting the morning sunlight, flashed in my eye. I bent down and brushed the sand away. Then I picked up the delicate object and slid it into the palm of my hand for a close look. It was a gold ring, crudely made, and so soft that the large diamond it held was mounted halfway down in the setting.

The stone was about 2½-carat size, and surrounding it, around the sides of the band, were six tiny diamonds.

This proved to be the major find of the campsite, though I also unearthed 13 silver pieces of eight. From the clusters of the cannonballs and the bricks, I could almost draw a diagram of how the fortress had been set up, complete with gun emplacements at strategic points. Another, enormously large puzzle piece fell into place.

When treasure fever strikes, you sometimes do some funny things. At the time I didn't see anything unusual in my action, but I guess it did seem weird to others, and poor Alice must have thought I'd lost my marbles for sure. I had seen an ad in a trade magazine for metal detectors. Some guy up North was selling out, and there was a real good buy in a quantity purchase. My old machine, faithful as it had been, was on its last legs, and I figured I could use some new ones. I sent off for a whole dozen of them.

They arrived one day when I was painting a church in Wabasso. The express deliveryman drove down and told me he had them, and asked for payment. I was broke, but I promised him if he would leave them at the house I would pay him the next time he came through. Bless his trusting soul, that's just what he did. My wife was out shopping when I got home, and I tore into the carefully packed crates with eager fingers. These detectors were real beauties. I went out again, and when Alice got home she saw all these boxes and crate paper scattered all over the front step and inside the house.

He remembered my birthday and bought me something nice, she thought to herself. What a shock she was in for, and she gave me hell that night, not only for forgetting to buy her a present, but for messing up the house. I eventually wound up selling most of the detectors at a handsome profit, so maybe I wasn't such an old fool after all.

As I've mentioned, my diggings at the Spanish campsite took place over a period of several months, and the finds, encouraging as they were, often were widely spread in point of time. Doc Kelso had his hands full with his busy medical practice and his family, but I would let him know what progress I was making, and now and then Doc would come over on weekends to look at my diggings and lend encouragement. My searching was manual labor, and it often grew tiresome. To break the monotony I'd occasionally swim in the surf, opposite the campsite, when the water was clear. I'd go out a couple of hundred feet or more, just lazily paddling around. Often I'd take my son Tom, who was just a little tacker then, and he'd play on the beach while I investigated the reefs lying in shallow water.

Sometimes I swam out with nothing more than my homemade face mask. Other times I took out an old inner tube. Then I felt creative one day and designed a crude wooden surfboard—and remember this was years before "Surfer Joe" and the surfing craze. My board would hardly pass muster among the teen-agers today, but it served my purpose. I simply cut a hole in one end of it and fitted it with plain window glass. With this inspired invention I could paddle out and put my face down next to the glass to see what was beneath the surface. Remember also, this was still before scuba equipment received the national popularity boom it has enjoyed in recent years.

Anyway, one afternoon I was floating around casually, when suddenly I spied something on the bottom. I dived down for a closer look, and sure enough, there, uncovered, lay four or five ship's cannon. Each one was about eight or nine feet long. Had they fired a cannon ball at that moment, I don't think I could have been more astonished. I free-dived down—they were only in about eight or nine feet of water—and poked around them until my breath gave out and I had to surface. I also found a huge anchor. Without doubt this was a wreck site—the first I'd found. I knew the ships had to be close by the campsite, and now, after all this searching, I'd discovered one. I was thrilled beyond words.

To make sure I wouldn't forget precisely where the location was, I lined it up with several markers on land. Then, after I got ashore, I took the bulldozer I had rented to clear the campsite and dipped a wide arrow through the underbrush, pointing directly to the wreck site. This gave me markers I could follow by land and by sea.

I'm certain one of the reasons I hadn't found a wreck site long before this was, once again, lack of experience. I hadn't really known what I was looking for. From old movies and books I guess I had halfway expected to see a full-fledged Spanish galleon, its hull intact, masts erect, lying on its side on the ocean floor, with moss streaming from its rigging. It doesn't work that way in real life.

In the first place, practically all wood on any ship that has been underwater in this area for a great length of time has been eaten away by the insatiable teredo, or shipworm. It is a rare piece of timber that escapes this hungry parasite. For the same reason, the traditional wooden treasure chests and barrels are virtually nonexistent. This pertains to wreck sites in the sea, under normal conditions. I understand vessels have been found in well-preserved condition in fresh water lakes in the northern United States, as well as in the Baltic Sea, where the salinity of the water is too low for teredos to thrive.

What one is more likely to find—and what I came to learn were just as helpful as clues even if the entire vessel wasn't there—are cannon, anchors or huge piles of ballast stones. That is really all a treasure hunter can hope for. And, if he knows his business, it's all he needs.

It was shortly after finding the first sunken wreck site that I got the wild idea I could cover more ground faster, and thus locate more sites, by flying over the water's edge. I leased a single-engine Taylor-craft, and, with the usual amount of anticipation, made my first run with a pilot friend of mine. We cruised so fast the entire sea bottom appeared as a confusingly featureless mass of grays and blacks. We landed on the beach—not recommended by the Civil Air Patrol—revamped our plans, and then took a second swing down the ocean front—this time at damn near stalling speed. I hung out the cabin door as far as I could to get a better view, and the pilot kept one hand on the stick and one on my belt.

After several trial runs, I gave up this method of search as too impractical. Oh, I sighted some interesting-looking objects. And when I did, I'd drop weighted coconuts—makeshift buoys—then circle and land on the beach, and swim out to the coconuts to see what was down there. But, overall, from the air it was impossible to tell an eighteenth-century galleon from a twentieth-century wreck. The coastline seemed to be littered with bones of unfortunate ships, and from the plane there was simply no way to differentiate.

I had learned, through our endless nights of pounding the books, that metal which remains immersed in salt water for a long period of time, particularly off the coastline this far south, becomes coated with a natural coral cement. Scientists speculate that this forms from the corrosion products of the iron combined with the coral sand that abounds on the ocean floor. Thus, nature seems to protect even man-made objects by providing a natural-color camouflage for the metallic pieces—as if they weren't hard enough to find anyway.

To get a bit more specific, the timbers of a ship are saturated with salt water soon after sinking, and become almost immediate prey for the teredo, and possibly fungi and bacteria as well. Then the constant, unrelenting wave action takes over. As the timbers rot and weaken, they are

3*

broken off by waves and by current action, and are scattered on the bottom. Some wood is soon covered by layers of sand and may survive down through the years. Mahogany lasts longest. Other pieces are soon completely destroyed by sea life. Only the heaviest beams, from the keel of a ship, have a chance to evade this slow but inevitable devastation. This occurs occasionally, when a ship impacts with enough force to bury the keel in the sands.

After the wood is gone, electrolysis sets in on remaining metal objects. Iron and silver, for instance, acquire a crust of deposits, either sand or other calcareous matter from the bottom. These particles cement themselves to the metal as corrosion sets in. Once the metal is thus encrusted, coral becomes attached also, and the object's original shape becomes completely hidden in disguise. Take, for example, the silver coins concealed in the heavy clumps Dan Thompson found. He had brought those up through sheer curiosity, not knowing at the time what they were.

Silver, incidentally, converts to silver sulfide, and iron to an oxide in this intriguing underwater chemical process. A silver piece of eight, in changing to sulfide and chloride, becomes a black mass, sometimes two or three times as thick as its original size. Gold, on the other hand, can lie on the ocean floor or buried in sand for centuries without tarnishing a bit. It is found as shiny as the day it went down, no matter what the time element.

Brass cannon suffer only slight corrosion, and often turn green after a long period of submersion. Despite the length of time underwater and the consequent oxidation, iron cannon, by their sheer mass of ferrous material, generally remain well preserved, yet will deteriorate after considerable exposure to air. The same is true of anchors, some of which exceed a length of 20 feet and a weight of four tons. It is hard to tell in what condition pewter will be found, since one piece may be corroded beyond recognition and the next one virtually untouched. Porcelain remains intact, though it and other ceramic materials are often covered with coral encrustations and other sea growths.

We learned all this from our researches, and I was soon to confirm the findings with real-life examples of these various objects. Steel, for instance, having little exposure to oxygen while buried under sandy bottoms, often is found in an amazing state of preservation. A steel sailmaker's needle we subsequently recovered at one site—measuring seven inches long and one inch across at its thickest part, showed no evidence whatsoever of oxidation after being removed from its coralline shell under a foot of sand. I have even seen paper—pages of an early Bible—in perfect condition after centuries under the sea. Figure that one out.

One other point here is noteworthy. Even when one finds scattered cannon and ballast and other obvious clues to a wreck site, there is no certainty that it is the grave of a treasure ship. On the contrary, the odds are much greater that it is a man-of-war, a frigate or any one of a number of other vessels. But somehow I felt my wreck belonged to that 1715 fleet. After all, it was lying only a few hundred feet off the salvage camp-site, and I had found a number of coins on the beaches directly opposite its submerged cannons. It just *had* to be a treasure galleon. I wouldn't even consider any other possibility.

When I told Doc of my new find off the first reef, he clapped his hands in excitement. To aid my underwater probes, he bought my first diving outfit—standard flippers, regulator and air tank. I had to try the factory-made face mask on in front of a mirror. I was sure proud of that outfit, and I itched to get back to the site.

After several trips with my new gear, I located other cannon and a few miscellaneous objects. One significant discovery was a fist-sized cluster of tiny silver coins, fused together in a shape that obviously indicated they had once been held in a pouch, the leather of which had long ago disinte-grated. It was a good omen, but if there was real treasure on this wreck, I realized I wouldn't be able to find it alone, or without some sort of sal-vage equipment. I could see even then it would mean moving huge mounds of sand, and Doc, Tom and I just weren't set up for it yet—either in terms of finances or manpower. So, I logged the perimeters of the wreck in my mind and moved on to newer pastures.

I had been told for some time of another wreck site north of Fort Pierce. It was, in fact, fairly common knowledge where this one lay. I used to drive down to Fort Pierce, fill up my single tank with air—it held only about an hour's supply—then swim out to the second site. Here, tons of ballast stones were lying in a great heap. Selfishly guarding my limited air supply as best I could, so I might stay down longer, I investi-gated the entire area. Again, I was thwarted by lack of men and machin-ery. I did manage to find a handful of coins, all of the 1715 era, but I couldn't move those massive stones by myself and make any appreciable headway, so I added another mental footnote.

I had faith the day would arrive when I could come out to these sites and others and work them properly. To prepare for that day I obtained from the Internal Improvement Fund of the state of Florida a nonexclusive salvage search lease covering a region extending 50 miles from the center line of the Sebastian Inlet to a point north of Stuart, south of Fort Pierce. I also got exclusive pinpoint leases on the wreck sites I had scouted. This move, as I came to appreciate later, was one of the smartest I ever made.

6 The Team Forms

Doc called me one day.

"What are you doing Sunday?" he inquired.

"Nothing special," I answered honestly.

"Let's go over to the beach for a picnic."

"All right with me, but let me check with Alice." She was all for it, but I couldn't get Tom interested, for Doc's seven children were all younger than my boy, and he was afraid of being stuck as a baby-sitter.

We were lying around soaking up the warm sunshine after lunch, and, full of beer and burgers, I folded my hands behind my head, stretched out, and prepared to take a snooze. Alice had other ideas.

"Why don't you dig for some coins?" she asked.

"Here? There's nothing here, Alice. Besides, I didn't bring my shovel." With that I promptly considered the matter closed, and shut my eyes. Alice was persistent.

"Here, Kip," she said, poking me in the ribs with a sharpened stick she had found. "Dig with this."

"But I tell you there's nothing here," I insisted.

"Dig," she replied. It sounded like an ultimatum. I had been near this very site often before on my beachcombings and had found nothing. This was silly, but damn it, I decided to dig a hole 10 feet deep just to prove to Alice there *was nothing there*. I'd show her!

I guess I hadn't gone down six inches or more when, bless my bones, there was a blackened piece of eight! Son of a bitch, I thought to myself. Doc pitched in then, as did our wives and the kids. In less than an hour we had uncovered more than 70 silver pieces, including a perfect eight real specimen spooned up by Becky Kelso. I was flabbergasted. Damn, I'd rather have Alice's intuition than a dozen metal detectors.

The next day I came back with a Negro helper, shovels and sifting screens, and we found another 70-odd coins. It was the richest lode I'd ever seen on the beach before or since. As Doc and I fingered through the silver that night, we wondered what the hell our next move would be. We knew these coins were from a shipwreck of the 1715 fleet. We knew we had found at least two wreck sites offshore from that fleet. What we didn't know was how we were going to get the treasure from those ships.

As fate would have it, our dilemma was being solved at that very minute, by men Doc and I had never met or heard of before.

Louis J. Ullian, possibly more than anyone else, was the catalytic agent who set off the sequence of events that led up to our team's formation. A powerful, huge hulk of a man, Lou was born in Boston, but moved to Fort Lauderdale when he was only six months old, and considers himself a native Floridian. In this melting-pot state that qualifies him as a native.

He grew up on *Treasure Island*, and other stories of pirates and sunken galleons, and with the golden sands of Lauderdale Beach nearby, he could swim and dive and let his imagination run. It wasn't long before he started finding artifacts off old wrecks along the coast. In fact, he says he began looking for treasure when he was 12 years old. I have to admit that's even before I got interested.

Later, he got more serious and pursued his hobby whenever he could spare the time and dollars. Off Pompano and Deerfield beaches he even found a few assorted coins, and he explored what he believes to have been a Spanish galleon that sank in 1733, off one of Florida's Keys.

Lou gained a mechanical engineering degree from Purdue University in 1955 and went directly into the Navy. He had some knowledge of explosives from his diving experiences, and was thus assigned to ordnance engineering, and put through an explosive ordnance disposal school. This training led to a job as an ordnance engineer at the Air Force Missile Test Range in 1959, after his service hitch was up. He is responsible for reviewing the destruct systems of each Air Force rocket launched at Cape Kennedy. He must see that all requirements of design are met, so if a missile goes astray once it leaves the launch pad, range safety officers can blow it up before it endangers a land area. It's an interesting, challenging job.

It was through his lasting love for diving that Lou met Delphine Long. Like Lou, Del had been born out of state, South Carolina, but his family had moved to Florida when he was less than a year old. They settled in Grant, a tiny community about 10 miles north of my house. Del has lived there ever since.

From childhood, he has loved to tinker with anything mechanical or electrical. He has been a welder, a sheet metal worker, mechanic and commercial fisherman. In 1950, the year America launched its first missile from the then Cape Canaveral, Del went to work at Patrick Air Force Base. Today, he applies his all-around mechanical knowledge as a ground power equipment supervisor. He has charge of all equipment of this type for aircraft.

He too has had a lifelong love affair with the ocean, and in 1956, together with an Air Force sergeant, he formed a skin-diving club and became its president. A couple of years later he and another fellow actually went out off Sebastian and stumbled onto a piece of a 1715 wreck. They even found some bronze spikes and ballast stones, but, of course, they had no idea at the time of the significance of their discovery.

Lou happened into Del's shop at the base one day in 1959, and found they had mutual interests. Del told Lou of the club and soon had recruited a new member. At a meeting, Lou met Ervin Taylor, a tall, native Floridian, born and raised in the hamlet of Micco, which separates Grant and Sebastian. Erv and Del had grown up together. A Mormon with serious religious beliefs, Erv worked with the Brevard County Mosquito Control District, and had joined the club out of a keen interest in diving. When Lou began telling of his treasure-hunting experiences off the south coast of Florida, Del and Erv listened with interest.

"I know somebody you ought to meet," Erv said. "There's a man down near where I live who's been poking around after treasure for years. I understand he's found a few coins, too."

"Who?" Lou responded with instant enthusiasm.

"His name is Kip Wagner. He's a peculiar cuss, but, if you like, I'll ask him if you and Del can come down and meet him." Erv didn't have to wait for their reply.

I didn't think Lou would ever stop talking the night I met him. He must have detailed every dive he had made, and described every rusted nail and broken chip of pottery he had found. If ever a man thirsted for sunken riches, it was Lou. We talked for hours, and when I showed him the coins and other objects I had accumulated, I could have turned out the lights. His face would have lit the whole house.

Over the winter of 1959-60, he and Del and Erv came down many nights, and we retreated to my little workshop behind the house for long chats before the fireplace. We smoked and drank brandy and talked all winter long. I told them of my hopes of finding gold and silver offshore, and they dreamed along with me.

Eventually, we got down to discussing ways of salvaging the sites I had found. None of us was very well to do at the time. I was broke, and they were all raising families on straight-salaried jobs. But if enthusiasm were money we'd have been millionaires. We agreed to pool what little finances we could scrape up, along with diving equipment. I needed manpower as badly as money, and, over the course of several weeks, we began mapping out arrangements to begin work the following spring, when the waters cleared up.

One of Lou's bosses at the cape was a man then putting the finishing touches on a distinguished, 24-year career in the Air Force—Colonel Dan F. Thompson. A native of Savannah, Georgia, and an electrical engineering graduate of the Air Force Institute of Technology, Dan had one of the most responsible jobs at the Air Force Missile Test Center. As director of operations on the 'range, he garnered broad experience in technical management, planning, policy-making, conference leadership, public speaking and engineering and managerial writing. He dealt with the highest level of leaders in government and industry. He directly supervised a highly skilled team of more than 150 scientific, engineering and administrative people, and briefed scores of visiting dignitaries, including the late President John F. Kennedy, and then Vice-President Lyndon B. Johnson. Dan is now an executive with IBM.

Lou went in to see him one day after quitting time. Dan sat in discomfort, one leg wrapped in bandages as a result of a diving accident off Ascension Island, one of the missile tracking sites located far down in the South Atlantic. He had gotten tangled up in some sharp coral reefs. Dan was, nevertheless, an expert diver, and when Lou told him of our discussions, he, too, asked to be included in the group. I was impressed the first time I met him. He not only would be a big help to us with his underwater knowledge, but he had a sharp mind that could prove invaluable in legal dealings and organizational work.

Now we had divers, but we were still sadly lacking in equipment. We needed a boat. Lou and Dan had just the man who could help us—Lieutenant Colonel Harry Cannon. Harry worked for Dan, as chief of the Range Safety Office. He had one of the most nerve-wracking jobs in the

Real Eight member Del Long brings up a cannon breechblock.

Silver pieces of eight with bits of the burlap sack in which they were originally carried still attached to them.

LEFT: Gold pendant bearing the head of a saint, found by Lou Ullian. Enlarged slightly more than twice natural size. BELOW, LEFT: This silver moth with coiled proboscis sat on the lid of a jar or urn.

The gold necklace found on the beach by Rex Stocker in November, 1962. Containing 2,176 handmade links, each faceted with rosettes, it has been appraised at $50,000. The dragon pendant has a toothpick in its belly, and its mouth forms a whistle. The chain is composed of four strands, over 11 feet long in all. The gold ring between the coins is set with a rough-cut diamond weighing 2½ carats, and six smaller stones.

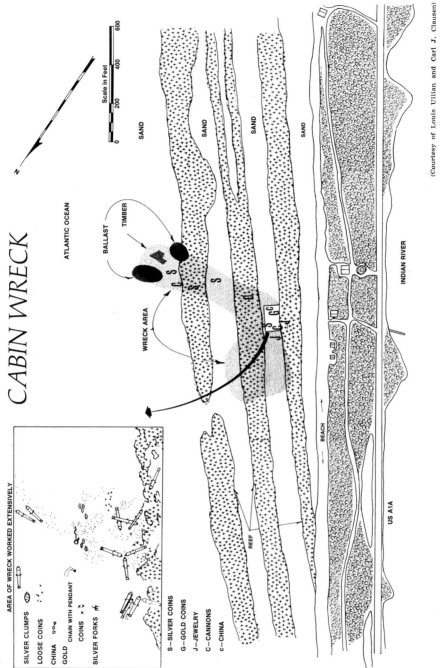

CABIN WRECK

ATLANTIC OCEAN

Scale in Feet
0 200 400 600

SAND

SAND

SAND

SAND

BALLAST

TIMBER

WRECK AREA

REEF

BEACH

INDIAN RIVER

US A1A

AREA OF WRECK WORKED EXTENSIVELY

SILVER CLUMPS	
LOOSE COINS	
CHINA	
GOLD CHAIN WITH PENDANT	
COINS	
SILVER FORKS	

S—SILVER COINS
G—GOLD COINS
J—JEWELRY
C—CANNONS
c—CHINA

(Courtesy of Louis Ullian and Carl J. Clausen)

Diagram of the cabin wreck, possibly General Ubilla's *capitana*.

Air Force: it was his responsibility to blow up rockets that wandered off their prescribed flight course. They tell me the first time he had to push the button, exploding a multimillion-dollar rocket into a thousand shreds of flying metallic bits, he turned ashen-faced white, and exclaimed, "My God, what have I done?"

Tall, rawboned and handsome, Harry is a native of Gainesville, Florida, and today directs a division at Radiation, Inc., an aerospace firm in Melbourne, Florida. During World War II he flew B-24's and C-47's over the Himalayas from India to China. After the war he graduated from a 42-week Air Force radar officer's course and the Air Command Staff College. He has vast experience in communications and electronics, and possesses the quickest natural reflexes I've ever seen. He had to have them for that ulcer-provoking job of his. Hesitation for only a few seconds on a runaway missile could spell disaster.

As if these awesome responsibilities weren't enough, Cannon was also in charge of a special recovery task force stationed at the cape each time an astronaut was flown into orbit. If trouble developed on the launch pad, or when the astronaut was over the cape, Harry was to direct rescue operations. Fortunately, these services were never needed during his tenure.

Harry had a boat—a 21-foot pleasure inboard-outboard. It seemed just right for our initial probes. The catch was, Harry wasn't a diver. Lou and Dan said they'd take care of this detail, and from what I've heard, Harry's initiation was a real wingdinger. It was probably the coldest night in January—about 30 degrees—when the three of them stepped out onto the patio surrounding the officers' club at the air base. Dan and Lou strapped diving gear on Harry's back and briefed him again on what to do. Then, without the protection of a wet suit, he was unceremoniously tossed into the frigid waters. When he came out he was blue. His skin was one giant goose pimple, his teeth were chattering, his lips were purple and his knees were shaking uncontrollably. But he passed the test.

This was the nucleus of our team. Del, Erv, Lou, Dan and Harry joined Doc, myself and Lisbon ("Libe") Futch. Doc, of course, had been in on things nearly from the beginning, and we had spent night after night researching or just plain talking—about the wrecks, about our plans and anything else pertaining to treasure.

Libe, also, is a longtime friend of mine from Sebastian. We had worked together building many a house. I was a block layer and plasterer who hated carpentry, and he was a carpenter who hated to lay blocks, so we got along famously. Libe, a few years my senior, had heard the stories of sunken galleons as early and as often as I had, but I guess I'm to blame for getting him keyed up enough to join in the search. We combed the beaches often, he and I—everytime rain halted our construction work or any time we felt like knocking off for a while. And I'll have to agree with Libe when he says we found a damn sight more bobby pins and beer cans with our detectors than we did coins. Still, he sensed my deep-rooted desire to search more seriously. He has been a true and valued friend as well as a trusted partner down through the years.

In mulling over the newly assembled team, I found we collectively had a wide variety of skills and specialized knowledge going for us. Libe, in addition to being an all-around handyman, knew the intricate network of channels and waterways in the Sebastian area as well as anyone I know. And he was an expert boatsman.

Del and Erv were mechanical marvels. They made practically every kind of pump, motor, dredge and what have you that we needed. In fact, I don't think there's anything they can't build themselves. Del constructed his own home in Grant for about $7,000. It would have cost him $25,000 or more to have it built by a contractor.

Dan and Lou were both expert divers—as were Del and Erv. Lou was also handy with explosives and electronics, and he proved to be skillfully adept at designing things. Dan has a sharp legal mind to help us in these lines. Harry was fast becoming a good diver, and he was our financial wizard. He has a good business head, something we needed badly.

Indefatigable Doc, of course, was a walking-talking textbook of Spanish history and underwater archeology. I had experience in a variety of trades, and owned a strong back and a tough pair of hands. And, I had enough desire to weld the entire group together.

Socially, and education-wise, our backgrounds were as diverse as could be imagined. Some of us had never made it through grade school; others held a number of college degrees and honors. I don't know a black tie from a polo shirt, but to others in the group, formal dress occasions were a routine affair. But the important thing was that our skills blended well together, and we had the one, all-important common bond—a driving compulsion to find treasure.

7 The Trial Run

By January, 1960, our group had pretty well jelled. I had decided some-time ago to test them—as divers and as men—on the wreck site just north of Fort Pierce, about 20 miles below Sebastian. There, 900 feet offshore, in waters 18 feet deep, were the decayed bones of a galleon. There were no particularly dangerous reefs surrounding it, and the waters were gen-erally clearer than anywhere else along the coast, which would make div-ing a relatively easy operation.

The hooker was that because of the site's accessibility and the clean surf, practically everyone on the coast within 100 miles knew about it. And, quite a few amateurs had worked the wreck. In fact, I had dived on it some years before during my inner-tube days. So I was reasonably sure it would be quite unlikely for us to find anything of real value here.

Why then bother? I looked at it this way. I knew precisely where some unexplored wreck sites were that would have a far greater potential of yielding treasure, but before exposing my secrets to a group of men I had known only a few weeks, save for Libe and Doc, I wanted to see just how serious they were about this business. If they were just out for weekend larks, and when the going got rough they'd fold their tents and go home, I wanted to know about it. After all, I'd invested years on this search, and thousands of dollars, and I didn't want to blow it all now with a bunch of greenhorns.

I remembered all too well the abortive salvage attempt with Steadman Parker and the others. They had quit in disgust. I needed a team that would stick together no matter what obstacles arose, regardless of the odds against us. Working this barren wreck would be my awkward way of testing them on the firing line, of observing them in combat. This was to be their trial run.

Besides, though this site had been probed by a number of people over the years, it was still, by comparison, a fresh wreck when one remembers that the gold-bearing galleons of Vigo Bay have been ravaged by more than 70 organized salvage expeditions in the years since they sank shortly after the turn of the eighteenth century.

Such was the setting on a cold, brisk day in January. The ocean was calm and the water unusually clear for this time of year, so Dan, Harry, Lou, Del and I decided to take an exploratory run out to the site in Harry's 21-foot cabin cruiser. We carried no diving gear or salvage equipment, of which we had very little at that time anyway. Sure enough, we came upon the ancient wreck almost immediately. There, three fathoms down, were thousands of ballast stones—virtually all that remained of a great ship that had been battered to bits in the full fury of the hurricane 245 years before.

As we drifted over the area, I could see that the others were getting keyed up, chattering away, speculating about what could be found down there under the weighty ballast rock. Even though I knew better, I caught myself speculating, too. To be perfectly truthful, there *could* be some treasure hidden in the sands that might have escaped salvagers in the past. I was pretty sure no one had methodically worked the entire site. But I was also sure we would never get rich from this one.

Over the next few weekends we made several runs out to the site, more for personal stimulation than anything else, I think. Between trips we began pooling bits of equipment—wet suits, regulators, air tanks, pumps, compressors—anything that might prove useful when we were ready to tool up and start diving.

Our most pressing need was a boat. We had used Harry's cruiser for the scouting trips, but when the heavy work commenced, we'd need something more practical. Libe Futch solved this problem for us. He and I went to the Navy salvage yards in Norfolk, Virginia, and for $1,200, bought a 40-foot liberty launch. It was some sight. The paint had all been chipped off it, an exhaust line had broken, and the whole inside of the boat was blackened with thick layers of soot. It looked as though the hull had been used to cook on. It still used a coxswain's steering post, and how Libe managed to maneuver it several hundred miles down the coastline I don't know, but it should rank with the major navigational achievements of the twentieth century. I had damn near caught pneumonia in Norfolk and chickened out on the slow ride back in favor of warmer transportation.

I'll never forget the day Libe brought it into port, if I live to be 90! It was a riot. Here he came, chugging across the waterway in that gosh-awful abortion. The superstructure was black, the hull was black—everything was black, including Libe. Had it not been for the whites of his eyes, I don't think I could have seen him at all. I was torn with mixed emotions. I felt kind of sick at thinking this was to be the vessel from which we'd base all our operations, but on the other hand it was so funny, in a pathetic sort of way, that I couldn't help doubling up and laughing until my sides ached. So when I say I laughed until I cried, it has a double meaning. I really felt like crying, too.

Libe, who had suffered with the thing all the way from Norfolk, and had had about all he could take, didn't see anything funny about it. I thought for a minute he was going to punch me in the mouth. When the others saw it, they echoed my sentiments.

"Are we going to dive off *that* thing," someone screamed incredulously. "You've got to be kidding."

We weren't, though. For better or worse, we were going to have to sink or swim with it, and the smart money was favoring the former. We promptly christened it the *Sampan*, because it looked so much like a junk. We began scraping her down as soon as our shock wore off. I'd spend a few hours every day on the *Sampan,* and the others would drive down on weekends to pitch in. After we got her cleaned up, I began outfitting a deck, and as the days passed she slowly began to take shape. There was no cabin, not even any protective covering, so we bent some pipe into a U shape and stretched a tentlike canopy of sailcloth over it to shield us from the scorching sun.

We knew, from our scouting runs over the wreck site, that we would have to move a lot of sand if we were to find anything under all that ballast, so we began experimenting with a series of homemade dredges. Erv Taylor and Del Long were real handymen at improvising things, and the first invention was a two-inch sand pump run by a tractor engine mounted in the bow of the *Sampan*. We raided junkyards within a 50-mile area to outfit the contraption. Fitted onto the pump was an old piece of stovepipe with a nozzle, and fire hose attached to it. Water going through the pipe created the suction necessary to vacuum the sandy bottom.

By April we had gathered probably the oddest, most-patched-up assortment of salvage and diving apparatus ever assembled by a treasure-hunting team. Nevertheless, we felt we were ready for our initial assault.

There was a tremendous pile of ballast on the bottom. It stretched about 70 feet in length, 20 feet in width and was stacked at least 8 feet high. The rocks were in all sizes, from ¼ pound up to 50 pounds and more. These had lined the ship's bottom, beneath the cargo, supplies, drinking water and food, and gun powder. Ballast, of course, was used to stabilize the galleons. The smaller stones were carefully placed to keep the large ones from shifting while at sea. The more treasure a ship carried, such as heavy gold and silver bars and coins, the less ballast was necessary. This added to my contention that we would find little of value here, for there must have been at least 100 tons of rocks lying on the ocean floor.

From the arrangement of the stones, we theorized the ship must have hit the reefs full force with its bow, ripping a huge hole in the hull. If the water were clear enough for one to back off and see the entire length of ballast, and, of course, it never was, the stones would have outlined the form of a vessel.

After a few diving reconnaissance excursions, we decided our only hopes of finding anything would be to move the ballast. To begin, we chose to cut a swath across the midships area, perpendicular to the line in which the ship had gone down. Because we had no powerful salvage equipment, the stones would have to be moved by hand.

And so our task began. At first everyone worked with spirited enthusiasm. We moved ballast by way of an underwater bucket brigade. One man would laboriously pry the rocks loose with a crowbar. He would then pass them through his legs to a second diver, who would, in turn, hand them to a third man, whose job was to pile the stones carefully in an area already covered, so we wouldn't have to move the same ones again.

Had somebody tried to hire us at double construction wages to perform such manual labor, they wouldn't have gotten a single taker. But here we were, breaking our backs for nothing. It seemed ironic. The work was sheer drudgery. After tossing a few of the larger stones around, we'd have to stop and rest. By the end of a day, after moving 400 or 500 rocks, we'd be fatigued almost beyond recovery. Our backs ached, our arms ached, our shoulder blades ached, our legs ached, and more often than not, our heads ached. Had we not been underwater, everyone of us would have lost 15 or 20 pounds in sweat.

Laboring on the bottom ate up our air supplies a lot faster than normal, too, causing more frequent changes of tanks. We worked in shifts. When one of us got pooped out, we crawled aboard the *Sampan* to catch our breath, but it wasn't any softer topside. The relentless summer sun broiled us even through our makeshift canopy, so much so, in fact, it was a relief to hit the water again, no matter how hard the work was.

As we cleared a path across the midships area, we took our homemade dredge and tried to clean the sand away, but our machinery proved to be a real clunker. We'd fiddle with the pump motor, finally get things tuned, dive down and prepare to begin dredging, only to have it conk out. The engine was old and cranky and the pipe had poor fittings. Frequently, we couldn't get the pump primed. It seemed as though we were spending half our time making repairs. From a surplus yard at Patrick Air Force Base, we picked up some noncollapsible hose that had once been used for missile propellant hose lines. We had hoped this would improve our dredge, but even then it was, at best, a balky, unwieldy system.

Our progress in moving the ballast was also painfully slow. Libe and Doc Kelso didn't dive, and Lou, Harry, Dan, Del and Erv all had full-time jobs at or near the missile center, so we could only work weekends and holidays, or whenever they could sneak away from their desks for an extra day. Then, we could only work the weekends and days that the weather was calm and the water clear. Between times I busied myself repairing equipment and puttering around the *Sampan*. As the summer wore on, the work seemed to grow harder, the hours longer, the sun hotter, and everyone's patience shorter.

"Anyone who thinks treasure hunting is a glamorous profession is just plain crazy," Lou complained one afternoon. He had a point.

"I get up at 4:30 or 5 every Saturday and Sunday morning after working hard all week at the base," Lou said. "I rush through breakfast, cut myself shaving, then drive 60-odd miles to Fort Pierce so I can get here between 6 and 7. We get out on the site by 8 or 9, then we spend all day moving those damn rocks down there until our arms won't respond anymore. We don't get back to dock until sunset, then we have to secure everything before I can head home to Helen and the kids. If I make it by 8 or 9 at night I'm lucky. I just have time for a snack and then bed. I'm too tired even to watch TV. What a crock."

"Lou," I said, "I couldn't have put it any better." Anybody who wants to chase treasure because he thinks he can strike it rich fast, without working, has seen too many movies starring Gilbert Roland, or read too many books. It just doesn't pan out that way. Here we were busting our tails and we didn't have the first coin to show for it.

By the middle of the summer we had cut a 10-foot path across the middle of the ballast stones. Occasionally, there would be a mild stirring of interest when someone came upon various odds and ends buried beneath the sands. We had patched our dredge until it began working more often than not. Its principle was simple. We'd pump water into the open-ended pipe, creating a suction that vacuumed seawater, sand, shell and anything else that might be lying around. This would all be discharged a few feet away.

The dredge began spitting up hundreds of tiny chips of Mexican earthenware potsherds, so many, in fact, that the divers soon began balking at having to bring them up. This job was given to 18-year-old Mike Hrebec, an apprentice, who had asked to dive with us just for the experience and thrill of it. The thrill soon wore off for poor Mike as he brought up load after load of the potsherds, but archeologists at the University of Florida Museum wanted all we could find. I was glad, at least, that we were making somebody happy.

We also found hundreds of cannonballs on the bottom. We would have souvenirs for our efforts if nothing else. There were, too, tiny chips of blue and white porcelain scattered on the bottom. We found none larger than a half inch or so, and didn't learn till later that these were remnants of rare K'ang Hsi china. There were other metallic objects under the ballast, but they were decayed beyond recovery—probably iron that had deteriorated through an oxidation process.

Del Long moved the last chunk of ballast from a section one Saturday, and underneath were exposed timbers of black, rotting wood. He grabbed a piece of it, and the fragile material dissolved into an inky cloud before his eyes.

"I've found the captain's easy chair," Del shouted, as he tossed a handful on the *Sampan*'s decks. "Here's some of the stuffing."

Later, we packaged it up and sent it to Mendel Peterson at the Smithsonian Institution for analysis. He wrote back explaining that Del's "stuffing" was actually a mixture of cow hair and tar. Peterson surmised that the Spaniards must have used it to coat the wooden hulls of their ships in desperate attempts to discourage the insatiable teredo worms. To the best of our knowledge this was the first recovery of such a mixture from a sunken ship.

From the shape of these timbers, buried beneath the ballast, it appeared that the vessel must have rolled over on its side in the storm and settled that way on the bottom. The planking ribs of the ship were locked together in such a manner.

We were finding cannonballs, potsherds, porcelain chips, rotten timbers, a copper rim and handle, and a handful of small brass nails—but no treasure. We had, by this time, cut all the way across the midsection of the ship, and we now regrouped our forces and decided to dissect the stern. We were learning through trial and error. Experience was teaching us about the decaying processes of a ship. It was obvious that the superstructure could survive in these waters only a few years, and thus was gone centuries before we had arrived. Likewise, anything light would have been salvaged early, or lost. But, we calculated, much of the cargo, particularly precious metals, which were heavier, might well have settled on the bottom, under the ballast, out of the reach of Indian divers who had to hold their breath and could stay under for only a few minutes at a time. They wouldn't have had time to move the ballast about. Thus, as we shifted attention to the lower area where the ship's ribs connected to the keel, our hopes rose again. We set up the ballast bucket brigade with renewed vigor.

But more weekends passed. June lapsed into July, and then August, and still nothing. To take a break from the monotony of lifting stones and riding the dredge, we would occasionally swim away from the immediate wreck site. Del had a habit of chasing lobster, or Florida crawfish to the purist, and he found one under a ledge one day. He tried to entice it out by scratching in the sand—we've found the creatures to be overly curious—but this one wouldn't fall for it, so Del shot his spear under the ledge and hit the lobster. But his spear got wedged in the rocks. He then got down on his hands and knees to work it loose, when he saw a flash out of the corner of his eye.

He looked around in time to see a 12-foot shark bearing down on him like a runaway freight train. It paralyzed Del with fear. At the last possible second the huge predator swerved away, but it passed so close Del was knocked flat on his back by the surge of water. Instinctively, he grabbed for his knife, which was in a sheath tied to his belt buckle behind his back. He had it drawn in an instant, ready for another dive-bomber attack by the shark, but it never came back. I don't know what good the knife would have done, for you only kill these monsters with blades in movies. Then Del noticed puffs of darkened ooze drifting up toward the surface. Had the shark clipped him somewhere with such speed and sharpness that he hadn't felt it? He quickly inspected his body and found he had sliced himself on the back when he drew his knife. Afraid of attracting more sharks, he hastily surfaced and took a long rest aboard the *Sampan.*

Sharks are not uncommon in these waters. Most of them are sand sharks, and, over the years, we have fostered a sort of mutual understanding with and respect for them. They have never attacked us, but there have been some rather unnerving experiences.

There is probably more free advice dispensed on sharks, their habits and mannerisms, and how to escape from them or frighten them off, than on any other phase of diving. I've personally heard hundreds of wild yarns, as have Lou, Dan, Del and the others, concerning experiences with sharks. Some say to flail arms and legs wildly when a man-eater is circling nearby. Others say remain motionless. Some recommend a heavy release of air bubbles, or tell you to shout and make loud noises underwater. From our encounters with the evil finned monsters, we can only conclude that we know as little about them as everyone else. Though they've been in the seas for probably 300 million years or more, man still is seeking the shark's well-kept secrets.

We once threw cherry bombs from the *Sampan* at a couple of black fins we saw circling in the water, but it had no effect, other than to send the divers scurrying to surface wondering what the hell that racket was. The one thing to remember above all about sharks is never to take one for granted. They are completely unpredictable. You might swim up on 19 of them and nothing will happen. The twentieth, as likely as not, will attack you head on. Some wise diver put it succinctly when he said, "The better acquainted we become with sharks the less we know about them, and one can never tell what a shark is going to do."

It's a gruesome thought, but each time I see a shark I cannot help wondering if its ancestors somehow might have passed along a story of a great feast of 1,000 or more men who drowned in that devastating hurricane of 1715. Try as I have, I can't seem to push that thought from my mind when I see fins slicing the water.

Harry Cannon had as much trouble with a variety of tiny fish that summer as he did with sharks. He had gotten a bad case of sunburn, and, when he started peeling, these fish would nibble at his dead skin, nearly driving him crazy. We often had armies of drum, sheepshead and grouper for company as we worked on the bottom. They would swim under our arms, between our legs—all over. But try as we might, we never could catch one of the rascals, and somehow whenever we went down with a spear gun they were never around.

Del thought he had a real prize fish one afternoon, but wound up with the fight of his life. He tells it better than anyone in that inimitable drawl of his:

"I was paddling around on the bottom when I saw this eye peering at me from under a reef. It was eerie, but I was sure it was just a snook under there. Now, to anyone who knows Florida fish, I don't have to explain what good eating one gets from snook. So I aimed my spear gun dead center at the eye and popped it in the head. I was free diving, without scuba gear, and could only stay down about three minutes at a time. So after firing the gun, I headed straight for the surface, pulling the line after me. When I broke water—I had been about 15 feet down—I hadn't budged that fish. I hollered to the fellows on board the *Sampan*, 'Hey, I've got me a big snook down here,' and stretched my hands wide apart in the classic fisherman's pose. I went back under for another look, tugging at the line as hard as I could the whole time. Then I saw this head come out of the reef and it had huge teeth showing. I'd never seen a snook that looked like that.

" 'Hey fellows,' I called out again, after resurfacing, 'this ain't no snook. I think I've got a big barracuda down here, and . . .' Before I could finish the sentence—ka-wham—something hit my leg like a bolt of lightning. I looked down, and the sight raised the hairs on the back of my neck. It was a greenish-brown, spotted moray eel, about five feet long. Its fiendish mouth enveloped my entire knee, and it felt as though someone was stabbing it with ice picks. Instinctively, I went after it with both hands and grabbed it just behind the head. We turned over and over in the water, like Johnny Weissmuller wrestling an alligator in an old Tarzan movie, only my monster didn't have its mouth taped shut. Its powerful jaws and double row bands of pointed teeth were locked on tight in a viselike grip. Finally, with a desperate lunge, I freed my leg and flung the moray—and a chunk of my kneecap along with it—as far as I could. It was all happening so fast there was nothing the guys on the boat could do, so I headed for shore as hard as I could swim. It was about 200 feet off. I hadn't gone more than 10 yards, when—ka-wham—the damn eel hit me again full force, this time farther down on my leg, driving its needle-sharp teeth deep into my calf. I grabbed it again, and over and over we went once more, until I could shake it loose. This time I hurled the moray and what was left of the spear gun line as far as I could toward the rocks. I think I must have eclipsed one of Weissmuller's old records making it to shore. Not only was I afraid of another knifing attack by the eel, but it was now trailing wide streamers of blood from the spear gun wound I had inflicted, and I was bleeding pretty badly myself. And no one knew better than myself that I was swimming right through 'shark alley.' We had sighted hundreds of sharks in this particular area, and a scent of blood was all they'd need to hunt me down like dogs after a cornered fox. But I made it to shore this time without getting hit again, and limped up on the beach, where my wife Betty was waiting. My knee was ripped open where I had yanked the moray off. He had taken the skin with him. My whole leg was full of deep punctures. We drove down to the hospital at Vero Beach, and I got bandaged up and they gave me a booster tetanus shot."

Of all the terrors of the sea—shark and barracuda included—I think we have come to respect the snakelike moray eel more than anything else, and not just solely because of Del's terrifying experience. I know of fishermen who have pulled these hideous creatures up on the end of cane poles, only to have the eels literally crawl up the line and savagely attack their captors. There is only one thing to do when you hook on—cut the line, and quick. In fact, I've read that Romans once threw slaves into waters infested with morays to watch the slaughter. Perhaps only the giant manta ray is more fearsome to look at. You can ask Dan about that. He swam right over one once. Its whiplash tail could flail a man to death in minutes.

But with all the dangers, there is also a unique beauty in the ocean. It's a world all its own underwater. I can't help but marvel at the artistry with which Mother Nature has carved the ocean floor, and wonder at the same time why she didn't make the splendid scenery more easily accessible to everyone. But in many ways the undersea world where we dive does resemble land areas. Actually, it's indescribable, but my son Tom makes a pretty eloquent attempt:

"The world in which we work is as diverse and changeable as the one above. You swim along great grassy plains that are reminiscent of Kansas wheat fields at harvesttime. Then you come upon canyons and ledges and caverns that remind you of the West's immense gorges. Suddenly, giant boulders rise like submerged mountains—these could be the Rockies. Forests of coral stand like Oregon's tallest timbers, and rolling sand dunes are almost identical to the vast desert lands of the Southwest.

"To me one of the most striking features about the underwater life is the fascinating kaleidoscope of colors that seem to pop up everywhere. Sunlight, refracting through the water, filters down in a shimmering rainbow of colors. It is like looking through a giant, submerged prism. Coral colors range through the entire spectrum, and the fish flit by in vivid golds and blues, brilliant oranges and silvers. Even the tiny parasites that hug the ocean floor blend their various hues into the overall color spectacular.

"Animal life runs the gamut. One becomes fascinated with the rapid-fire tail fanning of the tiny sea horses, three to five inches long; or awed by the sheer brute strength and size of the awkward, immense, 1,200-pound sea cows. I find myself comparing fishes to people. The sharks, barracuda and moray eels are the Genghis Khan types—the barbarians. They prowl and lurk and strike fear. The huge jewfish, the grouper and the snapper, though, are more civilized and easygoing.

"There is beauty, as in the gorgeously colored Queen Angel fish—and ugliness, as in the fierce-looking Florida crawfish, which glares beady-eyed at you with its menacing feelers and legs sticking out.

"There are the comics—the little, playful fish that dart in and around you, playing a game of tag. Then there are the smart fish. They wait until you fan the sand on the bottom or move a rock before swooping down and devouring the minute animal life that has been uncovered. Hundreds of these fish follow every movement, like a great, expectant audience. The world is alive down there.

"And, there are other dangers, like the spindly sea urchins—the porcupines of the ocean—which lie on the bottom minding their own business. But step on one, or brush past it while swimming, and its razor-sharp spines slash at you, tearing through protective suits and skin alike. Brush past a jagged edge of red coral with an exposed arm, and it feels as though someone has set fire to your skin. But, all in all, when the water is clear, it is a beautiful world, and the dangers are fast forgotten."

It was late summer and the diving season would soon be over, but still we had found nothing of value. As each weekend passed, the grumbling began to get louder. Dan and Harry were questioning whether there ever was any treasure out here. They were catching hell at home from their wives, as were the others. All summer they hadn't been home for a single Saturday or Sunday. They were becoming strangers to their youngsters. Wives were shouldering double responsibilities, and marital relations were beginning to wear thin. Little League games were missed; dentist appointments postponed, then cancelled; beach outings were put off; visits from neighbors discouraged. The sacrifices were many.

"You're a kid, an overgrown kid," one wife screamed at her husband one night after he had dragged in late. "You spend all day looking out in that lousy ocean for treasure and then you're too tired to take me out to dinner. Well I'm tired, too. Sick and tired. Treasure, that's a laugh. When are you going to grow up and forget about this fiasco?"

In all fairness, our families had put up with an awful lot. If we had had something to show for all the time, I'm sure it would have eased things, but there was nothing. How can you explain to an irate wife you worked for 12 hours that day and found only cannonballs and potsherds? The team was wearing rough on the edges, too. One or two of the boys liked to hit the cocktail circuit on Friday evenings, following the week's work at the office, and more often than not they'd wake up Saturday morning nursing one hell of a hangover—not recommended for a diver.

By early August we had reached a low point. Relations were becoming seriously strained, and we practically had to force ourselves to go down and move those cursed, ever-present ballast stones. One particularly unproductive Sunday, Dan, Lou and Harry—bone-tired and disgusted—crawled into their car and headed home.

"I've had it," Harry said. "Kip can take his treasure and cram it." Dan and Lou nodded in agreement. Had it not been so near the end of the diving season anyway, I don't think I would have ever seen them again. They had lost all confidence in finding anything.

My team was now teetering on the breaking point. Then our luck changed.

Harry Cannon had found his own little digging hole on the bottom. "It just looked interesting to me," he'd tell us when we queried him as to where he'd been. Harry would paddle off to it when he wanted a break from the monotony of the ballast brigade. Once it damn near got him in a peck of trouble—this swimming off by himself with no "buddy" nearby. On that occasion he inched along the sand with elbow-length visibility, when he peered around a large coral clump into the steely eyes of a 10-foot-long shark. He did an instant freeze, and the shark remained motionless, too. For a few minutes it was one hell of a staring battle—Harry and the shark—and the shark seemed to be winning. Harry's nerves were about to crack.

"I thought it over," he recounted to us later. "If I started to backstroke away so I could keep an eye on him as I did, I'd make a lot of motion, which might incite him. But if I turned and swam normally, I'd have my back to the beast. I didn't know what to do."

Harry finally decided to inch backward slowly on his fingertips, pushing off with his flippers. It was agonizingly slow, but he soon lost the shark in the murky waters and took off. We have a ladder running down one side of the *Sampan*, but Harry happened to surface on the other side that time, and rather than swim under the boat, he leaped over the side, carrying weights, air tank and all. It was quite a gymnastic feat, inspired, I'm sure, by the frightening mental picture of that 10-footer snapping massive jaws at his ankles.

One morning about mid-August, Dan and Del and Harry were hard at it on the ballast pile, when Harry silently slipped off again. He began poking around in his favorite spot, when something half-buried in the sand caught his eye. It was a lime-encrusted, fist-sized bar. Harry picked it up. It was heavy enough to be some kind of metal. A lump swelled in his throat and his first impulse was to surface, shouting, "Look, I've found something." But by now so many of us had done this, only to realize, in the bright, unveiling sunlight, that what we had was some worthless object.

On second thought, Harry vowed to himself to make certain he really had something of value before he came up to show the rest of us. He took his crowbar and began scraping the encrustations away. Underneath the coating he fingered the scratch marks he had just made. They shone bright silver, even in the depths 20 feet below surface. Harry began sifting the sand all around him, and tossing off ballast stones. He soon uncovered five more of the wedge-shaped objects. Then he tucked them under his arms and went up.

"Is it anybody's birthday?" Harry asked, as he poked his head above surface. Ironically, it actually was Libe Futch's birthday, and he responded automatically, "Mine."

"Well, here," Harry said, handing him a silver wedge, "here's a present for you."

Pandemonium would be a mild word to describe the scene that followed aboard the *Sampan*. Everyone whooped and hollered and stomped around so that I was sure we'd kick a hole in our boat and sink on the spot.

Harry said he felt as if he could walk on water, and I believe I would have bet he could. After everyone had examined the bars, divers grabbed regulators, face masks and flippers, strapped on air tanks and scattered into the water like buckshot.

For months we had been methodically moving ballast stones in an orderly manner, carefully stacking them in areas already covered so we wouldn't have to move them twice. Now the scene on the bottom looked like the clowns' finale at the circus. Divers were heaving stones every which way. Within minutes, our neatly dissected paths through the pile were a littered mess of rocks. And no one paid any attention to the next man. It was almost dangerous to work down there. You practically had to dodge the raining storm of rocks. We found three more wedges before we called it a day. Laid in a circle eight inches in diameter, the blackened wedges formed a silver "pie." We guessed three such layers would have filled a keg weighing about 100 pounds, the standard load for an Indian carrier. Two such kegs would have made a mule load.

Lou Ullian wasn't with us to share in the thrill of the find, and it was too good an opportunity to pass up, so on the way into port we hatched up a devilish scheme. At the prodding of Harry, Dan and the others, I put through a long-distance call to his house.

"Lou," I inquired. "This is Kip. You'd better get down here right away. There's been some trouble."

"What do you mean? What kind of trouble," Lou shouted into the receiver. I could tell by the high pitch of his voice that we had him hooked.

"We had another bad day," I began, biting my lips to keep from breaking up. "We didn't find anything. Harry had a few beers, and on the way in he and Libe got into an argument."

"Over what?"

"Well, Harry had brought up some junk metal to take a look at, and coming in Libe wanted him to clean it up. Harry told him if he wanted it cleaned, to do it himself and they had an awful scrap. Finally, Harry said he was fed up with the entire operation anyway and he was ready to quit. Libe said go ahead, no one will miss you.

"Then on top of that we ran onto a reef coming in and punched a hole in the boat. We almost didn't make it to the dock. Dan's teed off too. So

ABOVE: Bringing ashore an anchor, encrusted with shells and coral, from one of the lost treasure ships. BELOW: A member of the team uses a suction pipe like a vacuum cleaner on the ocean bottom, to clear away sand and bring up objects. Another diver, who does not appear in the photograph, inspects the debris that emerges from the device.

Kip Wagner examines one of the old muskets recovered from the ocean floor.

A diver brings up a bronze bell.

are Del and Erv. You'd better come on down, Lou, and see if you can do anything. I think the team is ready to bust up. Everybody's mad and they won't even talk to each other."

"But I don't have my car," Lou pleaded. "It's in the garage."

"Well I don't know, Lou. It looks as though they're going to break up tonight if something isn't done."

"Wait a minute." He sounded frantic now. "I'll see if I can borrow my neighbor's car. Look, Kip, hold them together until I get there at least. Don't let anyone leave. I'll be down as fast as I can."

I'm almost ashamed to admit it, but I doubled up with laughter before I could even hang the phone up. He had taken the story hook, line and sinker. Poor Lou must have broken land speed records that evening, for from the time we had driven the few miles from Fort Pierce to my house, it was no more than five minutes later that he was skidding into the driveway. Harry and Dan were standing outside in the yard, and Libe was inside with Del. Lou ran up to Harry.

"Look you guys, let's talk this thing over," he appealed to them. "We've got too much time and effort in this to blow it all in one day."

"Hell no, I've had it," Harry snorted, portraying his role of an angry man to perfection. "You can have this so-called treasure and all its heartaches," Harry continued, "but not me. No more."

"Well, just wait a few minutes, Harry," Lou said in desperation. "Come on inside and let's talk to Libe."

Finally, Harry shrugged, and said, "Okay, Lou. Just a few minutes. But it won't do any good."

Inside, Lou asked Libe to re-create what had happened aboard the *Sampan* that had caused the trouble. We had all gathered around now for the payoff.

"Well," Libe began, pointing at Cannon, "he brought up this junk— we've got it here in a bucket, and when I asked him to clean it, he wouldn't. Here, Lou, look at this crap," Libe said, handing him the bucket containing the silver wedges. For a second Lou fumbled with the heavy, encrusted bars. Then he saw the silver shining through and his eyes lit up like light bulbs.

"You dirty scoundrels," he howled, and, as if on cue, everyone broke up.

When Harry got home that day, in the middle of the afternoon, he tiptoed up to his front door and rang the bell. His wife seemed surprised to see him.

4

"What have you got behind your back," she wanted to know.

"Just this," Harry countered, and handed her a wedge.

"What is it?" she asked.

"Treasure," he replied.

She gasped, then looked at her watch. "It's only 3:30, Harry; why aren't you still out there in the ocean?"

Doc Kelso was hospitalized in Tampa at the time, recovering from an eye operation. We wrote him a note describing our find, and I understand it caused all sorts of hell. Doc was supposed to have absolute quiet, but when he got our message, the excitement was almost too much for him and he drove the nurses crazy trying to keep him in bed. But I guess he had waited too long to take such news lying down.

Over the next few weekends we found a half-dozen or so more of the silver wedges. I even got rambunctious and bet the boys a fifth of whiskey I could find one. Sure enough, I came across one on the bottom, and, after inspecting it thoroughly to make sure it was silver, I triumphantly brought it aboard ship. They paid their debt with surprisingly little whimpering, but, damn it, they stayed at the house that night until they had killed the whole bottle—*my* bottle!

By the end of August, the waters had muddied up and the diving had to be called off until next season. But this late summer find of silver—each wedge was worth maybe $500 to $600—had solidified the team. They had been put to the supreme test and they had made it.

"You'll never know how close we came," Dan told me later. "We were all ready to give it up, until Harry brought up those wedges."

There is one additional episode concerning the 1960 season which I feel is noteworthy. Prior to this team's formation, I had worked with a few other people on helter-skelter diving operations. One of these men was a longtime friend of mine, and in the early days he proved to be an able and helpful companion. One day he came to me and said he couldn't dive anymore. He was going into business for himself. I questioned the wisdom of his move, but couldn't stop him.

I thought nothing about it until he showed up with another fellow at our wreck site. By this time, of course, we had obtained our lease from the state for exclusive rights to salvage the ship. This didn't seem to faze them in the least. They anchored a few feet from the *Sampan*, suited up and dived. I told my son, Tom, to go down and signal for them to come up so we could explain that they were, in fact, trespassing. Tom tapped them on the shoulder underwater, but they shrugged him off. We finally had to go down and tear off their regulators to get them up. Our lecture fell on deaf ears. They not only ignored us, but came out again on the site. After repeated warnings came to no avail, we had no recourse but to write the state, and they subsequently told my erstwhile friend and his partner in no uncertain terms to get out or they would be prosecuted.

This did the job, but it was not the last I heard from them. They informed me they had three silver wedges to sell. Apparently they had obtained them from our site and now they had the audacity to offer them for sale. Rather than press charges, which would have resulted in sensational publicity—something we didn't want at the time, not to mention a lengthy court battle—I made them a fair offer of $250 per wedge, which they accepted. I then sent the wedges to Mendel Peterson of the Smithsonian and he bought two of them for the same price I paid. But he sent the third one back with a note saying it was a counterfeit. Apparently, these two connivers had taken some silver coins, melted them down, and poured them on the surface of a useless chunk of metal. They did a good job of it, because I couldn't tell this wedge from the others. It was a $250 lesson as far as I was concerned, and it taught me never to underestimate the extremes to which a man will go when treasure is involved.

The next few months were the longest in our lives. We had sampled the sweet taste of sunken riches. We knew they were out there, but there was nothing we could do until spring came, with its warm weather and clear waters. We were helpless. Over the weekends we passed the time as best we could, fixing our rag-tag equipment and working on the *Sampan*. Often we'd walk along the beaches and sigh, longingly, as we looked out to sea. We literally ached to get back out in the water.

Confident now that my team would hold up no matter what the circumstances, I made my decision to lead them to another site, farther north, the first time the elements eased up. This wreck, I knew, would yield a far better chance of finding important treasure than the one we had worked. We had found silver, true, and it was probable there was more down there somewhere. But we had pretty well cleaned that wreck, and I felt any future returns wouldn't justify the efforts we would have to expend.

Then on January 8, 1961, the waters cleared enough for us to make a scouting run, and that was the day Dan Thompson found the coin-clustered clumps.

The trial run was over. Now it was time to get down to serious business.

8 In Business

It was a good four or five weeks after Dan's find before we could get back into the waters, and those weeks seemed like months, even years to us. Can you imagine? We had a fortune in coins lying a few hundred feet offshore, begging for us to scoop them up, and all we could do was sit on the beach and wish. The winter winds kicked the sea up too much for us even to attempt taking the *Sampan* out. To say we were helpless would be an understatement for the way we felt—particularly the boys who drove down every weekend. By now I had pretty well developed enough patience to tide me over such periods, but even so I could hardly wait to get back out there between the reefs.

When we finally did get back to our site, it damn near resulted in a major disaster that could have halted our operations altogether. By mid-February, the seas had calmed enough to allow us to pass through the Sebastian Inlet without grounding—an accomplishment of no small merit in itself—and we headed straight to the buoys we had set out to mark the wreck site. Visibility in the water was only about 12 inches, but even that was enough with the stuff lying on top of the sands, as it had been on our last outing.

We maneuvered into the trough separating the two reefs, and several of the boys suited up and went over. For the most part we were using Desco rigs. These are shallow-water Navy diving outfits with air hoses running from a pump on board the boat to the divers below. It allows the diver to perform heavy work, but restricts freedom of movement to the length of the hose.

Dan and Lou surfaced within minutes, and their expressions were grim. "There's a coating of sand over the cannon and other things down there," Dan told us. Even in the few short weeks since we had been here, the wave and wind action had reshaped the bottom. Over the years we have, in fact, rarely seen the same ocean floor configuration twice.

The divers went back down and began their search. Despite the new sand piles, they found silver coins almost immediately. These weren't lying in the open, but we had a sand dredge operating, and the fellows also fanned the bottom with their hands, to uncover them.

Lou Ullian came upon a lumpy object that caused him to take a heavy intake of air. It was a rock similar in appearance to the coin-clustered clumps Dan had found in the same area the previous month. Lou excitedly examined its purple outer crust, and, finding nothing, took his crowbar and began chipping away at it. Still nothing. Convinced it was no more than an ordinary chunk of coral, he used it for a stool, while fanning for coins, lazy-man's style.

We had been on the site only a short time when the wind kicked up from the northeast and began whipping the waves. It was getting pretty choppy, and I was ready to call it another day, even though we had found a number of coins. I was thinking about signaling the men to come up, when fate stepped in and made the decision itself.

The fluke on our anchor broke. Normally, this wouldn't upset us too much, but with the wind and waves slapping hard on our bow, I was afraid. The *Sampan* was yawing toward shore—toward the first reef. If something wasn't done, and fast, we'd wind up the same as the Spanish had in 1715. I rushed to the stern and pushed the boat's starter button. Luckily, the engine fired right up, and just as we were drifting dangerously close to the reefs, I steered eastward, back into the trough.

Then naked fear froze me. I had acted instinctively when I cranked the engines, but now I suddenly remembered I was motoring right over the divers. Dan, Harry and Lou were on the bottom. If I hit a line, it could cut their vital air hoses. Despite the chilling wind, large beads of sweat popped out on my forehead. I had a hand tiller on the stern and I jockeyed the *Sampan* as best I could. You have to experience, to feel the action of a boat really to know what I mean. I don't think we could have been bounced around anymore without something giving, and despite the *Sampan*'s ungainly looks, doggone it, she was really getting a test of her seaworthiness, and she was holding up. But she was bucking like a freshly lassoed wild stallion, and my mind couldn't help but conjure up all sorts of ghastly thoughts of divers grabbing at their throats and gasping for breath, looking up at neatly severed air lines.

Fortunately, there was no time to dwell on this nightmarish line of thought. I had my hands full. We yanked on the divers' lines—four tugs on each one—to signal them up, but there had been no need to. The minute I had turned the engine they began to surface, wondering what the hell was going on. As their heads popped out of the water, one by one, I breathed a heavy sigh of relief.

"What the hell's going on?" Dan demanded. "You trying to saw us in half?" They were mad, but after we got them aboard and they learned what had happened, things cooled off. It was really kicking up now—breakers were slapping the boat like a giant playing bongo drums—and I suggested we call it a day, figuring I'd get no arguments on that one. But I was wrong.

"Let's stay a little while longer," Dan said. "I saw something down there that looked interesting."

"Are you crazy?" I shot back at him. "You may think it's fun to keep this tub from cracking open on the reefs, but I don't. No sir! Let's go in."

Dan was just as adamant. He wanted one more crack at that ocean floor. We finally settled for a compromise. I maneuvered the *Sampan* out of the trough between the two dangerous reefs and stopped a good 200 feet away. Dan and Lou slipped into their scuba gear for one last dive. They would have to swim to the site and back. I wasn't about to endanger our boat again, particularly when I thought the whole thing was a waste of time anyway.

Back on the site, visibility had worsened to only a few inches, and the combers were raising great clouds of silt and sand. How Dan and Lou managed to keep from being torn apart under there was beyond me. Serious treasure searching in such water was virtually impossible. It was foolish.

They had been gone only a few minutes when Dan reached up and tapped Lou. He pointed down to the floor, at a large purplish clump. Lou recognized it as the underwater stool he had used when he had been working the area earlier in the morning, and he shrugged his shoulders in the traditional "so what" manner. But when Dan rolled it over on its other side, it exposed a face that Lou had somehow missed examining. There, in a little pocket carved in its underside, were the unmistakable irregular cuts of metal, half buried in oxide-blackened fusion.

They surfaced and waved for the boat to come over. I waved back for them to come our way. The hell with trying to navigate in that trough again. It was too damn dangerous. Lou then swam over and grabbed a line, disappearing again beneath the rollers. Pretty soon he and Dan reappeared, lugging something on the line.

When they broke surface with it, I thought it was just an interestingly shaped chunk of coral for Dan's rock garden—they do make nice decorations—but, hell, this was no time to be bringing something like that up. Disgust must have stood out on my face like a neon sign. How stupid can they be, I thought, endangering the boat for a coral rock? I was steaming. I guess they could see this, for as soon as they got aboard they brought it over and showed me the coins. What could I say? Erv Taylor fingered the clustered pieces of eight and then said it for me.

"Now I know why they made you a colonel, Dan."

Lou had a more succinct comment.

"I'll be a son of a gun," he mumbled over and over, and we didn't get the significance until he told us he had seen that same clump before and passed it up, using it to sit on down there. He backed up his story by showing us the scratch marks he had made with his crowbar.

It was undoubtedly the most expensive seat Lou ever had. We found nearly 2,000 coins in that clump, and estimated its value at between $30,000 and $40,000! When we got into port, I didn't even take time to participate in the usual post-discovery celebration. Del and I worked for hours repairing that anchor. We had found more treasure, but it had been a nerve-wrangling experience, jockeying the boat in those swirling waters, and I didn't want to go through it again.

Once more, as if Nature were logging our every find so she could tease us all the more, a prolonged spell of bad weather set in, and we couldn't get back to the wreck for several weeks.

Harry called the house one day and he sounded serious. "Kip, can you get Doc, Libe and Erv over to your place tonight for a meeting? Dan, Lou, Del and I want to come down and talk something over with you."

"Guess I can. What's up?"

"I'd rather wait till tonight and discuss it when we're all together."

"All right, Harry, I'll see you tonight."

I think this must have been our first formal meeting. Oh, we'd gathered numbers of times to talk about the boat, equipment we needed, when we'd dive again, or various other things, but it was always informal. There was something in the air on this occasion, and it didn't take long to find out what it was. As the eight of us sat around my kitchen table, Harry opened the meeting.

"We've been thinking this whole thing over, our situation I mean," he said. "And we feel, now that we're beginning to find some important treasure, we need a little better organization."

We had discussed this briefly before, after finding the first two clumps of coins, but everyone had been drunk then and nothing was settled. I listened without comment as Harry continued.

"We've got a few thousand coins now, and the silver bars from last summer. But more important, we're probably going to start finding a hell of a lot more once the waters clear up this spring.

"Now here's what I'm getting at. We all entered this venture on handshakes and our words, and no one is saying he doesn't trust anyone else, or anything like that. Don't get me wrong. But with a possibility of us bringing up a fortune out there, I . . . we . . . feel we should draw up something on paper—just so there'll be no arguments over the splits or anything else. You'll have to admit our operation has been run pretty loosely."

I had remained silent long enough.

"If a man's word and his handshake is no good, Harry, then what the hell good is a piece of paper?"

"It's not a matter of distrust, Kip. We just feel we need some kind of protection for our interests; something legal and in writing, so there can never be any questions or any confusion."

"Look," I pointed out, "we've been working as a team for several months now—we've known each other for over a year. I don't think there's any need for all this."

"That's just not good business sense," Dan said, and he proceeded to give me a rather strongly worded sermon on my business naïvety and why they wanted something drawn up. I guess I'm just plain old-fashioned, but I still didn't see the need. I think Harry got right down to the bone of it though, in language no one had difficulty understanding. He was laying it on the line.

"Damn it, Kip," he said, "my philosophy is simple. When money comes in the window, friendship goes out."

There was a loud silence around the table for a couple of minutes.

"I see," I finally said. "I see." It was beginning to look as though our friendship was already starting to break up on some verbal reefs.

"Don't get things wrong," Dan said, sensing the tension. "We're not afraid of getting gutted or anything like that. We just feel, for our own safety, we should put something on paper. This doesn't mean anyone is doubting anyone else."

"Well, I'm still not sure we need to do this," I said, "but if you fellows are so set on it, let's see what you have in mind."

Harry produced some papers and explained they were drawn up from a sample corporation charter. By the time everything had been spelled out, and we got around to agreeing on it and signing, it was well past midnight, so I asked for an adjournment. My normal bedtime is 9 o'clock.

"But what about a name," someone asked. "What are we going to call ourselves?"

"How about Real Eight?" I said, thinking almost automatically of the old Spanish term for pieces of eight. What could be more appropriate? Everyone agreed. We had a name. "Now let me go to bed," I said.

I suppose they were right. In the light of what we have found since then, Harry and Dan insist we never would have stayed together without the papers binding us.

We met again on April 17 to elect the officers of our new corporation, and to split the 1,000 shares of stock. It was the first of the regular monthly meetings that we have held ever since. Our original bylaws were in line with existing laws of the state of Florida. Although we can name anywhere from three to eight directors to run Real Eight, we settled on three because of the limited membership. All normal rules of order and voting procedures are followed.

I was elected president, and, as such, am intrusted with the duties and responsibilities of the average chief executive officer. I report on the condition of business at each meeting and have the power to employ, appoint, remove, discharge and fix compensation for all agents and employees of the corporation. According to the bylaws, I must see that books, reports, statements and certificates required by law are properly kept, made and duly filed. Further, I sign all certificates of stock, notes, drafts or bills of exchange, warrants and other orders for payment of money drawn by the treasurer.

In the event I'm unavailable to perform these duties, Dan Thompson, our newly elected executive vice-president and treasurer, steps in. It's also his responsibility to keep up with the funds and securities of the corporation—and the books. Harry, as secretary, has the real workhorse job of the company. Keeping up with official correspondence is in itself a full-

4*

time occupation. I shudder to think of all the paper work he gets involved with.

One of our first orders of business was to reimburse Libe for the *Sampan*, which he had paid for out of his own pocket. We agreed upon $1,800. He had bought it for $1,200, but he was compensated for getting it to us from Norfolk. I don't think I would have done that chore for three times the amount.

I kept daily tabs on the weather. I nearly drove Alice crazy with the radio on all day, blaring out rock and roll, but I didn't want to miss any advisories. For a while the seas remained rough, the weather nasty. It was only a few weeks, but how gosh-awful slowly the time seemed to drag by, the treasure lying so near, yet unreachable until conditions calmed down. If I felt mental anguish during this trying period, Dan, Lou, Harry, Del and the others were about to go out of their minds. Regardless of how rough it was, they'd drive down anyway, in the hope, futile as it was, that we might be able to sneak out even for an hour or two. Fate seemed to be playing a continuing game of tease with us.

The couple of times we went out, things were so murky on the bottom we couldn't see our hands in front of our faces. And if that expression sounds trite, so be it. It's also true—that's precisely the way it was. But even then we found out something, and it was anything but good news. On one of the runs, Lou came up and shook his head in dismay.

"You can't even see the cannon anymore. They've disappeared," he informed us. We had marked the site with buoys, each with a line running down to the cannon and tied around it. The lines were buried under tons of sand. In January, when we had worked on the site, it had been in three fathoms of water. Now it was only two fathoms down to the floor. That meant the cannon, coins and everything else must be buried under a six-foot-thick layer of sand. We realized then what a long, hard pull this was going to be. King Neptune wasn't going to surrender his riches easily—at least not as easily as we had imagined after Dan's finds of the coin clusters.

"We're just going to have to find some way to move all that sand," Lou said in a classic understatement. Next came a procession of Rube Goldberg salvage devices that, looking back on them, I can't help laughing over, but at the time we'd have tried anything. Del Long and Erv Taylor are, in my mind, mechanical geniuses. They can work miracles with their hands, transforming the most useless bits of junk into a working machine that gets the job done. All of us chipped in with ideas of what we thought could move the sand, and Del and Erv would mold our word descriptions and drawings into material realities.

By the time the waters had cleared up enough to dive for the first time in the spring of 1961, we had come up with a two-inch sand pump. It ran on the principle of centrifugal force, with special blades powered by a motor that sucked in the sand at one end and discharged it at the other. It worked, but not well. It was too slow, and took an hour to scoop a hole three or four feet deep and about five feet in diameter. At this rate we wouldn't find enough to cover the operating expenses.

Another contraption Del and Erv came up with was a homemade airlift, using an old Model T Ford engine as a compressor. It, too, was discarded as impractical after several test efforts. We were learning by costly trial and error. As Del put it, "Without the right-type dredge our treasure search was comparable to hunting bear with a BB gun."

By early May, Mother Nature had again asserted her fickleness and swept most of the sand off the site for us. Maybe, somehow, she had seen our puny attempts to do this, and decided we'd never make it without help. But, after spending three or four days orienting ourselves with the confines of the wreck, and, incidentally, finding a number of things we hadn't seen before, the lady changed her mind once again and piled sand back on the site.

We had no recourse but to build a good, reliable dredge. We couldn't trust the elements to do our work for us. Erv had read in a skin-diving magazine of the dredges divers used in California when they searched for gold, and he snipped out a diagram. He and Del then set to work fashioning an instrument out of a six-inch-diameter aluminum water transfer tube, about nine feet long.

We tried it out one day in June when the water visibility was the best we had seen at this site. For the first time, we could look at one end of the cannon on the bottom, and see the other end—a distance of eight or nine feet. Remarkable! The dredge worked like a charm. In five minutes' time it could tunnel a hole deep enough to hide a Volkswagen. Eighty to 90 pounds of pressure were pumped into a 2½-inch fire hose to power the dredge. As the water jetted through the pipe, it created a suction on the bottom which siphoned sand, shell and, hopefully, bits of treasure. We attached a screen basket to the far end of it, so spewed-up coins and artifacts would be caught as the sand filtered through.

But it took us awhile to learn how to control it. In fact, the first test ended in a riot. Del was on the business end when Erv turned it on, and they had underestimated its power. For a frantic few seconds it whipped Del around as if it were a giant snake or moray eel gone berserk. He hung on like a rodeo champ, though—or maybe he was just too plain scared to turn loose, I don't know. So we learned some more. By sticking the suction head of the dredge into the sand, one man could control it easily, guiding it as one would a powerful vacuum cleaner. It was only when it was out in the open that it became unmanageable, because the fire hose we used had a tendency to straighten out and crack like a whip under the high pressure of water.

We soon had an affectionate nickname for our mechanical helper—the "hungry beast." It gulped anything in its path—sand, rocks, coral, fish, cannonballs—and then regurgitated everything at the other end of its nine-foot-long shaft. We even *lost* some gold to its high-powered vacuum. Ironically, Del got his hand caught in the mouth of the dredge, and it stripped off his wedding band. We have never found it.

The machine gulped everything except objects that measured more than six inches in diameter. These stuck in it like chicken bones in a dog's throat. We'd have to get a boat hook or a long rod to ram it through the tube, poking out what was wedged in. It also, by its swift suctioning, created cave-ins, making the area into a quicksand-like quagmire. This would sometimes bury the dredge, and we'd have to dig it out. Well, it was doing a good job for us, so an occasional turnabout was fair play.

One day in mid-June we brought up our first coins since February— about 50 to 100—all buried loosely in the sands and over a scattered area. We had no systematic way of working the dredge through the wreck site, and it was hard to tell if we had covered the same ground before. Unlike the silver wedge site, where we could move ballast and neatly stack it up so we could see where we'd been, the bottom here looked alike all over. Constant wave action in the trough between the two reefs stirred the sand so even if we could leave a pattern or trail of where we'd been, it wouldn't be there the next day.

We came up with another improvisation. We drove long iron rods into the bottom and tied lines to them. Then we took the dredge and slowly made a circle around the rods. At the conclusion of a day's work, we'd tie a knot in the line at the point where we knocked off. Next time out we just felt down the line till we reached the knot, then started in from there.

We found the best way to harvest coins uncovered by the dredge was before they went through the tubing. So we generally worked in pairs. One would hold the mouth of the dredge in the sand, and, as it bore down, the other man would keep an eye alert for coins. When some blackish-green shapes appeared, the dredge would be diverted while we picked up the coins. When a few got sucked up anyway, it was a simple matter to catch them. We even removed the wire screen at the tail end, for coins and other heavy objects went through the tube so slowly a diver could swim to the rear of the dredge in plenty of time to cup his hands and have the coins softly float down into them.

If this sounds like an easy, even lackadaisical method of salvaging, perhaps I'm oversimplifying things. We could take nothing for granted at this site because of the rough wave action. Let me reiterate how difficult it was in this particular spot even to stay right side up on the bottom. When the tide was right, it was almost like working under a pounding waterfall. To keep the dredge on target without getting knocked 10 feet away by each comber was, in itself, a full-time job. Swirling sand caked in our ears, stuck in our hair and even worked its way inside our suits, where it chafed like coarse sandpaper, rubbing our skin raw.

One of our biggest worries was seasickness. There was so much motion down there, it was hard to fight off the effects of vertigo. And when you have to bite into an air hose or breathe into a face mask to sustain life, how are you going to throw up? That's a real experience, certainly one of the most unpleasant in the treasure business. A novice could get in real trouble fast on this site.

Mike Hrebec, the youngster who had faithfully, if begrudgingly, brought up so many potsherds of archeological value from the silver wedge wreck site the summer before, was not a novice diver, but he had a heck of a scare one day that almost made him wish he'd never learned the profession. Mike helped us out whenever he could during the summer, and one day he was working his way along the bottom when something ripped into his leg. He thought sure he was in the viselike grip of a giant shark's jaws, and he turned white with fear. Then he looked around to see that a dredging ring had fallen, knocking his leg against some sharp coral, which had done the cutting. He had been so sure it was a shark that he came charging up to the surface and scrambled aboard the *Sampan*, huffing, puffing and holding his bleeding limb. It was probably a good thing he got out of the water anyway, because his blood might have attracted some real sharks.

Occasionally, to break the tedium or tenseness of our work underwater, especially on days when the recoveries were few and far between and our patience ran short, someone would dream up a practical joke or two. I never will forget the time, for instance, Dan and Del were working down below using Desco rigs. I was puffing heavily on a Dutch Master corona aboard the *Sampan,* and it occurred to me that I should share the delights of my leisurely smoke. So I slipped the air hose off the pump and blew a few smoke rings down it. Within a minute two green-faced divers surfaced, and the air turned purple with their profanity.

"What's wrong?" I asked as innocently as possible.

"You know damn well what's wrong," Dan snorted. "It's bad enough to sit in the same room with you when you're puffing on that piece of rope, but when you blow it down the hose it's suffocating."

I couldn't understand why they didn't think it was funny.

I include such a passage in this book on treasure, for were it not for such periodical pranks and icebreakers, I'm sure we would have been at each other's throats time and again. Diving for sunken gold and silver is, after all, a serious business. Thousands of men have been killed during searches—by drowning, being dashed upon jagged rocks, eaten by sharks or murdered in cold blood while chasing a pot of gold far smaller than the one we were after. So, in perspective, my gag and other practical jokes in a very real sense served a useful purpose. They made us conscious of the value of maintaining a balanced sense of humor despite the recurring dangers and disappointments of our trade.

As the summer passed, we brought up hundreds of coins—all silver. So far we hadn't found a single gold piece; an odd fact, I thought. But it would come. Sometimes we worked all day and only recovered 10 or 15 coins; some days we found none; and on other occasions we found hundreds of them. Our workhorse dredge also spit out silver buckles, iron ships' spikes, potsherds and other assorted items. We found, too, about 20 cannon over a 50- to 60-foot area along the reefs.

When the waters were too rough or unclear to work here, we made a couple of return trips to our site off Fort Pierce to seek the missing silver wedges we needed to fill our "pie." But we had little luck there, and the divers showed scant enthusiasm for moving that heavy ballast.

By September, as hurricanes began their northerly drifts, the diving season was shot, but this time, unlike the season before, we had much to show for our efforts. In the last few days before we called it a year, we came up with another, smaller cluster of coins, and our total take now numbered several thousand pieces of eight.

It was a peculiar phenomenon at the time that although we had been finding treasure fairly regularly and were well satisfied with our progress, no one really knew about it. Of course, our families and a few close friends did, but the secret was pretty well kept. We just weren't interested in any sensational publicity at the moment.

I recall a particular incident when we had found several hundred coins and other assorted valuables one day, and stored them in the back of an old panel truck we were using. On the way home Del and I stopped in a local filling station for gas.

"Well, did you find the pot of gold today?" the attendant inquired, with an unmistakable inflection of mockery. Everyone knew we had been diving.

"No," I answered as straight-faced as I could, "but we're still looking." As we drove off Del and I burst out laughing. In the back of the truck we had several thousand dollars' worth of silver—and that was only one day's take. Yet the whole town thought we were the biggest bunch of crackpots they'd ever seen. Treasure in the ocean. Indeed!

One of our priority items of business, now that the main diving season had ended, was to do something about the *Sampan*, so we could work from it during the winter if the waters cleared at all. The past January, when we found the clumps, we nearly froze to death because the boat had no cabin. I still remember Lou turning blue and shivering uncontrollably after being in the water for only a few minutes. We needed something more than that canvas shroud to help fend off the elements.

Even with a neoprene suit, one was only protected while in the water. After peeling it off on board the boat, the bone-rattling winds bit hard during the winter months. It was like coming out of an icebox and going into the deep freezer. How well I remember our trips from the site back to port. What little warmth we received from the sun was gone by dusk, and we'd almost fight each other to huddle around the *Sampan*'s diesel engine, sit on it or poke our feet on top of it.

So I was elected to carpenter up a cabin, and this busied me for several weeks. We also improved our dredge, bought a new engine for it, and acquired an air compressor to use with our Desco equipment. We wanted to get everything in A1 shape for the next season. We had wasted precious weeks early this past spring by trying out salvage equipment.

To raise money for new gear we voted to sell a few coins. We had been putting dough into operations on a monthly basis out of our pockets, and we were beginning to hang on by our fingernails. That's why the sale, small as it was, had a special significance to us. Naturally, the better we controlled the flow of such coins on the open market, the higher the prices we could command. If we flooded the market, it would only cut our take, so we doled them out carefully. You may remember the big news of a multimillion-dollar treasure find a year or so ago off the Bahamas. The proud finders of that one told of the thousands of coins they had uncovered. Immediately, the value fluctuated greatly, for dealers work under a strict law of supply and demand. It was smart business sense for us to see that the demand stayed constant.

For our silver pieces of eight—and remember, there had never been a collection of such coins to match ours—the price tags ranged from $15 to $100, with a dated coin in extra fine condition drawing as much as $150. Undated cobs were worth from $35 to $50, and the real "dogs" only drew $10 to $15. Dealers seemed amazed at the remarkably good overall condition of our coins. Most of them were clean, or had only a thin coating of oxide. We were pleased with the interest shown in our collection, and we made just enough to keep things going for a while.

As another convenience, we managed to gain permission to use a beach cabin that was directly opposite the wreck site we were working. We promptly referred to this area hereafter as our cabin site. We fixed the wooden cottage up with double bunk beds and stored air tanks and other equipment inside. It was a perfect place from which to headquarter our operations, and we've spent many a night there during busy periods, sipping beer and trying to rival each other's tall tales.

We even made a couple of significant finds over the winter of 1961 by swimming a few yards offshore, a practice we followed occasionally, when the waters farther out were too rough for a boat. Lou found three or four tops to silver jars while checking through the outer edge of the first reef, between the beach and the wreck site. There seemed to be an abundant supply of potsherds and fractured bits of blue and white china in the shallow waters, too.

It was Del who made the most interesting recovery. Here's how he describes it:

"The thing I remember most vividly was the icy-coldness of the water. I hadn't brought my wet suit, but I plunged in anyway. When the water is this chilly, you can't stay in too long. It quickly saps your energy, but I wanted to have a look at the second reef. I get hunches every now and then, and this was one of the times. In fact, I had told Kip and Lou earlier at the cabin that I was going to find something. I had a wooden paddle—

one of those things you bounce a little rubber ball off of on a string—and I waved it at them as I waded into the surf. 'This is going to bring me luck,' I remember telling them.

"I had a more practical use for the paddle than just as a good-luck charm. When I got to the reef, I used it to fan the sand away from the crevices and ledges in the coral formations. I had to keep surfacing and diving like a porpoise, for I hadn't brought scuba gear either. I was fanning in one spot when something bright began to appear beneath the sand. It looked like the top of a beer can, but as I began nudging it loose, I could see it was something more like a pot lid. It turned out to be a gnarled figurine of a silver moth—an ornamental stopper for some high-ranking Spanish official's brandy bottle. We'd seen nothing quite like it."

9 Characters and Shareholders

You meet some of the most extraordinary characters in this treasure-hunt game.

In the few years I've been at it I've run across Greek divers, Air Force generals, bank presidents, bums, soldiers of fortune, con men, celebrities, archeologists, and newspapermen, among others. Sit for a couple of hours in my living room at home, and any number of people of varying backgrounds and occupations will form a steady procession through the front door. But I love people, and I guess, from all they tell me, I'm somewhat of a character in my own right. Meeting people is one of the things that makes this business fascinating.

But of all those who have crossed lifelines with me since we've found treasure, none has been more interesting or more likable than the bright-eyed, moustachioed, bald-headed character I met one night during the winter of 1961.

"Kip, this is Luis Marden of *National Geographic Magazine*," Dan Thompson said by way of introduction. Luis, I learned, was covering the upcoming flight of astronaut John Glenn from Cape Canaveral (now Cape Kennedy), and through friends he had heard of our finds. He told us the *Geographic* was definitely interested in doing a story on us, and he would tell his editors more about us when he returned to Washington.

Sure enough, in the spring of 1962, after Colonel Glenn made his historic flight, Luis was back. By this time I had learned a little more about him. Many people, for instance, consider him the finest underwater still photographer in the field, and, after seeing him work with us, I certainly wouldn't dispute the claim.

He has traveled to every conceivable pocket of the earth on his writing-photographing safaris for the *Geographic*. I heard he once left on a five-week assignment and didn't get back to the magazine's home office in Washington for six months. And to top it off, no one even knew where he was! Now that's the kind of job I want.

Filming treasure recoveries underwater was nothing new to the irrepressible Mr. Marden. I doubt if even our awesome finds could have topped, for sheer thrills, his plunge into the sacred well of the Mayans at Chichén Itzá, on the Yucatán Peninsula. His account of that, "Up from the Well of Time," is spellbinding.

By now we had arranged a deal to tell our story exclusively to the *National Geographic*. I was to write it, which I subsequently did, and it eventually appeared in their January, 1965, issue. When I say the article was *eventually* published, let me explain. When we signed the exclusive publication contract, it meant none of us could tell any part of our story in print, on radio or television until 30 days after the *Geographic* had come out. Had we known they would not hit the stands with the piece for nearly *four years*, I doubt that we would have signed at all. It really tied us up.

Anyway, back in 1962, Luis wanted to re-create our finding of the silver wedges which we had recovered off Fort Pierce in the late summer of 1960. The waters were generally clearer at that wreck, so we drove down one morning after drawing 8 or 10 wedges and some coins out of our bank vault. Once on the site we lowered the silver down in a basket and scattered it around on the bottom, so Luis could picture us swimming upon it.

Now I have seen sharks, big-mouthed jewfish, barracuda, multicolored angelfish, spotted moray eels and any number of other odd creations of nature. But never in my entire life have I seen anything to compare with the likes of Luis Marden in full photographic battle dress underwater! I'll describe it as best I can, but I'm not even sure I believe it—and I saw it!

I *am* sure, however, that if I'd met this strange-looking phenomenon beneath the sea without knowing who he was or what he was doing, I would probably have had a heart attack on the spot.

We were already on the bottom when Luis jumped overboard. He had two or three cameras strapped around his neck; a shiny protective iron glove (in case of underwater flashbulb explosions); a red and white bag over his shoulder, full of bulbs, and floating up from his belt; light meters and reflectors seemingly coming out of every elbow and armpit; and an orange-phosphorus hammer and chisel, for chipping loosely encrusted artifacts.

Here he came. Every time he snapped a picture, a flash would set off and the bulb would float toward the surface. With his bald pate shining and his thick moustache flowing in the currents, he looked like some prehistoric, or maybe futuristic, monster, it didn't really matter which. Even the fish wouldn't get near him.

After he took a number of photos, we carefully placed the wedges in the wire basket and went up for some lunch. An hour or so later Harry Cannon noticed the weather was acting up a little.

"Let's get the wedges," he said.

"Not a bad idea," Lou Ullian answered, and we started hauling in the line that was tied to the basket. It seemed unusually light. When the basket broke surface, we could see there was nothing in it.

"That's not funny," Harry ranted. He thought one of us had hidden the wedges as a joke. We all looked at each other in complete surprise, and when we saw nobody was joshing, panic struck. Five divers hit the water at the same time—with and without face masks, flippers, regulators and air tanks.

On the bottom our mystery was quickly solved. Wave action had gently spilled the basket, dumping our precious silver wedges in a neat little pile. We wasted no time in bringing them up though. We had worked too long and too hard to lose them now. In fact, if you divided the total number of hours we spent in finding those wedges, into their overall value, they would probably be the highest-priced bars of silver in the world.

When Luis had to return to Washington for reassignment—his "beat" is the world at large—he turned the job of photographically documenting our work over to a young man named Otis Imboden. Otis was then assigned to a *National Geographic* field office at Cape Kennedy, and he covered all the major space launches as well as handling other chores from Florida to South America.

At first I think Otis doubted we had found any treasure at all. He would drive down to our cabin site every chance he got, loaded down with all sorts of cameras, lenses, filters and various other assorted pieces of gear. *Geographic* photographers certainly came prepared. But it seemed every weekend he came down, the waters were too rough or dirty to take any pictures. Then, when it was clear, we couldn't manage to find anything while he was aboard.

And when he first saw our boat I thought he'd cry. He had envisioned golden-haired girls diving off a beautiful white yacht. Otis told us the *Sampan* was the most unglamorous subject he had ever photographed.

Off and on, he worked with us for two years and showed as much stick-to-itiveness as any charter member of Real Eight had exhibited. We almost came to adopt Otis, in fact. His two youngsters, John and Jill, were both born during the period he worked with us, and he spent many an anxious weekend and even one chilly Christmas Day diving on the wreck site while his wife, Joan, was momentarily expecting.

For him it was a slow, frustrating and difficult task, because the waters were seldom clean enough for good color photography. But persistence paid off, and the photos he took, many of which appeared with the *Geographic* article, are real works of art. Altogether, Luis and Otis shot more than 3,000 photographs for their editors to select from.

The Luis Marden episode with the silver wedges somehow seemed to set the tone for our 1962 diving season. It was whacky and weird, and, before we were through, quite productive of unusual and valuable finds.

Occasionally, when the waters were very clear, we would knock off the salvage work and seek new wreck sites. This was still before we had access to such modern wonders of machinery as the magnetometer and other instruments, that, like computers, do man's work so much better and easier than he can do it for himself.

For our searches over wide areas of the ocean this particular season, I designed a device we came to call affectionately the "sled." Erv Taylor made my drawings into reality. It had a bottom of aluminum tubular conduit, with a plexiglass front, so a diver, with air tank attached, could lie down on the sled, look through the window-like shield and scan the bottom as we pulled him in back of the *Sampan*. There was a control stick on the sled that, for some reason, worked exactly the opposite of an airplane's stick. That is, when you pulled back on it, you went down instead of up, as you would in a plane, and when you pushed down, you went up.

After a couple of trial runs by Erv and myself, Dan Thompson climbed confidently aboard one day and we began trolling in an area north of our cabin site. That particular day, the waters were as clear as we have ever seen them. You could gaze around for 100 feet or more underwater. We were doing about four knots in about 35 feet of water, and Dan was zipping along behind us underneath, a few feet off the bottom, wagging his head from side to side, taking in the scenery, and looking hard for ballast, cannon or any other objects that would indicate the remains of a wrecked ship.

Things went pretty smoothly until, suddenly, he glanced straight ahead and saw he was heading into a large pile of rocks. Now Dan, as a retired Air Force colonel, has had years of flying experience. In fact, at the time he was still in the service, and I guess when panic struck him, he relied on sheer instinct.

Anyway, instead of pushing the stick forward to go up over the rocks, he reverted to his basic Air Force training and pulled back on it as hard as he could. The result was disastrous. Responding obediently, the sled nosed straight toward the rocks and smashed head on into them. The plexiglass shield ripped off, and the aluminum twisted like a pretzel, but, miraculously, Dan was not injured. On the *Sampan*, with the diesel engine chugging loudly, we didn't know of the underwater plight our friend was in, and kept going at a steady speed.

On the bottom, Dan was hanging onto that battered sled for dear life. He cleared the rocks and tried desperately to get the bashed-in nose of the device up so he could bring it to the surface, but it wouldn't budge, and scraped and bumped along the washboard ocean floor. He finally had to swim like hell to get around in front of it and lift it up forcibly. When he broke surface, holding the sled under his arm, we didn't know what to make of it.

After retelling his story on deck, everyone doubled up in laughter. Everyone that is except Erv and me. I had thought the sled was a pretty good idea. Erv, who had spent hours tinkering with it, looked as if he would cry.

Another bizarre search technique never got off the ground—literally. The idea was Dr. Gordon Benson's, a former chief of medical operations at the John F. Kennedy Space Center, and, as such, the man in charge of the all-important preflight physical examinations given America's astronauts.

Dr. Benson is a balloonist by avocation, and he proposed to rig a bosun's chair under his peppermint-striped balloon and float over our area with an eye peeled for scattered ballast stones or cannon. The technique is actually sound, and has been used by archeologists to spot lost, ancient ruins from the air. But persistently windy weather discouraged this project. I think it would have been fun, however. Maybe we'll yet use it someday. Certainly, after some of the wild devices we've tried over the years, I wouldn't discount the possibility of using anything.

It was Dan again who became involved in another hair-raising experience that summer. This time he and Del were hanging onto the end of two lines, being pulled through the ocean by the boat. This was one of our other methods of covering a lot of territory while looking for new sites, and I must admit it's normally a lot of fun being towed in this manner. We even squabble for the honor.

They were trailing 30 feet or so behind us and were down 10 feet in about seven fathoms of water. Things were quiet for a while, when Del saw Dan pointing down to his right. Del could see a nine-foot shark swimming slowly in the opposite direction, about 20 feet below them. They forgot all about looking for a submerged wreck and kept their eyes riveted to the metallic-gray monster. It seemed to be passing by without paying any particular attention, when, in a flash, it did a beautiful chandelle in the water and began closing in on Dan and Del. Terror drove its stabbing spikes into their hearts. They had a sudden realization that, in the eyes of the shark, they must appear as giant chunks of bait, being trolled through the water as a tempting dinner.

They started "walking" up their lines, with toes curled up, running hand over hand with such swift motion that all the shark could see was a blur of arms, elbows and flippers. When they broke surface, they kept coming, lickety-split. We had no way of knowing, of course, what was causing this flurry of motion, but it triggered instant hysteria on board. I think without question that seeing them flitting across the top of the water, pulling in that line for all they were worth, was one of the funniest sights my old eyes have ever seen.

"Laugh, damn you, laugh," Del shouted at us, and when he and Dan stretched their arms full length to show us how long the shark had been, it only seemed to set us off into more peals of laughter. We couldn't stop, and the more we wailed, the madder Dan and Del got. I guess if we had been underwater with them, it wouldn't have been so funny, but, likewise, had they been able to see themselves scrambling up that line I don't think they could have resisted a belly laugh. I'd have given a hundred pieces of eight to have that sequence on film.

One other tale is worth relating here. It concerned Erv's special shark gun. He worked for weeks rigging a spear-shooting contraption that would "protect us forever from the man-eaters." Finally it was ready for testing, and Erv proudly gave it to me since I was as fearless (and foolhardy) as anyone else. I went overboard and sighted a shark within minutes, and a good-sized one at that. I took careful aim, yanked the trigger, and—pow—hit home right below the dorsal fin. Then I got a rude shock. The damn shark didn't play dead. Instead, it took off for deeper waters and dragged me with it!

"Hang onto the gun, hang onto the gun," Erv was screaming from the boat. I did—for about another minute. By this time the predator had gotten up so much speed that I could have water-skied, had I had the skis. I had no choice but to let go, otherwise I'd have wound up on the other side of the Atlantic somewhere, but I had a hell of a time explaining this to Erv. He got even madder when I suggested that maybe a Portuguese fisherman would net the shark and return the gun. Some of poor Erv's prize inventions were sure meeting ill fates.

Between such hilarious adventures we did manage to get in some serious treasure hunting that season, believe it or not, and we brought up some unusual items to add to our growing collection. We continued to work the cabin site, and it was Erv who scored first. Perhaps Dame Fortune was at last looking his way.

We were using a heavy iron strap that was half buried in the sands as a marker. It was within a few feet of this that Dan had found his two silver clumps, and the general area nearby was a hot hunting ground for loose coins, too. Several feet seaward was what we at first thought was an anchor ring. We used this as a marker also, and tied buoys to it and the iron strap. After dredging around the ring, though, we discovered it was actually linked through a thick stock of wood that had been completely buried. This led us to believe it was part of a rudder rather than an anchor ring.

Anyway, Erv had kicked off a few feet north of these markers, and happened upon two long, slender pieces of iron, about eight or nine feet in length. He signaled me over to examine his find, and when I began chipping at them with my handpick, I bit deep into one end. We took them topside for a look in the sunshine, and, sure enough, they were two muskets, with wooden stocks at one end and iron barrels at the other.

We were finding loose coins with fair regularity, and Erv Taylor brought up a bronze apothecary jar and a little jewel box which we thought at first was made of gold. Under closer scrutiny we learned it was actually gold-plated and really made of pewter. I'll bet my last fiver some sly Spaniard was going to palm this off on an unsuspecting buyer as a solid gold box.

It was shortly after noon one day when Dan swam up to a coral-encrusted cannon that didn't look familiar. He poked his nose down its dark muzzle and felt around its long-barreled underside. Then his hand ran over something different. He peeked down and saw what looked like a lazy Susan attached to the great gun. It was a silver plate firmly bolted to the cannon by hundreds of years of coral growth. Centered on the plate was a silver cup.

Dan took out his chisel and hammer and began pecking away ever so lightly at the encrustations. It was a hard, tedious job, which became more difficult as he worked. The sea was acting up and he was at a point right where the breakers were crashing down over the reef. Dan tied two anchor lines down and wrapped his legs around them. When his head became dizzy from the relentless surf, and his arms ached from the tapping, John Jones took over.

John, a career captain in the Air Force assigned to Harry Cannon as a range safety officer, had agreed to assist in our operations. A native of Atlanta, he is a West Point graduate (adding further distinction to our group—what other treasure-hunting team can make that statement?) and a veteran jet pilot. He too, like Harry, has lightning fast reflexes. He once blew up a Polaris missile that was thundering off course *six seconds* after its ignition! A fine young man, John loves to skin-dive and welcomed the chance to help us out when Harry offered it to him.

Dan and John each surfaced several times to exchange tanks of air—one was good only for about 45 minutes—and went down again after we lent words of encouragement. Three hours later the stubborn plate loosened and they brought it up. It was a beauty, as was the cup affixed to it. They make a handsome addition to our Museum of Spanish Treasure, on highway A1A near Satellite Beach, Florida. We have been offered $150 for the plate alone.

A few days later the visibility was so bad on site—no more than a couple of inches—we put the six-inch dredge to work on the bottom and placed a croaker sack over the exhaust end. When the sack filled with sand, coral and, hopefully, objects of value, we took it up to the boat and dumped the contents out on the deck to filter through it. On the last sackful of the day, we found a formation of coral encrustation with the perfect molding of a plate in it. The dredge must have sucked the coral loose from the plate, leaving it intact down below. From its fine imprint it must be in excellent shape. We are still looking for the plate and will get it one of these days.

We continued to find loose coins and some silver forks, in both good and poor condition, but by September bad weather settled in, and I mean consistently bad weather. All during the diving season it's a touch-and-go thing in this part of Florida. We get about as many summer thunderstorms here as anywhere else in the nation. In fact, there's a place near Orlando, which is just a little northwest of Sebastian, that supposedly gets more such storms than any other geographical location in the continental United States. I certainly wouldn't be the one to dispute this, for I know we get our share.

It's nothing for us to go out on a beautiful June or July morning, under a bright sky with only lightly scattered clouds off on the horizon, and reach the wreck site on smooth seas, say by 10 A.M. Within two or three hours, which pass by like minutes when we're diving, a wind picks up out of the west, ominous black thunderheads close in fast, and the seas whip up into a white-capped frenzy. If we don't pull anchor and run for port at the first signs of storm activity, we're in for one hell of a buffeting out there. Those combers have nearly swamped us more often than I care to remember. Not only that, but during the 1962 season, the Sebastian Inlet channel had not been widened and deepened, and it was still a daring navigational feat to put our *Sampan* through in calm waters and at high tide. To try it any other time was flirting with disaster.

The same was true in placing our workboat in the narrow trough between the two reefs at the wreck site. It still is today. Even when we're positioned perfectly, it's only about 15 feet or so to the jagged first reef, and many is the day we scraped the second barrier of coral out there while trying to skirt the first one. Let me assure you, it's a pretty sickening feeling to know sharp-edged rocks are clawing at the underside of the hull. To tell the truth, I'm surprised we haven't gone down out there, with all the bumpings and scrapings and buffetings we've been through.

What makes those reefs so treacherous is the fact there are only two or three feet of water over them in some spots, so if a big roller picked the boat up and dropped it in just the right spot, we could wind up hanging onto a mass of good-sized splinters. It's an ever-present danger we have learned to live with, so it's quite understandable that we have the utmost respect for the elements, and when they feel like kicking up their heels, we call it a day.

I believe when most people think of the Florida coastline they envision a tranquil, blue-green sea with soft swells lightly lapping a golden stretch of beach. Twelve miles out, the water *is* beautiful and generally tranquil. This is where the Gulf Stream flows. But that's 12 miles out. Along a great portion of the East Coast the waves do gently rumble onto the beachfront; so gentle, in fact, surfboarders have a tough time finding one large enough to hitch a ride on.

But in our particular nook at the cabin site, it seemed as though fate had looked around for 100 miles to find the darkest, murkiest, most dangerous spot to sink a treasure-bearing galleon. Combers build up, foam over and then crash down upon the second reef, directly onto the wreckage. But then again, if this weren't true someone might have discovered the treasure long before we made the scene. Still, it is frustrating to work a site where, during the entire year, including a four-month prime diving season, there may be only a dozen or so clear, calm days when conditions underwater are ideal for salvage. That's why we've been working this one site ever since 1961. There's no telling when we'll finish.

So when we wrapped things up that fall, we expected to find little more until the waters cleared again the following spring. But in this profession you can take nothing for granted; you can rely on no hard-fast rules. You sometimes score the most when you expect the least. Such was the case one wintry day in November when my nephew, Rex Stocker, and I drove over to the oceanfront for a stroll down the beach.

Actually, it was just after a pretty good northeaster blow, so chances of finding something on the sands were relatively good. I had a metal detector with me and set to work immediately, following it as I would a straining dog on a leash, down close to the water's edge. Rex, who was 19 at the time, ambled up near the high-water mark. I'd only been going a few minutes when . . . zingggg . . . the detector whirred. After digging a few inches in the washed sand, I plucked out a rectangular cut of metal. It was a piece of eight.

I lost track of time, of Rex and everything else as I followed that detector down the beach. The coins were coming at a steady pace. Near the bluff, at the edge of the high-water mark, Rex was growing restless. Without a metal-finding machine, he had only eyesight to rely on, and why he was way up there I don't know. There sure as hell wouldn't be any coins there. He was getting bored with it all—if looking for treasure on a beach where you know it exists can get boring. Anyway, the next thing I knew he was jumping up and down and yelling as loud as he could.

"Kip, Kip," he shrieked, and he started running to me. I had a sudden fear. Had he been bitten by a snake that had slithered out of the palmetto brush for a sunbath in the dunes? As he neared, I could see something yellowish wrapped around his arm. He was bringing the reptile to me! It must be a pygmy rattler, I thought, and I looked around for a stick to bash in its nose. But then when he got closer I could see it wasn't a snake at all.

"Look," Rex exclaimed, between huffs and puffs. "Look what I found up there in the sand!"

I had to rub my spectacles on my shirtfront to believe my eyes. He handed me a long chain of finely wrought gold. It was the most exquisite piece of jewelry I've ever seen. Rex had found it knotted up lying in the open, where it obviously had been washed in by a high surge of water. The sun's reflected glitter had caught his eye. Otherwise he might have stepped right over it.

Later, at home, we examined it with great care and admiration. The chain measured an astonishing 11 feet 4½ inches in length, and was made up of 2,176 individual, flower-shaped links, each so finely designed and fashioned as to defy belief. It weighed nearly half a pound. The pendant from the chain is a golden dragon, or possibly a grasshopper, about the size of my little finger. The creature's back opens out to form a toothpick —a solid gold toothpick. What kind of dinner can a man eat to pick his teeth with a solid gold toothpick, I wondered. The tail forms a little spoon, probably for cleaning wax out of one's ears.

Rex blew into the half-open mouth of the dragon and a shrill whistle filled the room. It was in near-perfect condition after all these years. We guessed the storm had washed it in from the sea. We knew this was a magnificent ornament—the finest yet recovered in our searches either on the beach or underwater. Just how valuable a piece it was we didn't know. But we soon found out.

The first jewelers we took it to were completely baffled as to how such an intricate, delicate, beautiful piece could have been made. They had never seen anything like it. We have since had the gold chain appraised by three different museums—at $40,000, $50,000 and $60,000 respectively. So it is a fair assumption to say it is conservatively worth $50,000. But how can anyone, no matter how expert, place a real value on such an object? I contend it simply cannot be done, and I look upon this necklace not as a $50,000 piece, but as one that is, more accurately, priceless.

Now for the real corker! Rex thinks he may have casually kicked off a second chain just prior to making his rare find. He had been wading in ankle-deep waters and felt something wrap around his leg. Instinctively, believing it to be seaweed, he jerked his leg hard, sending the object sailing into the ocean. When, a couple of minutes later, he found the gold chain, a horrifying thought struck him: could he have, without looking, booted a second necklace into the sea? We scoured the shoreline in vain. If, in fact, it had been a gold chain that had wrapped itself around his ankle, it was taken out to deeper waters in the backwash.

Whether the experts agree or not on the value of the recovered piece, I don't care. But certainly no one can dispute that what Rex had found ranks among the greatest single pieces of treasure ever recovered— anywhere. The only comparable discovery that comes to mind was the finding of the fabled Bishop's Cross off Bermuda in 1955 by Teddy Tucker. He got his prize from a small pocket among the rocks beneath the sea. It is a gold pectoral cross studded with seven emeralds. Handmade by Indians, probably late in the sixteenth century, it also has two small golden nails that hang from the ends of the crossbar.

Like our gold chain, the Bishop's Cross has been appraised, and an expensive price tag placed on it. But I know my good friend Teddy would be the first to agree that both of these rare relics are beyond appraisal. It is almost blasphemous to attempt an assessment of their true value in dollar signs.

The origin of Rex's necklace remains a mystery to this day. We have shown it to state archeologists, to experts at the Smithsonian Institution in Washington, and to specialists at the Kensington Museum in London, and it has stumped them all. The best they could do was offer theories, and they're even divided on these. Some contend this chain is Chinese, and they have a strong point in their argument: the dragon pendant, which is certainly Oriental in appearance. Yet others steadfastly claim the necklace was handcrafted in Mexico.

In my unofficial opinion I have to go along with those who believe it to be from China. Somewhere in his voluminous readings, Doc Kelso came across a passage that told of Spanish traders in the Philippines. Among the items they bargained for in Manila were carved Chinese gold chains and necklaces. This is the closest we've ever come to tracing the exact origin of Rex's find.

Naturally we wanted to keep this brilliant piece of jewelry in our collection. Technically, it belonged to Rex, for anything found on the beach is finder's keepers. So at our next board of directors meeting we decided to offer Rex shares in our company in return for the gold chain. He agreed on our offering of 40 shares.

It was in this general time period that we had some changes in our team, so now would be as good a time as any to take a look at our company's structure. The Real Eight Corporation has 1,000 shares. At the first division of stock, after the finds of coin clusters and our subsequent organization early in 1961, the split went this way: Doc and I got 290 shares between us. Our five hardworking divers, Dan Thompson, Harry Cannon, Erv Taylor, Del Long and Lou Ullian each got 120 shares. Libe Futch, who didn't dive, got 110 shares.

To acquire the gold chain, we each contributed five shares to make the 40 we gave Rex. Then Libe's wife died, and he lost his treasure-hunting incentive. Libe was getting along in years, too, so he came to me one day late in 1962, before Rex's find, and said he'd like to sell out. I offered him a fair price for his shares and he agreed.

It may sound peculiar when I say we were in dire need of working capital, but it was true. Sure, we had coins by the hundreds, and numbers of other valuable objects, including the silver wedges. But we hadn't cashed anything in. They were stashed in bank vaults. We wanted to keep our treasure intact if possible.

I knew how we might raise some cash, so I approached the others. C. Robert Brown, president of the First National Bank of Melbourne, a city about 25 miles north of Sebastian, wanted to buy in. He knew of our finds because we had acquired a $5,000 loan from his bank to buy the beach cabin opposite our wreck site. As collateral we gave him 2,000 silver pieces of eight.

Now we have an agreement in Real Eight that if one of us wants to sell out at any time, the rest of us have a 30-day option to purchase the shares. But since everybody was paying operating expenses out of his own pocket, no one had the ready funds to buy up Libe's stock. I knew we could make a quick profit by selling it to Brown, and the gang gave me the go-ahead. I sold the 105 shares, and we had a new partner.

Within a couple of months Erv Taylor had remarried, and his wife put her foot down. He was spending entirely too much time in the ocean. Reluctantly, Erv decided to relinquish his shares. I told everyone of his desire and said we had 30 days to buy. I guess Harry and Dan and Lou and the others felt there was no rush, for a month passed and no action was taken.

Bob Brown, being the clever businessman he was, saw an opportunity and he pushed his advantage. He and I paid Erv an agreeable sum for his shares. With the 30-day deadline passed, I considered that the deal was closed. But when the others learned that Brown and I had acquired Erv's shares, they were fighting mad, and a board meeting was hastily called. The gist of the knockdown dragout that ensued seemed to center on the fact that they were mad because they considered Brown more or less an outsider. Everyone in our original group had contributed so much to the overall effort—in time, work and money—that it was looked upon as a rather tight-knit organization. Now, within a matter of several weeks, we found ourselves with a partner who had expended less effort, yet had acquired, through legitimate negotiations, more shares than anyone else in Real Eight but me. The others didn't like this one bit. Legally, no wrongs had been committed, because the 30-day option had expired, but, morally, the group felt they had been given a raw deal.

"Hell, if I'd known you were going to buy Erv out this quick we could have raised the cash," Dan pointed out. "We certainly didn't think, after all we've been through, you'd pin us down like this. We want to buy Erv's stock and split it among all stockholders."

He had a point, and I could see from the tone of the meeting that we were steering for serious trouble if some amends weren't made. I told them I'd see what I could do. When I later went to Brown and explained the entire situation to him, he understood, and voluntarily released his legally sound option to buy Erv's stock. We raised the cash and bought Erv out, with Brown adding ten shares in the transaction rather than the larger amount.

I learned much later that had the original transaction stood, whereby Brown and I would have acquired Taylor's shares, our company might have collapsed entirely. Dan, Lou, Harry and Del were ready to bolt. I guess I was the one being put to the test this time, and I'm happy to say the end result further solidified the team. There'll be no such misunderstandings again.

In May, 1964, we amended our structure to take in two new members —Bob Johnson and John Jones. Actually, they weren't new. They had both been diving with us for a couple of years, and the team felt their long, faithful service merited their official acceptance in the company. To make room, all original members donated enough to give them each 40 shares.

Tall, tanned and balding Robert (Bob) Johnson came to us by way of the oil fields of Texas and Arkansas, and the U.S. Army, with which he traveled extensively around the world. Bob is a tug master and an expert on salvage operations. He should be. He has had more than two decades of experience on all of the seven seas and then some. He has worked out of every exotic port in the world—from Capetown to Karachi; Murmansk to Madagascar; and Havana to Hong Kong to Hobart, Tasmania.

He knows boats and the sea as well as any man I've met, and he holds three licenses—small boat operator's; master of freight and towboats; and unlimited ocean. He can sail any vessel on any waters, and I wouldn't be afraid to ride through the worst hurricane or typhoon in history if Bob Johnson were piloting the craft.

To say he got involved with Real Eight in a roundabout way is understating the fact. He was a chief warrant officer at Fort Eustis, Virginia, in the twilight of a 22-year military career, when he was assigned to bring several LARC vehicles to Cape Kennedy in support of Project Mercury —the nation's first manned space program. The LARC is a ducklike, amphibious abortion that can maneuver on land, sea or in the marshiness that separates the two at the cape. These vehicles were needed in case an astronaut's rocket blew up on or near the launch pad—to motor medics and fire fighters quickly to the scene regardless of where he landed.

Bob ran into Harry, who was directing the overall astronaut recovery team. We got government permission to take a LARC down to Sebastian once to haul up some cannon for the Air Force, and Bob directed the operations. His all-around skills and savvy were so obvious we figured he would be a major asset to our team, and we invited him to dive with us. It was one of the smartest moves we ever made.

Bob and John later were given the opportunity to buy 15 more shares apiece, which they did. Then Lou and Del went one better, and gave their longtime friend, Bob Johnson, 30 additional shares for the token price of $1. So today, the split of Real Eight's 1,000 shares runs like this: I have 175; Doc, 100; Dan and Harry, 115 each; Lou and Del, 100 apiece; Bob, 85; Jones, 55; and Rex, 40. Bob Brown died in December, 1964, and his 115 shares are now controlled by his estate.

A Spanish cannon is deposited on deck after nearly two and a half centuries on the ocean bottom.

LEFT: Mel and Dolores Fisher examine ancient silver forks. RIGHT: Bob Johnson inspects a find of Spanish coins.

Pieces of eight, or cobs—oddly shaped because they were chiseled from the end of a bar of silver before stamping—and knife blade.

Kip Wagner with two gold eight-escudo coins, or doubloons. They bear the shield of Philip V of Spain on one side, a cross on the other.

10   Helping Hands

Things moved slowly early in the 1963 diving season, although we continued to exude confidence that we would soon make the "big kill." As usual, between our business affairs, which seemed to me to be taking up more and more of our time, we worked on our equipment and on the boat over the winter months. We went out on site a few times in May for short sessions on the bottom and found only sparsely scattered coins.

Then one morning early in June something completely unpredicted and unexpected happened. It was as if some great hand had passed a magic wand over the area. The sky showed nothing but blue, and the water was as clear and as calm as we'd ever seen it since we'd been diving as a team. Underneath, it was like a fairyland. We could barely believe our eyes. Visibility ranged from 50 to 100 feet, and all the cannon spread about the wreck site as markers were lying openly exposed on the sands. Conditions were near perfect for diving.

The actual site we had been working covers an area on the ocean floor about 100 feet long and 40 feet wide. Over the 1961 and 1962 seasons, we had confined our concentrated searches to a small zone about 20 feet square. Our salvage had been slow because the treasure was buried under several feet of sand and we wanted methodically to probe every inch of the wreck. Otherwise we might pass right over the richest portion.

But the water was so phenomenally clean we decided there would never be a better time to explore fully the perimeters of the wreck site, so we could accurately chart them as would a cartographer.

Mike Hrebec, the college student, was with us again for the summer, and he took off shoreward to see what he could find. A short time later Lou looked over the side of the *Sampan* and saw an excessive flow of bubbles streaming to the surface. It was Mike. He hadn't been down long enough to have run out of air, and it appeared as if he was struggling with something. With a desperate lunge, he made the rope ladder at the side of the boat. Now we could see he had something straddled between his legs, and we nearly fell overboard helping him up. His weighty object proved to be another healthy clump of silver coins—this one scaling in at about 70 pounds. Figuring roughly 20 coins to the pound, it contained something like 1,400 of those lovely, blackened pieces of eight. I had a feeling we were in for a string of good luck.

From the shape of Mike's clump, it was obvious these coins had been stored in a box at the time the ships went down. We found coins fused at 90-degree angles, where the chest's corners had been. We had learned that all of the large coin clusters had originally been stored in wooden containers or in cloth sacks. The sacks had rotted and the teredo worms had eaten the wood fibers, leaving the coins sealed together.

When, after a couple of days, the weather continued unusually calm and clear, Dan, Lou and Bob Johnson managed to wangle a couple of days off in staggered shifts, so we could work throughout the week. Normally, we were strictly weekend warriors, as Doc likes to call us, but this weather was too good and too scarce not to take full advantage of it.

Tuesday, Lou was off and he, Mike and I went out. The ocean was as flat and as beautiful as I've ever seen it. Its surface was a turquoise mirror. Lou and Mike went under while I tended to things aboard ship. They decided to retrace the steps Mike had taken when he brought up his clump, for often loose coins break off and fall to the bottom in moving such a cluster.

They had only been on the dredge about 15 minutes when before them shone a greenish hue—another clump of coins! They were working next to a ledge that dropped off abruptly, and this first find had been at the top of the ledge. As they carefully worked it loose—it was adhered to some coquina rock—they found another behind it. In fact, within a six-foot area, they brought up four large clumps and one small one, each weighing from 50 to 75 pounds, and containing a grand total of several thousand coins.

Unlike the solidified clusters Dan had found two years earlier, these apparently had been buried in the sands for a great period of time, and as Lou and Mike walked over to the boat, they left a wide trail of pieces of

eight on the sands. Dan's clumps had been cemented together more securely because they had been exposed to the seawater. These had not, and
were thus more loosely fused.

After securing the clusters, the divers went back down to vacuum the
corridor of coins they had spilled en route to the boat. During the
pickup, Mike found a beautiful silver crucifix, encrusted with multicolored shell fragments. On one of the last dives of the day, he came up
shouting excitedly and holding a square silvery object in his hand. Mike
thought it was a silver wedge, but instead it turned out to be a cube of
lead, probably used to make shot.

We were three tired treasure hunters that evening as we headed for
home. Those clumps are damn heavy, and it's one hell of a job to get
them up. But we were happy, too, and who wouldn't be, sitting on
$100,000 or so worth of silver coins?

Fishermen friends of mine say they love to ply their trade or their
avocation, as the case may be, in the ocean because they never know for
sure what they may bring up—a snapper or a shark, a snook or a sailfish.
The same is true in our business. It might be a ship's spike or a piece of
eight, a silver wedge or a chunk of useless metal, like Mike's lead box. By
now we thought we had seen just about everything, and felt that nothing
could surprise us anymore. We were wrong, however—dead wrong.

The weekend following the clump finds of Tuesday, the whole diving
crew was out in force: Harry, Dan, Del, Bob, Lou, Mike, John Jones and
myself. The weather was still ideal, and the honor of finding one of our
most unique and priceless treasures goes to Lou and John. They were
routinely sweeping the bottom with our six-inch dredge when they noticed something peculiar. About four feet down, the sand seemed to be
only loosely packed, then after layers of it were suctioned up, there was a
vein of gray-colored mud or clay. Strange indeed!

Studded in this mud were blue and white chips of porcelain, the discovery of which didn't create too much excitement, for we had found
hundreds of such chips before, no more than a half inch in diameter.
Jones was working forward, directing the hungry dredge, and Lou was
just behind him, when John suddenly turned around and rapped Lou so
hard it nearly knocked his face mask off. He held up half a cup of china.
Then, a second later, he produced the other half, making a perfect match.
An inch or two deeper in the sand, they found two cups and two bowls
intact, and then more.

"It looked just as though someone had opened up a china closet," Lou said. "We could see whole bowls and cups stacked horizontally, lying there as though they had been set out for an afternoon tea. John and I were dumbfounded," Lou continued, "but we were snapped back to our senses by a clanking, crumbling sound in the dredge. It had swallowed some of the chinaware and was spitting out broken pieces at the exhaust end. We quickly swung it out of the mud area and surfaced to cut the power down to a trickle. I took the two cups and two bowls up with me and challenged everyone on board to guess what I had. No one came close."

For the next hour or so the boys took turns working the porcelain out, little by little, lightly brushing the dredge over it to ease the pieces loose, and also clearing away the mud with their fingers. It was a delicate operation. Eventually, they brought up about 28 bowls and cups, all as perfect as the day they were made. Lou surfaced once with a stack of eight cups he had found just as they had been packed nearly 250 years ago. They also extracted a slew of bits and chips, and several large pieces of Mexican pottery.

When the waters started kicking up a little late in the afternoon, we decided to halt operations for the day, fearing the rough water would cause breakage. To protect the china, I emptied the toolbox on board the *Sampan* and painstakingly wrapped each piece with wads of toilet paper. We headed for port, but as we got to the mouth of the inlet, the boat's engine quit.

"What's wrong?" I snapped.

Bob Johnson and Del Long, our two expert boatsmen and mechanics, didn't know. As they began checking, the *Sampan* started buffeting in the slapping waves, and I got nervous. Here were these precious, fragile pieces of china being bounced all over creation, and we couldn't get the damn engine going.

But I wasn't taking any chances. The others eyed me curiously as I stalked around the cabin and gathered every life preserver I could find. When I had a double armful, I slipped them around the toolbox, shoved it forward and sat on it.

"What the hell are you doing?" Dan asked, half amused, half puzzled.

"If this boat sinks I'm going to make sure the china gets ashore," I replied. The words were greeted with a loud round of guffaws. Looking back on it, I guess it was a funny scene: me perched atop that toolbox swathed in bright-orange life preservers. But I wanted to keep that china if I had to swim in, lugging the box behind me; and if I looked ridiculous, so be it. Let them laugh.

After a half hour or so of tinkering, Bob and Del got the motor cranked up again, and we made it without further incident. Luckily for us, the tide was outgoing when we stalled at the inlet, and the current carried us seaward. Had we been swept into the channel, with its treacherous rocks, the *Sampan* would have been in very real danger of sinking.

When we unpacked the case later, I couldn't resist impressing the boys. Fingering a bowl with a beautiful design adorning it, I said, in as nonchalant a manner as I could manage, "I see this china is from the K'ang Hsi dynasty." Everyone was flabbergasted. Their mouths must have dropped three inches.

"How the heck do you know what this stuff is?" Jones asked incredulously.

The fact was Doc Kelso and I had known for years that there were quite probably cases of china in the wreck areas under the sea. We had found references to it more than once. I think Doc first learned of it in an obscure Florida historical quarterly, published in 1942. The author had found blue and white fragments in shallow waters near the beach, opposite the cabin wreck site, and had made an accurate guess that it was K'ang Hsi china. We had confirmed this later when we read the manifests of the *Principe de Asturias* and *Nuestra Señora del Carmen*—the two ships that had ferried salvaged treasure from the fleet back to Spain a year after the hurricane, in 1716. According to the manifests, a great amount of the china had been recovered, but it had not surprised us to find more.

Doc had even read of the type of mud or clay the porcelain had been packed in. It was called petuntse. What amazed me was how this fragile stuff could survive the full fury of the storm, the splintering of the great ships on the reefs and the pounding surf over all these years. It was indeed a miracle.

Doc wrote to Kammar Aga Oglu at the University of Michigan. She is a professor emeritus there and one of the world's leading authorities on such china. She easily identified the photographs we sent and told us it definitely was from the K'ang Hsi period (1662–1722). We had found three distinct styles: blue on white designs; pure white, with only a faint tracing visible where a decorative border once circled the rim; and bowls covered with black enamel with traces of gold decoration. The decorative trim, as best we can make out, was probably a gilded border of flowers, foliages, fish and shrimp. Mrs. Oglu wanted us to send some of the actual pieces to her, but we were afraid to press our luck. After all it had gone through, we didn't want to chance breakage now.

She also confirmed a fact Doc and I had previously found in our research. This china, delicate and beautiful as it was, actually was the five and dime store variety of its day. It was being shipped to Spain to be sold commercially. There was nothing rare about it in 1715. Mrs. Oglu placed an arbitrary value of $20 to $25 each on large fragments of the porcelain, and considerably more on each undamaged cup or bowl. But several museums, including the Prince Albert and Queen Victoria in London, say the china is priceless. It may have been garden variety 250 years ago, but today one cannot assess its true value.

Regardless of its material worth, it made a handsome addition to our collection. From an aesthetic standpoint it was one of our most important finds. My wife, Alice, spent hours of pleasant labor mending several of the broken cups, and the entire allotment is today exhibited in our museum. Since removing it from the sea, the china has aged a little, but it still has a rare beauty all its own. We have noticed a few hairline stress cracks in some of the cups and bowls, but it would almost take a microscopic examination for a layman to see them. Their chemical balance was probably upset somewhat when we brought them up, but fortunately it has been nothing serious. We've repaired the few stress cracks with glue.

I'm almost ashamed to say we never have gotten back to the area where we found the cups and bowls. In all fairness, though, it was either too rough, or we were busy on other recoveries. But we know where the spot is. There's a rich vein of mud there, and one of these days when the conditions are just right again, we'll open up some more of those china closets.

Bob and Lou made another significant discovery during this general time period. It was on a day when the tide was so low we couldn't get the boat into the wreck area, so they took a plywood raft, banked with blocks of styrofoam that Del had rigged up for such occasions, and swam out from the cabin. Bob had got us a six-horsepower Briggs and Stratton motor mounted on an aluminum block, and Del outfitted a centrifugal pump and a small compressor. We mounted all this on a float, and it enabled us to work in shallow and hard-to-get-to areas with a four-inch dredge. It also allowed us to get on site in minutes if there was a sudden break in the weather, whereas it took about an hour and a half to get through the inlet and into position with the *Sampan*. The whole contraption cost only about $125 in parts, and we got that back in silver coins the first time we used it.

This particular day Bob, Del and Lou swam out, towing the raft, and Otis Imboden, the *National Geographic* photographer, was along to shoot some pictures. They had found a few cobs, some silver forks and a couple of other trinkets, when, by three in the afternoon, it began to get choppy and they were ready to come in. Lou checked on the barge to make sure it wasn't drifting into the reef, then dived to see what Bob was doing. He hadn't been up for a while. On the bottom Bob tapped Lou on the shoulder and pointed down under the muzzle of a cannon. There were four or five links of a delicate gold chain. They gently fanned the sand away, and inch by inch, a lengthy necklace unfolded. It has a pendant with tracings of miniature paintings on both sides. The pictures under the glass were eroded by centuries of immersion in the salt water.

Over the winter of 1962, Lou made one of his frequent trips to the West Coast on missile business for the Air Force. By now we had heard of every serious treasure hunter on both sides of Timbuktu, and they had all heard of us, though at the time none of them had any idea of how much we had found. Lou made a habit of checking into skin-diving shops wherever he was to see what was new in equipment lines, and he happened into the Los Angeles shop of Mel Fisher one afternoon.

We had all heard of Mel. Treasure hunters are, in fact, much like professional pool hustlers. You may go for years and never meet, but you know the names and the reputations. There's not a billiard shark in the country who hasn't heard the legendary tales of Luther "Wimpy" Lassiter, Eddie "The Knoxville Bear" Taylor, or the storied Minnesota Fats. The same is true in our field, and Mel Fisher was one of the names we had heard frequently over the years.

In fact, he was somewhat of an underwater celebrity in California. He had become interested in diving years ago in Florida, and when he moved west he had opened the first specialized shop for skin divers in the world. He even had a weekly television program in Hollywood on which he showed movies of his subaquatic adventures. He had been after treasure for years, but was luckless. Though he had no gold, he had collected a number of experiences well worth retelling.

For example, he had taken an expedition to the sacrificial wells of the Mayans at Yucatán—the same ones Luis Marden had dived into. Mel had also searched for riches in the Florida Keys, Cuba, Haiti, the Dominican

Republic, the Virgin Isles, Panama, Colombia and Mexico, and he had worked a number of wrecked gambling ships off the coast of California. At one point he had gone $25,000 in the red, with only artifacts of historical value to show for the work and money invested.

After introducing himself, Lou noticed a Spanish half real piece under a counter and casually inquired where it had come from. Mel didn't know what the coin was. He had found it, he said, on a recent unsuccessful hunting trip to Panama. The coin keyed open a long conversation during which Lou told him of our finds. The next time Lou went west on a trip he called again. This time Mel was planning an expedition to the fabled Silver Shoals area off Puerto Rico where Sir William Phips had recovered his fabulous treasure in 1687. Again, Mel had bad luck, but he went back for a second try a couple of months later, and Lou told him to stop by my house on the way down.

I had an old map of a Silver Shoals wreck which I gave Mel. He is a balding, powerfully built man with as perfect a poker face as I've ever seen. We sat for hours spinning tales of treasure. He was very much impressed when I showed him some of our coins.

Mel worked his sunken ship off the shoals, but, unfortunately, he found no treasure, only olive jars, buttons, merchant seals of lead and cannonballs. In March, 1963, Mel stopped by my house again. He had a proposal. It was pouring brickbats outside, but I called Lou and told him to come on down and chat with us. What Mel said made sense to me, but I wanted another Real Eight member to hear him out.

Mel told us we were onto something really big, but at our rate of work it would take an eternity to realize it, since we mostly dived on weekends only. He proposed to form a hard-core team of experienced, professional divers to help us. They would pay their own way and provide their own equipment. In return for diving on our leased sites, everything they brought up would be split 50-50 down the middle after the state took its 25-percent slice off the top. Anything we recovered ourselves was still all ours. It sounded like a square deal.

We told Mel we'd kick it around at our next board meeting, and he said he'd see if he could assemble enough capable, eager divers. As we saw it, the entire risk was his. If they found nothing, they got nothing. If they found anything, we got half. I had to agree with him. It seemed as if we would take forever to get around to all the sites we had pinpointed. We had just spent two years on the cabin wreck and had barely made a dent

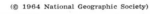

A silver crucifix encrusted with colorful bits of shells during its long immersion in the sea.

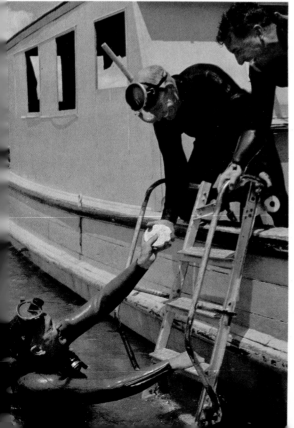

Harry Cannon passes a gold ingot to Bob Johnson aboard the *Sampan*.

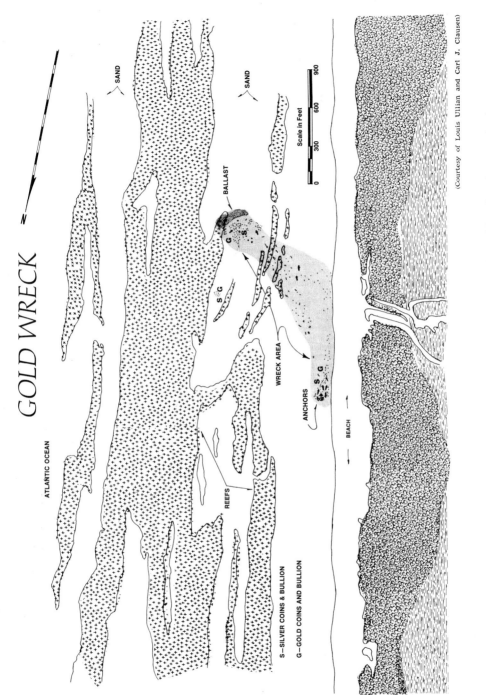

GOLD WRECK

ATLANTIC OCEAN

SAND

SAND

BALLAST

WRECK AREA

ANCHORS

REEFS

BEACH

S—SILVER COINS & BULLION

G—GOLD COINS AND BULLION

N

Scale in Feet

0   300   600   900

(Courtesy of Louis Ullian and Carl J. Clausen)

The Gold Wreck site, shown in this diagram, has yielded a king's ransom in golden doubloons and other treasure.

in the area. At our pace it looked as if we'd take years, and no one was getting any younger, particularly me.

Mel wrote a couple of weeks later from California and said he had found a team that had agreed to work one year without pay. If they hadn't done any good in that time, they would call it quits and write it off as another memorable experience. The board agreed it sounded like a winning proposition if we could get a few technicalities ironed out, but they were minor. Negotiations ran into the 1963 diving season, and it was just after we had found the K'ang Hsi china that Rupert Gates, Mel's right-hand man, showed up one day at my place.

Unlike the storied version of a treasure hunter—that happy-go-lucky soldier-of-fortune type—Rupert was a serious-minded, well-educated professional in the field. He is a graduate of Stanford and can offer as diving credentials experience on underwater safaris in such areas as the Italian Riviera, the gold-nugget-bearing rivers of California, Oregon and Alaska, and Lake Guatavita, high in the Andes Mountains.

"What are you doing here, Rupert?" I asked innocently.

"I just came down to tell you Mel and the whole gang have packed up and are headed down here to dive for you. Mel sold his boat, his home and his skin-diving business to raise cash for expenses."

The words dug into me like bits of shrapnel. We hadn't closed any deal or signed any contract with Fisher or anyone else. I got on the phone immediately and called a meeting of Real Eight members. After explaining as best I could what was happening, we decided to consummate the transaction. We had been close to agreement anyway, and the few details left could be worked out when Mel arrived.

Meanwhile, one sunny morning when the water looked good, we invited Rupert to join us on the *Sampan*. If he was going to be one of our partners, he might as well get his feet wet. He was initially surprised at how close to shore the cabin wreck site was, but this was to prove the least of his surprises that day.

Barely had we anchored when Mike Hrebec went over the side and brought up four pieces of eight that had slipped through the dredge exhaust the previous day and been covered by a pile of rubble. The night's sea action had washed the sand away, leaving them exposed, and Mike simply picked them up. Rupert had a skeptical look on his face. He honestly thought we had "salted" the area to make things look good. We had to take him down on the bottom and show him how things were before he would believe us. He had never seen coins lying loose like that in all his worldwide travels.

We also found some silver forks, but around one in the afternoon the compressor on the dredge broke down. Lou and I were tired and hungry and wanted to go in, but for some reason Del Long was hot to continue diving. He was, in fact, downright insistent. So while he started repairing the compressor with those magical hands of his, Lou and I swam in to the cabin for some chow.

Within 45 minutes, Del had the thing working again, and he and Dan went back under, using Desco rigs. On a hunch, Del had wanted to investigate one more spot, and Dan told him to lead the way. They were just over the first reef.

Lou and I were chewing food, and the fat, too, in front of the cabin, when Del's head popped out of the water, and he began whooping and hollering with such gusto I knew he had found something big.

"Son of a gun!" I exclaimed, more to myself than to Lou. "I'll bet he's found gold." Earlier that day Del had slapped me on the shoulder and said, "Kip, today I'm going to find some gold." I had shrugged automatically, and murmured something like, "Go to it, kid."

By this time he had reached the boat and it looked as if everybody on board were doing an Indian rain dance. They were shouting and stomping and laughing and patting each other on the back. Lou and I dropped our sandwiches and swam back out. Sure enough, Del had found gold. He showed us a beautiful eight-escudo piece as perfect and fresh as the day it had been minted. Poor Rupert was bewildered by now, and I couldn't blame him. I was a little excited, too. This was the first gold coin we had uncovered. But soon Rupe was diving and finding things right along with us.

Del said he and Dan had been working a spot in about nine feet of water when the sand parted and it looked just as though someone had turned a flashlight in their eyes. Shiny gold pieces stared up at them.

Everyone went over, and we formed a circle around the area and slowly worked our way in. In all, we picked up 23 golden doubloons, four- and eight-escudo pieces before the water got too rough for safety. Del also found a brilliant gold ring with an expansion band. He had dredged a funnel-shaped hole and saw the ring slipping down the sand at the side of the hole. Del applied the *coup de grâce*. He held out his little finger and let the ring slide right down onto it.

Rupert Gates was sure going to have a lot to tell Mel and his boys.

They arrived a few days later. It was quite a crew. Dick Williams, for instance, has been, at one time or another, a railroad diesel engineer, a welder and a radio electronics repairman. As a commerical radio operator he has literally sailed all the seven seas—and then some. He is also an expert hunter, marksman and outdoorsman, and is an outstanding instructor in survival techniques. He had accompanied Mel on one of his earlier, abortive treasure expeditions to Silver Shoals.

Walt Holzworth was a Pennsylvania Dutch farmer who migrated to California to become a construction superintendent, and wound up, through his insatiable interest in coin collecting, a full-time treasure hunter. He was 52 years old when he made his first dive in 1963, but has since become a proficient workman underwater.

Fay Field, a native of Fort Bridger, Wyoming, is Mel's electronics expert. He was formerly a project engineer on ground-controlled approach radar systems. His interest in diving began in a unique fashion. He is a shell collector par excellence, and he was eternally seeking the rare spiny oyster—Spondylus Americanus—which is seldom found in perfect condition, for its long, delicate spines are easily fractured. Luckily for Mel, and for us, these shells are found most often in wrecked iron ships. To cut expenses on his far-ranging searches for this curious specimen, Fay decided to build a supersensitive underwater detector that would distinguish between ferrous and nonferrous metals.

He tinkered with his "little black box" for two long years, but when he finally put it together, he had created a device that would revolutionize our salvage operations. It's called a magnetometer. When Mel heard about it, he outlined the treasure-hunting potentials of such a piece of equipment to Fay and persuaded him to join the Florida expedition.

Perhaps the most colorful diver on Fisher's team is Demostines Molinar —better known as Moe. Born in Colón, Panama, he was originally hired as a diesel mechanic for Mel's 65-foot, specially equipped boat, the *Golden Doubloon*, but Moe's enthusiasm was infectious, and he was later signed on as a diver, too. Incidentally, I often wonder why Mel named his boat the *Golden Doubloon*, for he never found a single gold coin while working from it in all his searches.

No mention of the Fisher contingent would be complete without a note or two on Mel's lovely wife, Dolores. Not only is she the mother of four children, but she also is an active participant in the team's hunts. In fact, she once held the women's underwater endurance record with scuba gear—54 hours and 37 minutes! I might add also she's a damn sight prettier than any other member of our team or Mel's.

The first order of business for Fisher was to find a boat from which to operate. He had sold his *Golden Doubloon* and needed something less extravagant. Even so, I don't think he was prepared for the homely, 50-foot craft—the *Dee-Gee*—he finally purchased at Port Canaveral, just south of Cape Kennedy. Lou Ullian had found an owner willing to sell, and although it suited the purpose, the boat was almost as unsightly as our *Sampan*. But Mel was eager and enthusiastic, particularly after seeing some of the gold and silver we had recently found, so it didn't deter him, nor did the fact that the engine acted up en route to Sebastian and he became temporarily grounded. It was rather an unglamorous beginning for his Florida treasure-hunting expedition. But I'm sure appearances didn't bother him as much as the fact that the *Dee-Gee* needed a hell of a lot of work to be converted into an operational salvage boat. Although his entire crew worked 12 and 14 hours a day to put it into shape, by the time it was ready the choice diving season was over. It was September.

They made a few survey runs using Field's magnetometer, looking for additional wreck sites, and they were eager to dive despite the adverse weather. So we put them on the silver wedge site we had labored so hard on during the summer of 1960. They knew there would be little hope of finding much there, but it would acquaint them with the ocean conditions and familiarize them with a wreck site. Besides, the water was usually clearer in that area late in the season than it was at our other locations.

Surprisingly, using a 10-inch dredge that required two men to hold it down, Mel's men turned up another silver wedge and several clay figurines. It was a start.

In the fall, I took them to another location—called the Sandy Point wreck. This one is just south of Vero Beach, about 15 miles below our cabin site. I had known of its existence for a number of years. A friend of mine named Otto Roach had originally told me about it, and I had spied ballast stones and cannon there during one of my plane rides. I had, in fact, helped bring up 18 cannon off the site for Art McKee's museum in the Florida Keys. But I had never seriously worked the area for treasure, nor would I have now had not Otto told me he had no plans to attempt salvage.

It's our guess that one of De Echeverz' ships, very possibly his *capitana, Nuestra Señora del Carmen y San Antonio,* went down here. We base this assumption, primarily, on documents from the Spanish archives and on eyewitness accounts of survivors which say this *capitana* sank off a point of land. Sandy Point is the only place between Sebastian and Stuart where there is such a noticeable landmark. Also, smaller cannon, seven and a half feet long, have been found here and we know from research that Ubilla's *capitana* and *almiranta* had larger guns, nine feet in length.

Real Eight had never worked this Sandy Point site simply because we didn't have the time. We still had long months, even years, of work on the cabin wreck, and it was yielding a steady supply of treasure. Why quit that to speculate on an unknown ship?

Ironically, it was one of our team, Lou, who found the first coin at Sandy Point. He went out on Fisher's boat one afternoon and was working the dredge with Holzworth, when, beneath a cannon, he discovered a badly corroded silver cob. In the days that followed, Mel and his divers brought up between 1,000 and 1,200 pieces of silver—half of which, by terms of our agreement, were ours. However, they were real "dogs." The sea and sands had been much rougher on them here than at the cabin site. Under thick layers of corrosion were thin sheets of silver, most of them worn smooth. Only a few had even a faint imprint on them. Three gold coins were also uncovered.

The harsh winter weather called a halt to all operations. It got too rough even for Mel's hungry band of divers, though they had to learn the hard way. They went out one day and were buffeted about so badly that Mel was thrown against the bulkhead and cracked a couple of ribs. Another time, when the waters had calmed somewhat, we led the Treasure Salvors team, as they called themselves, to our cabin site in hopes they would find enough to give them a morale boost. They found something all right, but all it gave them was a cold shot of fear.

Just as Rupe Gates was about to go over the side and check the bottom, a long, dark shadow sliced through the water. It was a huge shark—at least 12 feet long. Not only did it swish close by Rupe's heels as he scrambled back aboard, but it stayed in the area, circling the boat, for more than an hour.

Don't ask me why, I don't know, but for some reason the immediate area surrounding the cabin wreck site seems to be a favorite hunting ground for sharks. Dan Thompson once flew over this patch of ocean and saw two huge schools of sharks with about 150 in each school. I have seen one monster that was every bit of 20 feet long.

I nurture a pet theory that indigo and dye stuff somewhere in the galleon's scattered cargo attracts them. All of us have had experiences with sharks at one time or another. Personally, I was never that afraid of them, but in my advancing years I'm learning to respect them more and more. Dan has been hit in the face by miniature predators while dredging on the ocean floor, and Doc Kelso once broke his toe on a reef while scampering away from a shark in close pursuit. Foolishly, I suppose, I once smacked one on the nose when it got in my way.

But for pure madness, nothing can top the time Dan and I got plastered on a fifth of rum at our cabin one chilly day that winter. Offshore, shark fins were as thick as candles on an octogenarian's birthday cake. With courage and stupidity spawned of our alcoholic refreshments, I announced, in a Don Quixote manner, "Let's go get some shark fin soup," and Dan nodded approval.

We stripped to our waists, picked up handy two-by-fours and waded out into the icy waters. There must have been dozens of blacktip sharks, all about three- to six-footers, but by the time we got to the reef and started flailing aimlessly away with our makeshift weapons of lumber, the school swam off. Examining this questionable feat of heroism in the sobriety that followed, I shivered at the gruesome mental picture my mind conjured up.

With the rough weather, the muddied seas and the ever-present sharks, we had no choice but to wait things out. This was bad enough for us, but for Mel Fisher and his crew it was sheer torture. They were in this business full time, and when a treasure diver can't dive, what can he do? The time was beginning to wear on their nerves. They had agreed from the beginning to give this venture a year, and if, in that time, they hadn't done any good, they would go their separate ways. But now, like us, they had just enough taste of the sunken fortune out there to whet intense appetites.

It got to the point where Lou and I had to give them a peptalk. Mel is an eternal optimist. When everyone else is ready to toss in the sponge, he still searches for that elusive ray of hope, and often finds it. But now even he was discouraged. The elements were beating him down, and he was frustrated because there was absolutely nothing he could do about it. How can you fight nature?

Lou remembers one particular raw, biting winter day that he and Mel sat on the beach and looked out at an angry, churning ocean, driving mountainous, white-capped waves crashing onto the shore. Lou told him we had gone through the same emotion-draining experiences, but that better things would come with the spring; that there were millions in gold and silver out there waiting for us to reap the harvest.

I must give a lot of credit to Mel and his men. For they, as my team had done back in 1960, exhibited the courageous ability to stick things out. We knew that if they could weather the winter, they would be well repaid for their patience. How well they were to be repaid—within a few short months—surprised and delighted us all.

11 Gold
Is Where You Find It

One night in August, 1963, my front door bell rang, and when I answered, three strange faces peered at me.

"Kip Wagner?" one of them asked.

"Yes."

"We'd like to talk to you about some treasure we found."

Inside, they introduced themselves as Bruce Ward of Vero Beach, Don Neiman of Fort Pierce and Frank Allen of Orlando. They had some gold coins they wanted to show me. I looked at the bright doubloons, all dated 1714 and 1715. They were obviously from the Plate Fleet. What I didn't know then, but found out later, was that Allen had taken the coins to New York to have Henry Christensen, the noted authority, appraise them. Allen was shocked when Christensen told him this was the second batch of gold coins he had examined. I had shown him some of ours from the cabin wreck a few months earlier. Allen got my name and address from Christensen, and he, Ward and Neiman wanted to know where I had found them. I told them, without specifically identifying the site, and I also advised them of our 50-mile lease covering the area from the Sebastian Inlet to Stuart.

"Where did you find your coins?" I inquired after enough time had elapsed so I wouldn't appear too eager. Inside, of course, I was craving to learn the source of their gold. They were beautiful coins.

"Just this side of West Palm Beach," Ward said.

"That's not true," I snapped. I knew virtually where every ship in the 1715 fleet went down and there were no wrecks anywhere near West

Palm—a city about 90 miles south of Sebastian. My sudden accusation caught them flat-footed. They looked at each other as if to decide what to do next.

A few days later they were back, and admitted they hadn't got the coins down there. They wanted to know if we would work out a deal with them. They didn't have the manpower or equipment to salvage a wreck they had found, but they offered to put us directly on it for a percentage of the action.

"Did you find the coins on the beach or in the water?" I asked with specific intention. If they had found them on the beach, then they hadn't located a wreck at all and were just guessing where one might lie offshore. It could be anywhere over an area of several acres. On the other hand, if they had uncovered the coins in the water, they could well have pinpointed the site.

"We found them in the water," Ward announced emphatically, without a hint of hesitation.

"Let me ask you this, then. Did you find the wreck anywhere between the Sebastian Inlet and the Fort Pierce Inlet? If you did we can't make a deal, because I know every site in that area."

Their eyes lit up, and Ward said triumphantly, "Our wreck is not in that area."

"I'll check with my people then," I told them, "and I'll get in touch with you."

At a meeting of Real Eight directors we decided that if, in fact, they had found a wreck site bearing gold coins, it would be to our advantage to offer them a percentage deal—a finder's fee so to speak. We agreed upon a 60-40 split after the state's 25-percent slice, with Real Eight getting the long end, since we would put in the man-hours and foot the expenses. Ward, Allen and Neiman agreed to the terms and we signed a contract.

"Okay," I said eagerly, "now just where *is* this site of yours?"

When Ward penciled an X on a map of the coastline at a point a few miles south of Fort Pierce, I felt like kicking myself right in the tail as hard as I could. When I had asked him if it was between the Sebastian and Fort Pierce inlets, I had forgotten all about this area. Damn it all, I had known about this wreck all along, and I have correspondence with the state dating back to 1960 to prove it. We hadn't bothered with it because the specific location was hard to pinpoint. Further, in our researches, Doc Kelso and I had come across reference after reference that had indicated that this particular wreck had been completely salvaged by the Spaniards. According to their documents, there was nothing of value left. Why, then, spend the time, effort and money to explore such a site when we were making regular finds at the cabin wreck? But then there were the coins Ward had found, so maybe there was something at this site after all. Maybe it was unregistered, "bootleg" treasure. If Ward could steer us to it, we felt it would be worth the exploration.

In the meantime, while we had been ironing out the percentage arrangements, I had done some digging to get a line on the background of this strange trio. Ward, it seemed, had moved to Vero from Illinois in 1955, and had actively pursued skin diving as a hobby. He had found bits and pieces of artifacts on underwater scouting trips, and became so interested, after being fed the usual allotment of local legends, that he got a job as a night watchman so he could devote his days to beachcombing and diving. His methods were much like mine in the early days: he used face mask, snorkel and flippers and stored anything he found in a peach basket encircled with an old innertube.

Earlier in the year he had met a small, intense man—Don Neiman—during one of his lonely walks along the oceanfront. They were covering an area south of Fort Pierce that I had not traversed during my beachcombing days. Neiman was housefather at the Florida State School for Boys in Okeechobee, and collected fossils and Indian artifacts. He often prowled the beaches looking for anything of interest.

They struck up a mutual agreement, and began working together. Not long afterward, using a metal detector, Neiman found a perfect eight-escudo gold piece. They danced a merry jig on the spot and dreamed of sudden wealth. Within weeks they had a few more gold and silver coins. All of them had been found on the beach—not in the water!

Here's where Allen came into the picture. A heavyset man with jet black hair, he was a history teacher by profession and a coin collector by avocation. Allen had made some money and was looking around for ways to invest it. Ward and Neiman were looking for an investor to finance expenses for a more thorough search in the ocean. They needed a boat and diving equipment. Allen heard of their coin finds and agreed to pay costs for a third of anything found. They then bought a 14-foot boat and searched in vain for the wreck. That's apparently when they decided to come to me and offer their proposition.

Our deal sealed, we put Mel Fisher and his crew on the project. Bad weather hampered us from the beginning, and when the waters finally cleared, Ward led Mel to the "site" he had found. They struck out. Ward hemmed and hawed and stalled, and said he had gotten his directions crossed up, but would locate the wreck the next time out. More delays set in before the weather broke. Then another zero. At this point Ward admitted to us that he had found his coins on the beach and not in the water—a fact which we had guessed by now. He never had located a wreck site. He was only guessing and hoping.

For the next several weeks an angry Mel Fisher and his divers scoured the entire area, running their magnetometer full blast. They made several noteworthy finds—noteworthy in that they had no connection whatsoever with the 1715 Plate Fleet. They brought up some old landing gear strips, a strut assembly and a battery from an old Navy airplane. They found all sorts of odd pieces of iron—rusted bars and pipes, and even some World War II mines that had been set out off the Florida coast to blow up enemy submarines that came in too close.

To make matters worse, Ward and Neiman had originally agreed to help out in the search for the wreck. Now they fell back on every excuse imaginable to skip the grueling, all-day runs. By January, 1964, Fisher came to me, his fists clenched, teeth gritted and veins popping.

"We've had it, Kip," he said. "We've looked for that goddamn ghost wreck since September and haven't found a smell yet, and we've had it. It's just not worth it to go on."

I was, in fact, surprised that Mel hadn't come complaining to me sooner. Looking at it from his standpoint, it was a questionable deal even if Ward had led us directly to a gold-bearing galleon. Here's what Mel could expect: after the state took its 25-percent slice off the top, Ward's group would get 40 percent of the rest. That left Mel with half of our 60 percent on three-quarters of what was brought up. I have to admit it wasn't a very encouraging proposition.

"Let's work out a new arrangement with Ward, then," I offered.

"Okay," Mel said, reluctantly, "but it had better be a good one for us."

"It will be," I assured him.

When Ward, Neiman and Allen reassembled around the kitchen table in my house, I got right to the heart. I pointed out that we had already spent 600 man-hours looking for a wreck they were supposed to have shown us the first day, and we had nothing to show for it. And I outlined Mel's gripe at the meager percentage he would reap if he ever found anything.

"Boys, they're professional treasure hunters," I said. "If they don't find anything out in the sea, they don't eat. And they're certainly not going to look long in an area where they don't find anything but World War II relics.

"Now, we can do one of three things. You can either chip in to share the expenses of the search, or you can agree to a readjustment of the percentage split, or you can forget the whole thing. If you don't go along with either of the first two choices, we're going to pull out of the hunt altogether. So take your choice."

"What kind of percentage cut are you talking about?" Ward asked.

"We get 90 percent, you get 10 percent."

The words hung for a second or two before soaking in, then Ward exploded.

"Ten percent? Are you nuts? Ten percent," he repeated. "No sir," he raved. "Not on your life." He seemed to be assuming the authority of spokesmanship for Neiman and Allen, but they offered no argument to his attack. I let him go on for another minute or so, then reiterated the reasons for our decision.

"After all, when you get right down to it," I reasoned, "10 percent of something is a helluva lot better than 40 percent of nothing, isn't it?"

My philosophy was met with angry stares.

"No deal," Ward said with a tone of finality, and out of the house they stomped. Five minutes later they were back. They must have driven around the block.

"We've reconsidered," Ward said. "We'll agree to 15 percent."

"Sorry," I said, shaking my head.

"All right then, 10 percent!"

"Deal." The entire group—Real Eight and Mel's team—met later to confirm the transaction formally. Then we made a serious mistake.

"We don't see why there's any need to redraw any papers," we told them. "We've reached a gentleman's agreement, and your word is good." We shook hands, and I poured them a drink. We should have known better.

With the new agreement, Mel began "magging" the area again. This is a term we use, meaning that he used his magnetometer while trolling the waters. Fay Field's sensitive machine would record any ferrous metals on the ocean floor below, reacting somewhat as a compass would. It was still a trying period, for as if we weren't having enough troubles, the weather continued to halt our operations.

Finally, in April, they found some scattered ballast stones and a single cannon. They were located at a point nearly a half mile north and a considerable distance seaward of where Ward had first led us. This provided final proof that he had never had any idea of where the wreck was. He had simply surmised something must be out there after finding the coins on the beach.

It was another month before the water cleared enough to allow any diving. Mel had a different manner of salvaging than we had. We were still using our faithful six-inch dredge, but he had designed a special "blaster," capable of clearing an 8 by 10 foot hole through as much as 4 to 6 feet of sand, mud and loose rock in about 10 minutes.

Mel conceived the idea of using the *Dee-Gee*'s engines to power a propeller and thus divert a jet stream of surface water through an improvised, square rig in such a powerful concentration it would literally blow sand off the submerged reefs. The blaster, in effect, created a constant, forceful waterfall, straight down, which bored deep into the ocean floor.

Toward the end of April, Mel's team, with the help of Lou, Dan and Del, had found about 100 silver coins on the new wreck site. Then on May 8, Moe Molinar, the expert Panamanian diver, moved to an area about 15 feet seaward of where they had been working. He spotted a dull gleam in the sands, then another. He picked up two objects. They were heavy. In the brilliant sunshine they shone brightly. They were solid gold discs, each weighing about seven pounds. We had found nothing like them before. Mel later sold a similar 22½-carat disc, which bears a Mexican mint mark, for $17,500.

When Moe surfaced with his find, Rupe Gates nearly stepped on his head trying to get in the water. Divers made splashes in all directions, but no more gold was found that day. In fact, they got so engrossed in their work—and you have to remember this was the first real strike for Mel and his boys in almost a year—they didn't see an approaching squall. It was Mel who first noticed a swirling water spout nearby, and they rode out one hell of a buffeting on the way in. But in their state—and I know because we'd had similar experiences before—I don't think they would have minded too much if the *Dee-Gee* had sunk. They had found treasure—even if it had been nearly nine months after Ward had said he could lead us directly to it.

This time the party was at Mel's house in Vero Beach, and he invited us all down. It was another ripsnorter that lasted until the wee hours—at least for some of us. Others didn't make it past midnight. The whole affair was remarkably reminiscent of our coin clump finds in 1961; first the initial discovery, then the party, then a frustrating wait for the weather to clear again so we could get back on site. In Mel's case it was several days. When they did get back out on the water, their disc area was clouded in mud and visibility was nil. They worked it awhile, but couldn't see anything on the bottom. The divers wanted to go in, but Mel had other ideas.

"Let's go out farther and punch a hole," he urged. They shrugged, but agreed. About 50 feet to the east, they dropped anchor. "Let's try here," Mel said, and Moe went plunging overboard. Thirty seconds later he was up with a beautiful golden doubloon, dated 1698. They found a few more that day, and, on May 21, recovered over 200 four- and eight-escudo pieces.

Mel, as Del had done the year before, had moved on pure instinct—which bears out another one of my pet theories on treasure hunting. I'm convinced you could take the best financed, most fully equipped expedition ever, and lead it to the most thoroughly researched, richest wreck site under the seas, and still not find a thing—without the intangible, enigmatic element of luck. How often over the years we've been ready to call it a day, to give up, when someone's hunch has paid off in the eleventh hour. Without some amount of luck, no treasure operation will be successful. Ask Teddy Tucker or Ed Link or John Potter how important this factor is. Of course, through scientific procedure you can reduce your dependence on luck somewhat, but, nevertheless, without it, you're lost.

Three days later, on May 24, the big haul was made. Mel's blaster cut a hole about 15 feet long and 5 to 6 feet wide down a ridge between two rocks. Moe, Walt and Lou went down to see how it looked, and they were blinded by a bright-yellow glow. There, in all its magnificent splendor, was a veritable carpet of gold, the likes of which modern man had probably never seen before. The divers burned up almost a full tank of air just staring in awe at the sight. But then Moe grabbed a double handful and surfaced.

Even with the coins lying open on the bottom, it was hard work to recover them. First, gold is much heavier underwater than silver or other metals, and if a diver didn't have a good grip on a coin, it slipped right back to the bottom and camouflaged itself under a thin veneer of sand. Secondly, the blaster was still going to keep the hole cleaned, and the combination of its action, jetting a stream of water down, plus the natural motion of the sea, made it extremely difficult for the divers to maintain their positions. They didn't just drift from spot to spot plucking coins. They had to kick their flippers as hard as they could to keep from getting washed out of the hole completely. It required a great amount of physical exertion. Lou, for example, burned six tanks of air in five hours down there.

Because, in this instance, there was so much action on the bottom, it was not feasible to work with buckets. They would have been washed all over the place. Instead, Moe, Walt and Lou would grab a bare handful of coins and stuff them into a glove they wore on the other hand. They tucked each coin inside the cuff encircling the wrist. When a man had a gloveful, he would scoop up as many more coins as he could in his bare hand and then surface, spilling as many as 60 to 80 gold pieces on deck at a time. All day long that's the way it went—up, down, up, down, with not a break for lunch or even coffee. Not a second could be wasted now. They had learned in the past how fickle the seas were, and knew a storm could whip up in a matter of minutes, dumping tons of sand over the exposed gold.

By day's end the divers' wrists, where they had stuffed the coins, were raw and bloody. They had worn the skin off, and still carry scars from it today. But we had 1,033 pieces of gold to show for it—by far the best recovery to date.

Mel was beginning to think the entire bottom was paved with gold, and I was leaning toward agreement. I was even afraid that if we continued this pace long we'd ruin the world coin market for these rare specimens.

As it turned out, we had a more immediate problem. Now that we had found treasure, someone suggested we had better get that percentage revision with Ward's group in writing—just so there'd be no misunderstandings. Here, the picture gets a bit hazy, and I'm not exactly sure to this day just how the sequence of events unfolded, but to the best of my knowledge, this is what happened:

Ward, Neiman and Allen still acknowledged they were to get 10 percent of what had been found. We got their signatures on documents stating this, and we made a division of the coins after the state had taken its share. But the next thing we knew Neiman and Ward filed suit against us, charging they had received less than their share of the treasure we had found. Their complaint said they had discovered the wreck site—which they hadn't; and, furthermore, that they were supposed to receive 40 percent of what was found on the site. When Frank Allen refused to join them in this absurd action, they named him as a defendant in the suit.

In due course, Ward and Neiman admitted to us that they had agreed to the percentage cut to 10 percent, but now they felt they were entitled to more and were thus taking legal action. We, of course, felt the second paper that had been signed was a binding legal contract. So by the time we got over the shock, we filed a countersuit listing their charges as frivolous and a sham, and pointed out that they were falsely maligning our company and causing us to look bad in the press and thus lose sales of our coins. In their action they sought to restrain us from disposing of any part of the treasure—even though we had already given them coins exceeding the value to which they were entitled.

When we presented all the facts in court, I'm happy to say, even if it is somewhat trite, that justice prevailed. Their suit was thrown out. It was ridiculous from the start and they knew it. Not only had Ward's claims been set aside, but from our point of view the publicity given the matter was injurious to our operations. Moreover, we were still bound by the *National Geographic* contract and had agreed with Ward that they were to say nothing in print of any treasure find until one month after the *Geographic* article was published. The publication in *Argosy* magazine of an article sympathetic to Ward's cause injured our contractual relationship.

One other point is worthy of mention here. It concerns Rupe Gates, who deserves a lot of credit. After the gold strike he took every single coin, photographed its obverse and reverse sides, and catalogued it, listing its denomination, where it was minted, and its condition. This was a thankless, painstaking job that literally took days and days, and I can't praise him enough for it. I certainly didn't envy his task, but it put us in A1 shape, inventory-wise.

Weather-wise, the diving season of 1964 was the worst we've ever experienced. I don't think there were five good clear days all summer. Had it not been for Mel's ingenious blaster, we would probably have had to write off the year as a failure, for with the poor visibility our dredges wouldn't have done much good.

After the record day of finding 1,033 gold coins on May 24, we continued to work this hot spot. Del, Bob Johnson, Lou, myself, or one of the other Real Eight members would go out with Mel on the *Dee-Gee* nearly every day to spell one of his crew members. They had been hard at it seven days a week, and the occasional rest we could allow them was well appreciated.

On May 25, more than 900 doubloons were found, and in a single

The beach cabin of the Real Eight Company, about 2½ miles south of Sebastian Inlet. Note the buoys which mark site of wreckage.

Spanish coins of gold and silver salvaged from the wrecks. The gold doubloons are rounder and more accurately minted than the oddly shaped silver pieces of eight, some of which also show corrosion from the salt water. The coins display on opposite sides the Spanish royal coat of arms and the cross.

week's span, we brought up nearly 2,500 pieces of gold—a king's ransom in any country. After a few days, however, the source petered out. Doc Kelso and I had calculated that anywhere from 1,500 to 2,500 coins would have filled a chest and, in all likelihood, we had found one's contents nearly in its entirety. So we weren't surprised, merely disappointed, when the chest ran dry.

Then we began working patterns on the bottom to cover the entire wreck site systematically. This process is at best slow, tedious and bone-tiring work, and now seems a good time to cite the unsung heroes of a treasure salvage operation—the deckhands. I know of no better man at this job than Dick Williams of Mel's team. When we are working a hot spot, the boat is held stationary by four anchors—two off the bow and one from each corner of the stern—so the blaster can remain zeroed in on the productive patch of ocean bottom. But when we are probing, and finding only scattered coins, we keep moving the blaster and boat every few minutes during the day. To do this, the four anchor lines must be hauled in and secured anew every couple of feet we move, and this is where the muscle and elbow grease is needed. Sometimes, when those lines get wet with salty seawater, they burn right through the skin of the deckhand's palms. But he has no time to nurse his wounds. He has a number of other chores to perform, too, like keeping the air compressors running, and so on.

Diving is a tough job in these waters, but at least there's a bit of glamour to it now and then. For men like Dick Williams, though, it is mostly physical labor. Yet their part in the overall success of an operation is just as vital as that of the men down below. In fact, the deckhand must keep an ever-watchful eye over the side to make sure everything is all right with the divers. It is a responsible, thankless job.

I might add that in Dick's case he has another positive mark that renders him invaluable to our work. He is one of the best sea cooks I have ever run across, and believe me, this means a lot to a hard-working, hungry crew. Even in the summer, the divers get chills after being in the depths for several hours, and nothing picks them up faster than a heaping plateful of Dick Williams' mulligan stew.

Throughout the summer we kept our eye on the cabin wreck area, too, but the waters there were invariably rougher and dirtier than they were south of Fort Pierce. I don't think we dived off Sebastian more than half a dozen times throughout the 1964 season, and the finds there weren't too impressive now that so much gold had been discovered to the south. Off the cabin wreck we found only a few silver coins, a Mexican spice bowl, and a small gold pendant with the carved head of a haloed, bearded saint. Lou saw it underneath an encrusted cannon.

Both our crew and Mel's team concentrated on the Fort Pierce site all summer, and although things tapered off after our hot spot had been cleaned, we continued to recover scattered gold coins.

One morning when dredging operations were slow and finds were scarce, Mel and Bob slipped off a little north of the cabin wreck to search for a place I called my "mysterious sand spot." Doc Kelso and I had gleaned from survivors' eyewitness accounts the exact coordinates of one of the sunken ships—quite possibly, so the records we then had suggested, it might be Ubilla's *capitana*. We are now relatively sure, however, that this is incorrect, as I shall discuss further in a later chapter. At any rate, I had surveyed the specified area once from a plane and found a strange, unexplainable shallow spot in rather deep waters. Why was this specific site so different if there wasn't a wreck buried there? I wondered. But we had taken the *Sampan* out more than once to pinpoint the location and never found it.

Mel had his 14-foot skiff, and Bob drove up the coast, parked, and then swam out to meet him a short way offshore so they could motor out and "mag" the area with their magnetometer. A woman living in a beach-house nearby saw Bob swim out and get picked up by Mel, and she promptly called the nearby Air Force base to report saboteurs in the area. As it worked out, Colonel Dan Thompson, the Director of Operations at Patrick Air Force Base, handled the call and had half his security force digging until we told him in casual conversation that night about Bob's and Mel's trip. He put two and two together and figured the woman must have been talking about his partners. That's the nearest we've come to espionage in the treasure-hunting business. I really couldn't blame that woman for calling the authorities, however. Bob and Mel are both bald-headed and look every bit the movie-type spy, à la Yul Brynner. We certainly gave them the needle the next few days! What that strange sand spot out there is, though, remains a mystery.

Back at Fort Pierce, Lou and Mel were working a site among some ballast stones one day when Mel spotted a long object that appeared to be a piece of wood. He deftly picked it up, turned it, and tossed it to Lou for examination. It knocked Lou flat on his haunches. What he had thought was wood, felt like lead and turned out to be a silver bar. It weighed more than 35 pounds. Now we had found everything—gold and silver coins, wedges, discs and bars—except a solid gold bar. We're still looking for that.

Speaking of heavy objects, Del found a gorgeous, irregular-shaped gold disc one afternoon—complete with purity, mint and assayer's marks on it—and laid it on the bottom alongside a pair of other discs, one gold and one silver, that he had unearthed. Deckhand Dick Williams, in the excitement of things, dived down to bring them up. His head bobbed up, then down, above and below surface several times, then he slipped back down to the bottom. The discs were too heavy to carry all at one time, and Lou had to go down and give him a hand.

We got quite a chuckle out of this, but for laughs that summer, nothing could quite match the trials and tribulations of Harry Cannon when struggling with the sand blaster. Let me preface this by saying that Mel's powerful machine was a real ripsnorter. When it moved around, funneling that jet stream of water down to the bottom, it kicked up a king-sized cloud that looked and hit like a desert sandstorm. Revved up to full speed, the blaster can propel giant boulders in all directions. Not only does the sheer sound of it frighten the uninitiated, but even the divers used to working around it get caught up in the whirlwind rush of water occasionally, and, as Lou phrases it, "are chewed up and spat out."

Business commitments had kept Harry away for a few weeks, and when he came down to dive for the first time under the blaster, we all looked around at each other with a knowing smile in our eyes. Bob, Walt and Lou were on the bottom when Cannon's elongated figure appeared. In a second, the high-velocity shaft of water from the blaster had him in its steely grip. The expression on his face shifted between terror and amazement. The jet of water picked him up like a log and rolled him over and over and then bounced him past Lou and Bob. They caught him and clamped his hand on a large piece of coral to anchor him. Less than a minute later, he was in the blaster's clutches again. This time it rolled him up like a ball and sent him spinning to the edge of the hole. After that Harry kept a respectful distance from the area, a little the worse for wear, but wiser.

In a way we had nearly every storekeeper and self-service laundry owner in Fort Pierce working for us that summer. To mark the gold-yielding areas over the scattered wreck site, we placed buoys on the surface. The best buoys we could find, as we learned through experience, were common plastic bleach containers. So we had everyone save their empties for us, and I'm sure it must have been a curious sight to passersby when they saw Mel rambling toward the beach with the back end of his car loaded down with empty plastic flasks.

On June 19, after the big gold finds, we tore up our original agreement with Mel and drew up a new one. We felt it only fair, since he had not only pinpointed the Fort Pierce wreck with his magnetometers, but had also located the hot spots there. His crew deserved more. So the new arrangement called for us to split everything found—by either group—50-50 down the middle. After all, he was working at it every day while we were still weekenders.

Late in August two hurricanes, Cleo and Dora followed each other up the east coast of Florida, and closed our diving season. The year had been fraught with frustrations, intrigue, wheelings and dealings, and finally, I'm happy to say, with a rich assortment of treasure. We took inventory and only then did we realize just how successful the summer had been. We counted more than 3,700 gold coins and over 200 pounds of silver pieces of eight. There were six silver and six gold discs, or circular-shaped ingots, the heavy silver bar, 16 gold rings, eight pieces of chain, several silver forks, knives and spoons, two ornate silver candlestick tops and two silver plates.

Our coins were struck at four New World mints during the latter portion of the reign of Charles II of Spain (1665–1700), and the early part (1700–1714) of Philip V's rule. They represent a broad sample of Spanish colonial coinage, and have proved to be a real find numismatically as well as materially, for they are generally in excellent condition and include denominations and types previously unknown to historians and collectors.

From extensive studies, we have learned that most coins struck during the latter half of the seventeenth century and the first 14 years of the eighteenth—the time period covering our finds—were generally irregular-shaped. They were called "cobs" from the Spanish *cabo de barra*, or end of the bar, because they were clipped into individual planchets from the end of a strip of metal.

After being trimmed to the proper weight, these odd-looking blanks, of assorted sizes and thicknesses, but weighing nearly the same, were placed between two iron or steel dies into which the coin's designs had been driven. These dies were then forcefully pressed into the metal, but due to the careless work of ill-paid, hard-ridden mint employees, often only a portion of the die design left its imprint on the metals, and many of them came off the line undated. Efforts were made only to stamp each coin with the mint mark and assayer's initials.

We've frequently cursed those sloppy craftsmen, for a coin of this type, stamped off-center without a date, is worth far less than a perfectly marked, dated one. Odd, for with today's coins, of course, just the opposite is true. If the mint makes a mistake now, the error greatly increases the value.

Silver at the time of Philip V was struck in denominations of half, one, two, four and eight reals. Gold, valued at 16 reals to one escudo, was minted in one-, two-, four- and eight-escudo pieces—the eight being the legendary doubloon. It equaled 16 eight real coins, or pieces of eight. By United States standards, a real is worth approximately 12½ cents, and it is interesting to note that the old colloquialism "two bits" came from two reals, which equaled a quarter.

The Mexico City mint began operations in 1536, but didn't process gold until 1679. Coins struck here usually carried the crest of the King on the obverse side and a Jerusalem cross on the reverse side. The legend around the coins read "Philippus V [or Carlos II] D. G." on the front, with the date, and "Hispaniarum et Indiarum Rex" on the back.

Interspersed in our collection were a considerable number of imperial coins, or nearly round gold specimens evenly struck with the dies and in almost pristine condition. We found no such examples of silver, although contemporaneous records indicate they were fairly common in that long-ago era.

The mint at Lima, Peru, coined both gold and silver in most denominations during this period. Its coins carried pillars of Hercules and waves on the obverse side and a cross, usually with the arms of Castile and León, on the reverse. These coins appeared to have been minted to higher standards than those at any other New World establishment.

Santa Fe de Bogotá coined silver and gold in denominations smaller than eight escudos, but most specimens of its work were crude and irregular, and there were many errors. Often the entire crest was struck in reverse or otherwise incorrectly portrayed. We believe use of unskilled Indian labor caused the poor craftsmanship. Potosí coined only silver until late in the eighteenth century, and the design used there was similar to the one used at Lima.

Our finds in 1964 were impressive in terms of historical artifacts, too, including 5 iron cannon, 79 cannonballs, 9 examples of bar shot, 80 musket balls, countless fragments of pottery, olive jars and large ceramic containers, four pairs of brass navigational dividers, sounding leads, pewter plates, miscellaneous lead objects, including one crushed box, odd ships' fastenings, and a number of unidentified items.

Among the more interesting recoveries was a single, heavily encrusted sword handle and section of blade. Doc Kelso X-rayed it and found an S-shaped quillon and semicircular knuckle blow running from the juncture of the handle and hilt to the pommel.

Our biggest recovery wasn't found at the Fort Pierce site. Lou's family doctor, Herb Allen, while boating south of the inlet one day, sighted a huge anchor on the bottom, and told us about it. We found it some weeks later and rigged up a boom off the bow of the *Sampan* to bring it up—an operation that took about an hour. The iron anchor is 11 feet long and weighs close to a ton. We kept it in my front yard until Alice rebelled, and it is now a star attraction at our museum.

Our gold coins needed little if any cleaning up. They were almost always found in near-mint condition despite their exposure under the seas for so many years. The silver pieces of eight, however, were another story. They were corroded black with silver sulfide, and we tried nearly everything to get them polished and ready for marketing.

We experimented with steel wool pads, soda, muriatic acid—even scrubbing the coins in the sand, yet nothing seemed to work. We could get them shiny, all right, but it took hours to do it. We used to sit around in a semicircle, like so many washerwomen, and rub and scrub till our fingers and knuckles were raw.

Finally, Del and I solved the wash-day problems. He rigged up a little octagonal-shaped wooden box, based on my design, and mounted a one-quarter-horsepower electric motor to it which ran with an 18 to one gear reduction. He then dropped a couple of hundred coins in and added some rough steel shot—the same stuff that is used for jewelry burnishing—and some detergent, to act as a cushion between the encrusted coins and the shot. The little motor rotates the box with the same effect a squirrel running on a treadmill achieves, turning it about six times a minute. After two hours, the blackest, dirtiest coins come out as bright and shiny as the day they were stamped at the mint. This is one black box that really works—our own coin-cleaning machine. I'm sure thankful for it. We were beginning to get that dishpan-hands look.

During the fall of 1964 we decided to see what would happen if we tried to share some of our hard-earned treasure with the world. We elected to sell some coins. Henry Christensen, one of the most famous coin auctioneers in the world and a noted authority on Spanish pieces, was holding an auction in Hoboken, New Jersey, on October 8. After several rounds of correspondence, we agreed upon terms. He was to get

20 percent for selling them. Real Eight, Fisher's Treasure Salvors and the Bruce Ward–Frank Allen combine together made up a collective consignment of some 100 coins, mostly gold. Fisher sent another batch of coins, as we did, that were catalogued separately.

Circulation of the sales list caused a mild tremor of excitement among the select percentage of well-to-do numismatists who specialized in New World gold coins. We were offering something never before available on the open market. In fact, many of the pieces were so rare they were completely unknown to previous cataloguers.

I must admit I was probably the most nervous person in that crowded room when Christensen authoritatively banged down his gavel and opened the sale. Except for a few silver coins we had sold back in 1961, we hadn't disposed of any portion of the treasure. This was a real trial balloon. But I took heart in the anticipated prices quoted in the catalog. If the bidders would only come close to these, we would be more than satisfied.

Most of the pieces were expected to draw a few hundred dollars each, and we had several tentatively listed at well over $1,000. The coins had been minted at Cuzco and Lima, Peru, Santa Fe de Bogotá and Mexico City. Most dates were in the 1690's or early 1700's. None were minted later than 1714.

From the beginning, a small man with graying hair and a thin white moustache, puffing steadily on a pipe and eyeing the proceedings over a pair of half-lens glasses, dominated the bidding. He was F. Xavier Calico of Barcelona, Spain, one of the world's foremost collectors and coin dealers and president of the International Association of Professional Numismatists. On many items he received strong competition from John J. Pascale, president of the Quality Tool and Die Company of Hoboken, who was a relative newcomer to numismatics, but made up for it with his enthusiasm and spirited bidding.

As Christensen moved to the first of our real gems, a beautiful eight-escudo gold piece minted in Mexico in 1695, I could barely stand the tension. I wanted to get up and walk out of the room, but my legs wouldn't carry me. It had been estimated at $4,000, our highest, and when the final gavel rapped down, it brought $3,500. Not bad.

And so it went down the line. One of the most active bidders, surprisingly, was none other than Frank Allen, who had taken several thousand dollars in cash to the auction, and picked up quite a few of our gold pieces for his personal collection. A lot of our coins didn't sell. Interest seemed, rather, to center on a chosen few. Apparently, the buyers had read the catalog well and knew precisely what they wanted.

Then Christensen put up a 1711 four-escudo piece that weighed 13.615 grams (gold is $35 an ounce raw). It was a choice round specimen with full legends and in almost uncirculated condition. It proved to be the real sleeper of the sale.

"$2,200," Señor Calico offered. I thumbed through my catalog. Its estimated selling price was only $2,000. Hot dog, I thought to myself, keep going. To my delight, they did.

"3,000 . . . $3,200 . . . $3,400 . . . $3,500 . . . going . . . $3,600 . . . going once . . . going twice . . . sold for $3,600 to Señor Calico!" It was the highest amount paid for a single coin at the sale.

Still, the Barcelona collector felt he had a bargain. "It was a steal," he told newsmen later. The sale of that coin stirred my memory. At long last we were beginning to realize something for all the years of sweat and toil and frustration we had put in; $3,600 for just one coin—and we had thousands more back home. Things were looking up.

Altogether, just over 100 coins were sold, and we realized about $29,000 from the sale, although the papers erroneously reported the figure as $51,000. We had hoped to dispose of more, but it was our first real venture and there would be time in the future.

Calico was kidded by newsmen who pointed out that now, nearly 250 years later, the coins were going home to Spain, but he had an answer to that. "I bought only for other collectors," he told them. "Not one customer is in Spain. No collectors there could afford them. These coins are definitely lost to Spain."

Back home we gathered the clans for a full report of the auction and for a division of the take, after first paying off some accrued bills for operating expenses. All along we in Real Eight had kept tabs of our individual expenses, everything from wear and tear on vehicles and boats and other pieces of equipment to time put in and gas mileage in traveling to and from the diving sites, and so on.

My poor pickup truck had literally been run off its wheels, and the group awarded me $15,000 in expenses to replace it and to compensate me for the time I had put in, which was far more than anyone else had worked, since they came down mostly on weekends. With me it was a full-time job. We went around the table totaling time, expenses and depreciations, and divvied up the rest of the money. Del got about $3,500, Dan and Harry $1,000 each, and so on.

This large cylinder is used on the Real Eight boat *Derelict* to blast sand off the ocean floor and uncover treasure.

Thousands of beautiful gold coins, like the doubloons (eight-escudo pieces) and coins of smaller denominations shown here, have been recovered by the diving teams.

Handmade silverware from the cabin or cargo of a Spanish galleon.

Some of the rare and delicate pieces of K'ang Hsi china recovered from the sea floor.

It was the first material return that any of us had realized. It seemed ironic that we had recovered a fortune in treasure, estimated by some to be in the millions, but these few thousand dollars were all we'd been able to stuff into our pockets.

12 Treasure
the Legal Way

Legally, our treasure finds have set a number of precedents, caused more confusion, created new laws and challenged old ones, and triggered suits and countersuits in a maze of court entanglements, some of which remain unsolved to this day. I'm not even sure I can present a clear picture of our transactions with the state of Florida, simply because I'm not sure I understand everything myself, but I'll try.

The law of the state governing salvage operations along the coastlines, effective January 1, 1958, reads in part as follows:

"The Trustees of the Internal Improvement Fund of the state of Florida, as owners of the submerged lands under navigable waters and under waters connected with navigable areas, may lease the same for salvage operations and explorations for sunken treasures.

"A single lease may not include more than 50 square miles total of submerged land, in not more than three counties. Leases are non-exclusive, but in the event of a 'find,' the lessee may define a one-acre area and request that his lease be exclusive as to the one acre, remaining non-exclusive in the remainder of the leased area. Annual lease rental is $100 per year, payable in advance.

"Quarterly reports are required of lessees, unless specifically waived by the Trustees, stating what operations, if any, are underway, listing all relics and material recovered. In addition to the rental, there is a royalty of 25 percent of the material taken (subject to selection by the Trustees) or 25 percent of the fair market value of the items. No sale of items taken is to be made until report of the taking has been reviewed by the office of the Trustees and lessee has been notified in writing whether royalty payments shall be in materials of archeological or other peculiar value, or in terms of 25 percent of the fair market value.

"The lessee is required to furnish to the Trustees written consent of all upland owners of lands in front of whose property lessee shall operate within 500 feet of the upland shore. Surety bond of $500 or more, depending on location and extent of the lease area, will be required of lessee.

"Leases shall be on a year-to-year basis, for not more than three years. Lease will require compliance with all laws and regulations concerning navigation and conservation of marine life, and no operations will be permitted which interfere with or impair the statutory riparian rights (ingress, egress, bathing, boating, and fishing) of upland owners.

"Lease will contain provision for forfeiture and cancellation, with right of Trustees to recover under the bond in event of failure of lessee to comply with the provisions of the lease, or in the event of willful neglect to truthfully report operations or recovery of materials.

"Applicants must define the submerged area sought to be leased for exploration, by legal description or marked U.S. Coast Chart, which will be checked to verify state ownership and identify any already outstanding leases or interests."

The state's authority covers the standard three geographical miles into the Atlantic Ocean off Florida's east coast, and extends nine geographical miles off the west coast into the Gulf of Mexico.

As early as 1959 I had contacted Van H. Ferguson, director of the state's Internal Improvement Fund—the agency charged with the handling of salvage rights. By this time Doc Kelso and I were sure from our extensive researching that the sunken 1715 fleet was off our shoreline, and we told Van of our interest in working the sites, and of our intention of preserving anything found of historical value. Within a year we worked out an agreement and on March 11, 1960, we were issued exploratory search lease number 1329, covering the 50-mile area from the middle of the Sebastian Inlet south to Stuart. We also got pinpoint salvage leases on the wedge wreck off Fort Pierce and the cabin wreck south of the Sebastian Inlet. But Van had gone a step further. He told us we were the only people he had ever dealt with who were sincerely conscientious in respect for the law and in cooperating fully with the state. He said he would not let anybody else work the entire area covered by our exploratory lease.

Van Ferguson then assigned Dr. William H. Sears and Dr. John M. Goggins, both of the Florida State Museum in Gainesville, to work with us. They came over several times during the 1960-61 period to see what progress we were making, and to inform us of what the state was interested in in the way of artifacts. It was a very informal, first-name arrangement, but one that fully satisfied all parties. We accepted the terms Van had proposed in good faith, and the state in turn trusted us implicitly. To me, as I've said so often before, this is the best way to handle business—by a handshake and a man's word.

Things were running very smoothly during this time, and no one had any problems. Whenever we found any coins or artifacts, we'd call Goggins or Sears, and they would come over. Then we'd spread everything out and ask them what they wanted. They would select a fourth of each find, and I'd load it up in the back of my pickup truck and drive it over to Gainesville. We also religiously filed quarterly reports, detailing what we had or hadn't found over the past three-month period.

The state was completely pleased with the manner in which we carefully recovered any item we thought would be of historical interest. In fact, we brought up countless musket balls, cannonballs, fragments of china and thousands of pieces of pottery—all for the specific purpose of turning it over to the state. It even got to the point where it was costing us time and money to recover some of the objects, for we could not sell them for profit. They were of no material value.

Goggins and Sears both expressed this point, and their overall satisfaction with our operations, in official correspondence. It's on record. In a letter to Van Ferguson, dated January 13, 1961, for instance, Sears said:

"The Real Eight Corp. is doing its work in a scientifically impeccable fashion. Detailed drawings, photographs, and other records have been made, and correlated with the specimens recovered. To our best knowledge, this is the first and only wreck in Florida to have been properly investigated, scientifically speaking.

"This company is apparently the only one to attempt to fairly meet their contractual obligations under a salvage lease."

Our unusual lease arrangement and full cooperation with the state was also duly recorded in the official minutes of one of the Internal Improvement Fund's board meetings in 1962.

When Goggins died later that year, we began dealing exclusively with Sears. We took great pains to inform him personally of each major find we made. We wanted him to hear about it from us rather than read about it in the papers or to get the news secondhand via the rumor mill. So when we found the first gold and the K'ang Hsi china, and other important items, we called him directly.

Then late in 1963 something happened that changed the entire outlook on things. Van Ferguson retired. We talked with him before he stepped down, and once again he assured us he would try to see that our rights were protected in every way possible.

His successor, appointed by then-Governor Farris Bryant, was a short, balding man—William Kidd. For several months nothing changed. We continued to deal exclusively with Sears. Then Mel Fisher made the big gold strike south of Fort Pierce. As always, we immediately called Sears in Gainesville and told him the details and that we were putting a fourth of the gold in the bank in escrow for the state until the actual division could be made at a later date. He acknowledged this in a return letter, and said it was fine with him. Not only that, but a couple of state representatives under Kidd had been at Mel's house the night of the gold disc finds —so the state had to know what was going on.

Hereafter things started to get muddled. Unknown to any of us, state agents began spying on Mel's crew, and documenting their movements. All sorts of clandestine measures were employed. It smacked of James Bond. Highway Patrol Captain Ed Reddick, dressed in civilian clothes, would hide in the thick palmetto brush, blanketing the sand dunes fronting the beach, and focus high-powered binoculars on the *Dee-Gee*, anchored only a few hundred feet offshore.

At Kidd's request, Reddick and Paul Baldwin, of the Internal Improvement Fund's staff, began questioning everyone around Fort Pierce about the treasure hunters. They talked to storekeepers, gas station attendants, local photographers, beachcombers, and even express agents who might have received gold shipments. They wanted to know who Fisher was and what he was up to. I could have saved them all the trouble, but apparently Kidd had directed them to see me last.

Reddick had more disguises than Lon Chaney. Once he appeared on a sailboat moored near the *Dee-Gee*, sporting a flowing beard. He even struck up an acquaintance with Mel's divers and was welcomed aboard, where he made discreet yet probing inquiries about their operations.

One day about three weeks later, the state officials finally showed up at my house, and told me they had a full case against Mel for poaching on my lease site and illegally extracting treasure from the ocean. If I would press charges against these highjackers, they told me, they could lock up

Mel and his whole crew. I had to fight back the temptation to laugh in their faces.

"I don't quite understand what's going on here, fellows," I said, "but I'm certainly not in a position to press charges against Mel Fisher. He works for me. We've hired his crew to dive for us. Someone must have given you the wrong dope."

This really set them back, and when the first wave of shock passed, they mumbled a few abrupt words and went out, slamming the front door.

Then we began getting hit with a barrage of totally unwarranted bad publicity in the state's newspapers, intimating we were stealing Florida blind. In Tallahassee, the state capital, Kidd contended he had never gotten word of our gold recoveries from us, and that only by sending agents down to the area did he find we had placed everything in the bank. He went a step further. He wrote a letter to the head of the Florida Highway Patrol, commending the investigative work of Reddick, whom he had sent to check on us. In part, here is what he said:

"This is to advise you that Captain Reddick and a representative of my office have during the last week located sizable recoveries of gold and silver, which have been removed from state-owned property. They are now in the process of inventorying and collecting all of this material and storing it in a safe location.

"Let me say," Kidd went on, "that through the efforts of Ed [Reddick] I believe that the state of Florida will recover two or three hundred thousand dollars that otherwise would have been lost."

Kidd's letter was subsequently quoted in a front-page splash in the *Miami Herald*, the state's largest newspaper, and in other papers all over Florida. We were beginning to appear, in the eyes of the people, as the biggest band of thieves since Henry Jennings and his cutthroats.

Had Kidd checked with Sears in Gainesville, he would have known that we had reported the gold finds. Why this fact wasn't brought out in the turmoil that ensued I don't know. We continued to get bombarded in the press. Kidd reported that we didn't even have an exclusive salvage lease to work the Fort Pierce site; that we had only a search lease covering this. Therefore, any recoveries made in the area were, in the strictest definition of the law, actually illegal.

Dr. Charles Fairbanks, chairman of a special advisory committee set up to look into the matter, then jumped on the bandwagon that was now apparently out to steamroller Real Eight. He publicly charged that the state should get 100 percent of all we had found at Fort Pierce, because we had worked it without the exclusive salvage lease. Others said we should be openly prosecuted for this flagrant violation of the law. Dr. Hale Smith, a Florida State University anthropologist, came out with the statement that the state, "employing ordinary recovery procedures," could have found the wreck site itself.

The mass attacks stemmed from the fact that Van Ferguson, acting in good faith, had told us back in 1960 that we could have carte blanche on working any site in our 50-mile zone. We hadn't applied for pinpoint leases at each site then because he had assured us he would allow no one else to hold concurrent leases in this area. We had even offered to pinpoint all our wreck sites and get coverage on them individually, but Van didn't even want to know where they were. It was a fine agreement as long as he held office. Now it was backfiring in our faces. Clearly, through Kidd's charges and the newspapers' campaigns—and oh, what a just crusade they thought they were riding—we were losing the faith and trust of the state.

I had worked too long and too hard to let things slip through my fingers now, so Mel and I went to Tallahassee to lay things on the line with Kidd and work out an arrangement. I don't think Kidd trusted Mel from the moment he saw him. There was a lot of shuffling and fast talking on both sides, and, unfortunately, I think we did more harm than good.

Kidd next announced he was not issuing any more leases to anyone until the whole affair could be straightened out. He called for a full investigation, and it began to look as if he would even revoke our existing leases. Things were getting gloomier than ever.

Then Dan Thompson, Harry Cannon, and John Jones came to the rescue. They had pretty sharp business minds and also personal connections in Tallahassee, so they flew up there on June 11, 1964, to see Kidd and try to make some sense out of the proceedings. Kidd's secretary said he was too busy to see them. They went across the street to the governor's office, where Dan knew Bryant's secretary. She managed to work them in for a few minutes, and they told the entire story to the governor, who listened very attentively. They recounted our agreements with Van Ferguson, how we had told Sears of the gold—everything. Bryant assured them he would take a personal look into it, and sent them to see Jimmy Kynes, then the state attorney general. Jimmy and Dan were friends, and this time it was a case where "it's not what you know, it's who you know," really paid off.

Jimmy was up to his ears in problems, for this was the day Martin Luther King had been jailed in St. Augustine for leading a civil rights demonstration. Kynes had hot lines buzzing incessantly, and told Dan and Harry he was glad to see them but could spare them five minutes at the most. Harry cut right to the quick. He told Kynes that Real Eight's position was clear and firm. We held a legitimate lease, and if it was revoked and reissued to another party, we would have to sue the state.

"And $25 million might be a good figure to start with," Harry tossed out, to emphasize the point. Kynes is nobody's fool, and he quickly saw they meant business. He told his secretary to cancel his appointments and hold all calls. They huddled behind closed doors for more than two and a half hours.

After a thorough briefing, Jimmy picked up the phone and said, "Get Kidd over here right away." He told Kidd he had known the Real Eight members for years and that our integrity and honesty were beyond question. He said the state had acted hastily, and he wanted Kidd to work out a mutually agreeable proposition with us. Kidd then invited Dan, Harry and John to his house to discuss it over drinks. Kidd is an intense man, with a penetrating personality. He was overly enthusiastic about treasure. During the talk, they learned a number of things. Kidd told them he had reason to suspect some sort of intrigue was going on in regard to the coins; that we were selling them on the sly. Dan assured him we weren't. He told them he distrusted both Mel and me, and that he had hired an underwater archeologist, and that all our operations from now on would be openly monitored. We had no objections to this.

The crux of the whole matter, Kidd felt, centered around our 50-mile lease, which was legally for exploration only, but morally for salvaging, too. He was being pressured from all sides to open the area up to other interests. Our gold finds had made front-page news around the world, and hundreds of amateur and professional salvagers wanted in. Politicians were badgering Kidd on behalf of well-heeled constituents—and they were hammering away on sound legal grounds. Something, Kidd emphasized, would have to be done. We believed that even then he had committed himself to other concerns, and this later proved to be true.

Dan told him we had no objection to relinquishing our rights in the 50-mile area—we never had any objections to this, even under Van Ferguson—so long as we were granted exclusive leases on the eight wreck sites we had pinpointed in the area. We were interested in working the

1715 fleet wrecks only. We knew there were a great number of other sunken ships in our area, but we had plenty to keep us busy, and if our rights to these eight locations were fully protected, we didn't care who else came into the area. We would even welcome them and wish them luck.

Dan, Harry, John and Kidd agreed to set up a full-scale meeting at Melbourne the next week, with all members of Real Eight and Treasure Salvors present, so we could resolve the issues and lay them to rest. It would be a summit conference.

At the meeting we formalized, with Kidd and Kenneth Ballenger, an assistant state attorney general from Jimmy Kynes' office, all that had been discussed earlier in Tallahassee. We agreed to opening the Sebastian Inlet to Stuart area in exchange for exclusive leases on the eight wreck sites. We pinpointed the locations to Kidd, and asked, despite our protection from the state, that he keep them confidential. The following Sunday the *Miami Herald* ran a map listing every one of our exact sites!

Even after this, the cloak-and-dagger activities continued to a lesser extent. One night Kidd summoned all of us to report to the sheriff's office in Fort Pierce. He wanted us fingerprinted, so he said, for identification cards that would say we were bona fide treasure hunters. Wouldn't old Henry Jennings have choked with laughter on this? Anyway, we showed up at the sheriff's and had to wait until well past midnight for the fingerprint man to get rustled out of bed and down to the office. After all this trouble, we never did get the cards Kidd was so hopped up about.

But at least we had official sanctioning now, fingerprints and all. Kidd issued a memorandum to his people that stated: "Our objective is to develop with Real Eight and Treasure Salvors an atmosphere of mutual cooperation and respect. A contract is no better than the contracting parties, and I propose to see to it that we develop an attitude of 'fair play' on our part."

Now he was talking!

Charley Herring, our lawyer in Vero Beach, formalized the new arrangements. Subsequently, another treasure company, headed by a man named Oscar Ewing of Carrabelle, Florida, filed for salvage licenses adjacent to each of our eight sites. When he was denied, he filed suit against the state. We hope the state's action stands because it is impractical for two outfits to work side by side over ill-defined perimeters. How do you draw an exact line on the bottom of the ocean? As Mel Fisher pointed out, al-

6*

lowing two firms to compete on a wreck where gold and silver are involved could lead to everything from cutting air hoses to actual bloodshed.

Under the new terms of our leases with the state, we got a renewable six-year contract on our eight sites that, with options, will run until 1975. These terms were approved by the Internal Improvement Fund's board of trustees, which included Governor Bryant, state comptroller Ray Green, treasurer Ed Larson, Jimmy Kynes, the attorney general, and agriculture commissioner Doyle Connor.

Originally, our pinpoint leases covered about one acre each, but wrecks are scattered over much wider areas, and we have since been granted permission to work a much larger zone at each of the eight wreck sites. Generally, each lease covers an area with perimeters running like this: 660 feet due north of the starting reference point (center of site); then 660 feet due east, or seaward, from the point of origin; 1,320 feet, or a quarter of a mile south; straight west to the beach; and, finally, northwest on the beach to the north limit line. The total area may span 30 or more acres. However, to be covered from 500 feet in to the shoreline, we also have to have written permission from the owners whose property fronts the wreck site. We have acquired this permission on several of our locations, and, of course, we own the property adjacent to the cabin wreck.

Shortly after our meeting in Melbourne we had another gathering of state and company officials—this time in Vero Beach—to divide the gold and other valuables that had been found south of Fort Pierce. I'm sure no splitting of the spoils by pirates centuries ago was done with more flourish or intrigue. We took everything out of the bank vaults and spread it all on a table in a conference room. Otis Imboden wanted to shoot color pictures for *National Geographic,* so he spread a green velvet cloth over the table.

Treasure fever was running rampant. This was the richest accumulation we had acquired to date, and when we laid it out altogether, I must admit it was a tremendously impressive sight. I glanced around the room. Mel Fisher's eyes looked as if they'd pop out any minute. Frank Allen was sweating. Rupe Gates was fidgety. Even the staid accountants present were in awe of the fortune so eloquently stacked before us.

Just how the division was made is an interesting story. We think it was the fairest way possible, considering all the circumstances. Some people have criticized us about it, but they have never yet offered a satisfactory alternate method that would please all sides. Actually, it was simple. We placed all gold coins in stacks of four by denomination, date and condition. Mint-fresh eight-escudo pieces, for example, were separated and sectioned off, four to a stack, and so on down the line. Then the redoubtable Captain Ed Reddick of the Highway Patrol took his choice of the piles. If there were four equal stacks of eight-escudo pieces, he had his choice, for the state, of any of the four. Granted, he was not a coin expert. But we felt, by picking arbitrarily, he would give everyone a fair shake. He had just as much chance of selecting a stack containing a $4,000 coin as he did of choosing one with coins of lesser value. This way there was no chance of any "sleepers" being concealed. We had no way of knowing which pile he would reach for. Had experts been appointed for the division, it is conceivable we'd have taken months to split the treasure. With great aplomb, Reddick chose the state's fourth of the gold, and he did a damn good job.

It wasn't quite as simple with the other valuables and artifacts. For this part of the transaction, he and the other state representative left the room. Then Allen, Mel and I, and other members of our groups, set about to make four equal piles. We sorted chains, gold discs, silverware and everything else for an hour or more, until we had four stacks we pretty well agreed upon that were of near-equal value. Then Reddick was called back into the room. He had his choice of the four piles. Reddick conferred with other state people present before making his selection, and he picked the one containing a number of rare artifacts of rich historical as well as material value.

With the state taken care of, Mel and I worked out our split after more hours of sorting, horse trading, haggling and bargaining, and then set aside 10 percent for Allen's group. It was a full, memorable day, and everyone went away happy.

A few days later Governor Bryant flew to Miami when President Kennedy came down to make a speech, and showed the Chief Executive some of the gold coins we had found. Kennedy expressed great interest in them, and listened intently as the governor told him our story. It made us proud when we heard about it.

The state, after receiving their quarter of our treasure, agreed to sit tight on it until the *National Geographic* was ready to release its prepublication publicity. When the story broke, on September 21, 1964, the state arranged a simultaneous exhibit and press conference in Tallahassee.

It was a smash hit, for which we, in Real Eight, had mixed emotions. It was nice, naturally, to have the admiration and respect of friends and neighbors who had for so many years thought we were crackpots, but there was another aspect to all this newspaper play, too. To top things off, the state announced it had insured its portion of the treasure for $400,000. How they settled on this figure, no one knows, but they did, and we were stuck with it. It didn't take the headline writers long to calculate if the state's fourth was worth $400,000, the entire take must be $1.6 million, and they had a field day with the figure.

From Washington, the *Geographic* sent out numerous releases detailing the forthcoming magazine article, and outlining our operations. They also mailed several color photos—free of charge—to the nation's newspapers. We were plastered all over front pages from Walla Walla to Key West, and from Phoenix to Portland, Maine. "Millions in treasure brought up from the sea": that was the theme everywhere.

What followed in the next few weeks would have made the California gold rush almost seem tame by comparison. Treasure hunters, pro and amateur, legally armed with new leases and illegally trespassing, loaded down with equipment or with no more than a curious eye, descended upon my sleepy community of Sebastian in force.

For a while at this time they very nearly trampled over each other along the oceanfront, particularly after a storm. The fact that Rex had found his $50,000 necklace on the beach spurred them on. One day, from the steps of our cabin, I counted 14 people with metal detectors, and a dozen others with shovels. Most of them wouldn't have recognized a piece of eight if it dropped into their hands. We had to shoo swimmers and scuba divers off our wreck site, which was marked by buoys. We even found some boats perched there—shades of Hoyo Solórzano. It was almost comical. We really weren't afraid of losing anything to the Sunday divers, but they were becoming more and more a nuisance.

Skin-diving equipment houses sold out, and had to reorder new gear. Most of the people purchasing the expensive suits had never dived before, and also had to pay for lessons. Mail-order metal-detector houses did a landoffice business selling everything from $25 machines, good for beer cans, to $1,200 beauties that sorted out only precious metals. Local libraries had to take copies of John Potter's *The Treasure Diver's Guide* out of circulation, so great was the reader demand. Someone even offered me $45 for my copy of the book. Its publication price was only $9.50.

A few people were getting rich quick, but it wasn't the gold hunters. One was Ralph Odum, a state official who years before, as a hobby, had produced a copyrighted map which he entitled, "Ye True Chart of Pirate Treasure lost or hidden in the land and waters of Florida." The maps proved popular enough in gift shops to net Odum several thousand dollars over the years, but with this new boom, his sales skyrocketed, and he kept printers on overtime running off more copies. Scalpers bought these up by the dozen and sold them dockside for exorbitant prices.

One man walked into a local fish camp and asked the operator, a friend of mine, if he would show him where the treasure was, because he didn't have much time to look for it. Another man appeared in Fort Pierce with a "gold-finding machine." Like the snake-oil peddlers of the late nineteenth century, he gathered groups around and went into his well-greased spiel. Then there was the slicker who tried to foster off a magic pendulum, which he claimed would swing at random until it detected gold, then it would quickly lock onto the source.

More serious hunters lined up financial backers for expensive expeditions. Almost all of these glory chasers were doomed before they began. If it took me years to find my first coin and a decade and a half to make a major strike, how could they hope for success in a couple of hours, a day, a week, or even over a period of months? We would spend longer than that on just one phase of our research alone.

Skilled con men appeared in droves too, promising all sorts of fantastic riches to anyone with enough money to back their action. They expended nothing from their own pockets, but assured others they could lead them directly to a gold-laden galleon—for the right price, of course.

Unlike the California strike more than a century earlier, where even the most naïve novice had a chance to stumble onto gold, an underwater search is not for the unknowledgeable, or for those on a shoestring budget. It's a job for experienced professionals who have the money for the right equipment. You can't take a pickax and make a lucky dig here. A proper salvage operation beneath the sea is a costly venture, and one that requires a lot of previous study and in-the-water experience even to know what you're looking for. As any career treasure hunter will tell you, there are no perfectly preserved wrecks just sitting on the bottom waiting to be plucked clean. You have to know what might be left in the way of debris—and you have to know how to follow invisible paths across the ocean bottom to the actual wreckage itself, which is often buried beneath tons of sand.

To launch a treasure hunt in the state now, you have to prove you are serious, with the finances and the planning to back you up. If the state issued a lease to every eager fortune seeker who applied, there wouldn't be a whole artifact left along the coastline.

With the 50-mile area from Sebastian to Stuart now open, save for our eight 1715 wreck sites, a number of legitimate concerns were granted leases and began work. As long as they didn't bother us, we didn't mind at all. A lot of big money was spent to back these expeditions, and only one has paid any substantial returns. It was a venture headed by Ken F. Gordy and Albert Ashley of Fort Pierce. Working a site near our wedge wreck off Fort Pierce, from a beautifully equipped, 72-foot boat, they located an American shipwreck of Civil War or earlier vintage, and brought up some $50,000 in U.S. gold coins, according to newspaper accounts.

Mel Fisher, in a separate deal, has found an old paddlewheeler on the bottom which he thinks may be loaded with rich cargo, and is hopeful that he'll soon bring something up from it. Mel, incidentally, also works a location in the Florida Keys during our off-diving season. There, he has zeroed in on a Spanish treasure galleon—the *San Fernando*—that sank during the historic 1733 hurricane, which drowned a fleet of 21 ships carrying some $68 million in gold. Historians record that only $12 million was ever recovered. Mel has found silver plates, china and assorted pieces of silverware, and hopes to strike gold soon.

Our publicity sent the fortune seekers scurrying to other wreck sites in the Keys, too, and all along both coasts of Florida. At one time more than a dozen charter-boat captains in the Keys were making their entire income by directing divers to known wreck sites. Most of these, of course, had been worked over before and held nothing of value, but try to discourage someone afflicted with treasure fever. It can't be done. I ought to know.

It didn't take long for the tribe of transients to come and go. A few hours of nonproductive searching and digging under the broiling Florida sun sweated the enthusiasm out of them fast. Yet, as one batch left, another would arrive, in an almost continuous stream, and I know now I'll probably never again be able to roam the beaches in the blissful solitude I enjoyed years ago when I began all this action. Each time another major find of ours is announced, the parade starts anew. It's like the fisherman who makes the first catch of the day. Before he can bait his hook and toss it out again, a dozen other anglers have blanketed his spot with a snarling entanglement of lines. Such is human nature.

Apparently, there are no limitations to the extremes to which people will go in efforts to deceive others where treasure is involved. A story broke in Florida newspapers early in 1965 about a large find of silver pieces of eight from a wreck off the west coast of the state. We followed the accounts with keen interest, but strangely, heard nothing more for several months.

Then one Sunday the papers headlined the account of an elaborate fraud uncovered by state officials concerning this alleged treasure discovery. It was reported that U.S. coins were melted down and then made into counterfeit Spanish cobs. Experts found many obvious flaws in them. Two small statues, supposedly brought up from the wreck as having been originally produced by the Aztec Indians, were exposed as actually being mail-order bookends from Mexico. And a knight's head that had been said to have adorned the hilt of a sword found at the site was believed, by the investigating officials, really to have been a replica of a cap from a popular brand bottle of men's cologne.

William Kidd, who gave us cause to worry, left the scene late in 1964, and was replaced as head of the Internal Improvement Fund by Robert Parker, who was not unfamiliar with our operations. He had met Dan, Harry and John when they were in Tallahassee seeing his old boss, Jimmy Kynes.

He's doing a creditable job, but things will never be the same as they were back in Van Ferguson's days. There is too much at stake now. There was a time when we went about our business without fanfare, but that day is past.

Parker has a tough job. He gets attacked from all sides. Puritans accuse him of not protecting Florida's rights, claiming the state should get all treasure salvaged. They do not take into consideration the very principle upon which our nation was founded—free enterprise. To reap all the spoils, the state would have to go into the business full time, and this is something it is not prepared to do—nor should it be. As it is, the state gets one-fourth of all the treasure and a much larger percentage of artifacts with only historical value. Look at it this way: if it hadn't been for us, for our initiative and endurance, the state wouldn't have gotten *anything* from the 1715 fleet. I don't believe for a minute that worn-out adage that someone else would have found it if we hadn't. After all, the stuff was out there 250 years untouched!

Parker also gets pressured by private concerns, some with financial and political power behind them—and he is in an appointed (and thus vulnerable) position. He has all sorts of legal brain breakers to contend with. One man, for instance, is suing the state, claiming it has no right, title, claim or interest in offshore treasure-salvage operations.

His suit states that Atlantic Ocean waters come under the jurisdiction of the Federal Government. Further, he charges, the only right the United States granted to Florida was the right to lease or recover natural resources lying within the three-mile limit, but no right was granted for the state to lease to others who desired to search for abandoned property.

I almost shudder to think what would happen if such a suit is ever upheld by the courts. It could overthrow state control on salvage operations, and conceivably open the door to all ocean treasure seekers.

In January, 1965, the new Florida governor, Haydon Burns of Jacksonville, issued a moratorium on treasure leases. No new ones were to be granted for an indefinite period, although existing leases, including ours, would continue to be honored. Burns wanted to take a long, hard look at the state's policies and operations.

The most noteworthy outcome of this intense study was the creation of an Antiquities Commission. Although this would still be under Parker's Internal Improvement Fund, the actual administration of granting treasure leases and seeing that the state got a fair shake would be directed by the chairman of the commission.

The antiquities law of 1965 covers treasure trove, marine salvage, artifacts, historic sites and objects, fossil deposits, documents, books and all other personal or real property of scientific or historic value. Basically, the rules and regulations governing salvage operations remain unchanged. The antiquities board consists of the governor and his cabinet.

An Antiquities Commission was also established, to advise and assist the board. Commission members include the state archeologists, the director of the Florida State Museum, the chairman of the Florida State Historical Society, the director of the State Conservation Board, the state geologist, anthropology and archeology department heads at state universities, the chairman of the Florida State Library and Historical Commission, and the president of the Florida Anthropological Society.

The commission provides technical and professional assistance to the state board of antiquities in arranging for the salvage, protection and preservation of all objects and sites covered by the law. As in the past, the salvager retains 75 percent of objects recovered under the new law.

Dr. J. C. Dickinson, director of the Florida State Museum, was elected chairman of the commission. We have known him a long time. Drs. Sears and Goggins worked for him at the museum, so he is fully aware of our methods of operation and our interest in preserving artifacts of historical significance. In fact, we cooperated closely with Dr. Dickinson to set up a state exhibit of the major finds we recovered from Fort Pierce in 1964, and other rare pieces in our collection, including the $50,000 gold necklace.

After the announcement of the creation of the Antiquities Commission, new attorney general Earl Faircloth ruled that our leases would be valid when the authority for treasure supervision was transferred to the commission from the Internal Improvement Fund.

By the time we got back into the waters at the beginning of the 1966 season, the state had organized a marine salvage patrol. Made up of conservation officers trained in diving, the patrol has been set up to oversee and supervise treasure-salvaging operations conducted under state leases. It is these officers' duty to catalog each artifact lifted from the sea bottom, and to watch for illicit salvage activities. The 10-man patrol will have quite a job keeping up with things if all serious requests for leases are granted. I understand that during Governor Burns's moratorium a backlog of nearly 100 such requests accumulated.

Today, as we continue our searches, we operate on sound legal ground, and once again enjoy mutual trust and respect with state officials. Regardless of what new developments arise, our aims and operations are on record. We have cooperated fully with the state in the past and we will continue to do so as long as we dig for riches in Florida's offshore waters.

13 Underwater Bonanza

For some time we had looked for ways to replace our beloved, but bedraggled *Sampan*. For sentimental value it was irreplaceable, but for practical salvage operations it left a lot to be desired—a helluva lot. It just wasn't cut out to be a treasure-hunting boat. Even with our long hours of revamping it from stem to stern, it still fell short. Bob Johnson, in fact, called it unseaworthy, and there were many times when I actually thought we'd go down in it, trying to maneuver through the narrow Sebastian Inlet.

But it wasn't until 1964, when this salvage operation began to take considerably more of our time, that we seriously looked around for a replacement. I think it was Mel Fisher's *Dee-Gee* that helped spur us. It was no beauty by any stretch of the imagination, but it was equipped for the job—something the *Sampan* wasn't, nor ever would be.

One day Bob ran across a boat up on Merritt Island, near the Air Force base, and gave it a good going-over with his inspection-experienced eye. It looked just right for our purpose, but on closer examination he had vetoed it, because there was a copper bottom sheathing. When salt water gets under this sheathing, the ever-persistent teredo worms get at the wood, and you have a first-class maintenance problem. Otherwise you might go out one day and find leaks springing out of a hundred tiny holes.

But after thinking it all over, Bob decided we might be able to convert the vessel anyway and dry-dock it periodically to keep the salt water out. Actually, it was nothing more than an open hull, but it had no bad wood and looked to be seaworthy. Besides, Bob figured we could pick it up for a good price. The owner, however, had other ideas. He wanted $3,000. Bob turned him down, and after a day or two of dickering, the owner asked if he would accept the boat as a down payment on Bob's beautiful, 63-foot yacht, the *Sea Dragon*. We had used this jewel of the ocean a few times on seek-and-search patterns off Sebastian when we were looking for new wreck sites. Built for the man who has everything, it was complete with three separate staterooms, a bar and lounge, and every conceivable piece of equipment a boat would need for ocean voyages. And if anyone knew what was needed, the man was Bob Johnson. He's sailed them all.

Eventually, they got together on the price and made a deal. Real Eight now owned a 50-foot hull with a 13-foot beam. We planned to rebuild it, from the hull up, to suit our particular type of salvage operation. It seemed a terrible shame that Bob had to part with the *Sea Dragon* at a bargain price, for no greater sacrifice has been made in the Real Eight cause. It was a yachtsman's yacht. We pretty well stripped it clean of anchors, lines, ship-to-shore radios, winches, binoculars, compasses and dozens of other items that would prove useful on the new acquisition.

Del said he nearly cried when he saw the 50-footer for the first time, and I have to admit it did have a ringing resemblance to a garbage scow. But it belonged to us now, for better or worse, and its maiden voyage under the company banner made me think it would be nothing but the worse.

We sailed it down the Indian River to the Eau Gallie Yacht Club and stopped there—near where Harry and Dan live—to take on fuel. When we cranked her up again, a piston must have blown, for huge clouds of billowing, black diesel oil smoke began pouring out the exhaust. While we fiddled with the engine, the hostess at the exclusive yacht club restaurant came out waving her arms frantically.

"Please, please get out of here with that tub!" she wailed. "You're driving all my customers away." The wind was funneling our smoke right through her establishment, and believe me there is no blacker, dirtier, more-choking smoke than that from a sick diesel oil engine.

We got back into the middle of the river's channel, and the engine quit altogether. Almost spontaneously, we christened our boat the *Derelict*. It seemed most appropriate. We had to bring the faithful *Sampan* up from Sebastian to tow it to dock. By now we were in the height of the 1964 diving season, and there wasn't much time to work on the *Derelict*. And it needed work! How it needed work. We pitched in nights, and weekends, and days when the water was too rough to dive. What a job that was! The entire hull of the boat was lined with a foot-and-a-half-deep pile of leaves, pinecones, papers, dirt, old bottles and all sorts of other junk.

Toward the end of the summer we began making progress. We pulled the main engine and replaced it, cleaned out the knee-deep crap in the hull and built a main deck and pilothouse with steering apparatus. Then the mast and boom were fitted. We worked on that boat until I got sick of seeing it. Mostly, it was Bob, Del, Lou and myself, with Rex pitching in. We must have averaged four hours' sleep a night during this period, burning the midnight oil far into the wee hours. When the hurricanes began approaching, calling a halt to our diving in the fall, we turned full attention to the streamlining of the *Derelict*.

Some days I think we worked too hard for our own good—like the time Bob was putting down the fiber-glass deck. It was a blistering hot day, and he was downing liquid refreshments one after another. The next morning when we inspected his handiwork, here were his bare footprints all over patches of the now-hardened fiber glass, like an actor's prints at that famous Chinese restaurant in Hollywood. Bob swears up and down it wasn't the excessive amount of liquid he consumed that had caused his fancy stepping, but, he claimed, the resin had made him dizzy and he didn't know what he was doing. It made a good story, but when we re-surfaced the deck, we kept the ice cooler out of his reach.

Our last major project on the outfitting of the *Derelict* was the installation of a new blaster. After seeing Mel Fisher's machine in operation throughout 1964, we knew this was the most efficient manner to move sand on our wreck sites, and Del and Bob set about to design an improved blaster specially for the new boat. They fabricated a quarter-ton steel cylinder eight feet long and three and a half feet in diameter. Then we purchased a 1935 Ford rear end transmission, ran its shaft down the cylinder, and mounted a four-bladed propeller. Del's long experience in welding and pump building really came in handy here. They then cut three holes in the side of the cylinder and mounted the engine sideways on the boat and welded universal joints and couplings to it.

The principle of the blaster is simple. As clean surface water rushes into a six-foot tube, the whirling propeller forces a 30-inch-in-diameter jet stream of water down the steel cylinder, which literally blasts the sand away on the bottom. It is just the opposite of our dredges, which suction the sand up through pipes. The 500-pound blaster creates a powerful circular movement, much like a hurricane's winds—or at least it did on paper. As there had never been a machine quite like it ever created before, we weren't sure just what we could expect on our first trial run in the harbor at Wabasso. Everyone had his fingers crossed when we cranked it up.

I don't think any of us was prepared for what happened next. To say our test run was successful would be grossly understating the fact. That damn homemade blaster—which had cost only a couple of hundred dollars to piece together—blew mud off the bottom of the Wabasso harbor for 200 feet or more. It sounded like 16 jet fighters roaring off the runway at the same time. It was far more than we had dared hope for, and we felt as happy as we would have had there been a big gold strike.

The blaster turned out to be a real lifesaver. We know of nothing else that can move sand fast and furious, yet can be idled down so it gently uncovers the most delicate artifacts without injuring them in the slightest. It can dig a hole big enough to bury an elephant in minutes, and it can be slowed down, when we hit a hot spot, to fan light layers of sand away without disturbing the treasure. As we subsequently were to find out, the blaster cut years off our salvage operations. During a single day, it opened up huge pits in areas that would have taken us weeks to cover with the conventional dredges, and it was actually a safer, more thorough operating procedure.

Still, the *Derelict* needed work. We had toiled endlessly since July, 1964, but Bob wouldn't take it out until everything was shipshape. When the final repairs were made it was April, and we had sunk about $15,000 in the project.

With the start of the 1965 season, we went into the treasure-hunting business full time by putting Bob and three young divers, my nephew, Rex, Mike Hrebec, and his friend, Bob Conkey, on salary. We had decided to do this some time before in order to take full advantage of the lucrative wreck sites at the cabin, and south of Fort Pierce, that were now yielding steady supplies of gold and silver coins. Bob was the perfect man to direct our operations. He had all the necessary skills, and licenses, to master the *Derelict*, and he resigned from his job at Cape Kennedy to concentrate on diving. We financed the operation through the sale of coins and via a bank loan which we had obtained by putting up gold doubloons as collateral.

On April 22, the first finds were made off the new boat. They were far from impressive—two silver coins and the base of a silver candlestick—

but they were a starter. Bob promptly nailed one of the four real pieces to the cabin of the *Derelict* as a memento.

For the next month he took his hungry young divers on a merry chase from the cabin wreck site, 30 miles south to the one past Fort Pierce. Weather had a lot to do with the hopscotching. If the waters were rough at all, he'd go south, to Fort Pierce, where it was generally clearer. If it was calm, they'd take the boat out off Sebastian. Mostly, it was too dirty for practical diving at either site.

Then on May 19 they made their first significant find, and, like so many others, it almost came about by accident, after everyone had wanted to quit for the day. Young Bob Conkey, our greenest diver, went down on the Fort Pierce wreck, about 500 feet or so north of where Mel Fisher's people were working, and he came up shaking his head in dismay.

"Mr. Johnson," he wailed, "it's so black down there I can't even find the bottom. We'll never get anything today." Rex and Mike concurred, so Bob suited up to see just how bad it was. Normally, he would have given up for the day, but the ocean was unusually calm, and if there were even the slightest ray of hope for the waters to clear up, it would have been worthwhile to stay on site. Bob could see patches opening up here and there, and told his divers to keep searching until they hit one of these open spots and then work it.

A little later Conkey surfaced again. This time it looked as if his arm was 15 feet long. He had a gold coin tightly clenched in his fist.

"How wrong can I be," he shrilled. They brought up 19 doubloons that day. Over the next week or so, a few more were found, along with several "new" cannon, two anchors, some pewter plates, musket balls and other assorted pieces of wreckage.

Although they were working quite a way north of Mel and his crew, it was still the same wreck. Again, I emphasize the fact that when the ships went down in that vicious storm of 1715, many were ripped to pieces on the reefs, and wreckage was strewn over a wide area, often covering several acres. Sea action over the years further spread the sunken remains. So we were finding a few coins here, and Mel was also scoring on the past season's gold hot spot, to the south.

We have no rabbit's foot or horseshoe or magic divining rod—or anything else of superstitious nature aboard the *Derelict;* only scientific gear. We have no need for such lucky charms—not with Del Long around. In the past he had miraculously led us to one productive site after another through some sort of uncanny perceptive knack. He didn't get hunches often, but when he did they were real lulus. No one laughed at him anymore. We sort of held his prognostications in admiring reverence.

Del was out with us one weekend—we all joined the full-time crew on Saturdays and Sundays, or whenever we could—and toward the end of the day he pointed off to the south.

"I've got a feeling, fellows," he began, and we all gathered around to glean whatever prophetic pearls he was about to spill, "that we're going to hit it big again soon—right over there." We estimated the spot he aimed at to be about 800 to 900 feet south of the area we had been working.

"Yep," he drawled with a note of assurance, "if we go over there we'll find a heap of gold."

Sure enough, and may I be struck on the spot if it's not the gospel, Bob and the boys motored over to the location in the next couple of days, and on May 30, found 130 gold coins four fathoms down—not 50 feet from the site Del had pinpointed! It was phenomenal. How can you explain it?

As everyone was off work the next day, Bob called and told us of the strike. Everyone but Harry was aboard the next morning when we sailed at 8:48 A.M., and anchored a little over an hour later, about 1,000 feet offshore. Within 20 minutes Conkey came up with a gold doubloon. His find opened the floodgates to the most fantastic single day we have ever recorded. I hadn't been diving lately because of a bad back, but I couldn't resist the temptation, and down I went. It was a beautiful day, and the waters were as clear as any I could remember. Visibility was 40 or 50 feet in all directions. Conditions were perfect. The sands were so white it looked as if the surf had scrubbed the grains with detergent.

And then I saw it—a sight every man should see just once in his life. The blaster had cut a hole about 30 feet in diameter, and there, in this vast pocket of the ocean floor, lay a carpet of gold; believe me, a carpet of gold! It was the most glorious picture one can imagine. Not even Hollywood could have upstaged this natural underwater scene. Off to one side, against a rock-coral formation, the coins, so help me, were even lying in neat stacks of three and four. The water magnification made it seem as though the entire bottom was lined with gold.

We were spellbound. Here was a bunch of seasoned, hardened treasure hunters who had been making finds for more than five years, and we couldn't move. It was like a great painting by one of the old masters. It just held us in awe. When we finally did snap back to reality, we surfaced and made sure everybody on board got a chance to view this wonder before we began picking up the coins.

So abundant were the doubloons that we literally scooped them by the double handful and loaded buckets to the brim with them. Not only were the coins plentiful, but they were in mint condition—and they were big ones—mostly eight-escudo pieces, about the size of an American silver dollar. Most of the gold we had found the year before was smaller—one- and two-escudo pieces.

Before we had vacuumed the area clean, we hollered to Mel, Rupe and the others on the *Dee-Gee* to come over and join in the fun. Moe went down and came up with gold glistening in each of his palms and a smile splitting his ears. All day long we poured the coins onto the decks of the *Derelict* in a steady cascade of gold. We were one tired bunch of divers when we finally knocked off at 5:20 that afternoon, but we had the comforting knowledge that we had recovered more treasure in one day than anyone in history—in recorded history at least.

We entrusted the day's take to Lou and Dan for sorting and counting that night, and when they arrived at Dan's house, he told his wife Jane, "We hit it pretty good today, honey. Get out the card table." By now she had gotten used to seeing silver coins by the bushel and other treasure, but gold was still a relatively scarce commodity in our group. Jane later described the scene to me, and I think it's worth recounting from her point of view:

"When Dan told me they had made another strike, I was happy, of course, but then Lou went home for supper so I figured it wasn't that important, and I scurried off to our kitchen. A little while later Lou came back and I could hear a lot of clinking on the table, so I went out to see what they had found. It took my breath away. The tabletop was completely covered with coins. I thought at first they must be counterfeit. There couldn't be that much gold in the world!

"The thing that struck me more than anything was the nonchalant manner in which my husband and Lou were counting and stacking the coins—as if they were so many buttons or pennies from the piggy bank. Everything was so matter-of-fact to them. Here was, by conservative guess, several hundred thousand dollars worth of gold on my card table, and they could still maintain poker faces! Eagerly, I helped them sort and catalog each coin, and if you can imagine the sensation, my fingers actually got tired from counting doubloons."

Few people, I'd venture, have experienced fatigue from such a chore, nor would they have minded it. Neither did Jane. It was one in the morning when everything had been properly assessed and stacked. The total count from our record day was 1,128 gold coins.

The breakdown went like this: 351 eight-escudo pieces, 378 four-escudo pieces and 215 two-escudo pieces from the Mexico City mint; 167 eights, 3 fours, and 13 twos from the mint at Lima, Peru. There was also one four-escudo imperial. This is a coin that workers took extra care to strike from new dies, so as to form as near perfect impressions as were possible. Imperials were then presented to royalty. This one was dated 1711. Its value is estimated at from $2,000 to $5,000.

Not only had it been a banner day for quantity, but also nearly half of the coins were eight-escudo pieces—which are worth more on the market. In good condition, and these all met that qualification and more so, this denomination sells for $1,000 to $3,000—and we had 518 of them! How much was our total take worth for the one day? You figure it out.

With most treasure hunters, like fishermen, they see the big take and are ready to haul it in when the elements, or luck, engulf them, leaving only the tall stories to tell again and again. I've heard countless tales of divers getting within close range of a recovery only to be thwarted by bad weather or some similar misfortune. With us, the story had a new twist. We had found treasure, and *then* the conditions worsened, leaving us with tongues hanging out and fingernails bitten to the quick. Such was the case on our first coin clump finds in 1961, and on so many other instances—and such was the case the day after this fabulous gold recovery. The waters kicked up, clouding visibility, and told us in no uncertain terms that we had found enough for a while, now sit back and cool it. We had no choice. The whitecaps would have slapped us all over the ocean had we tried to go out. We could only wait. What a great equalizer nature is.

It was June 3 before we could get out again, and we found only six gold coins, adding five more the next day. The obvious question again is how could we bring up more than 1,000 one day and so few the next. The answer is simple. We had cleaned our hot spot in that one day. Those gold coins were undoubtedly from one chest—the wooden confines of which had rotted long ago, spilling the doubloons over a specific area. Remember, these were mostly large coins, and our total find probably filled

one entire Spanish chest. I might add, by way of footnote, that we didn't
pick up a single silver piece of eight during this whole period. After a few
more days on the site, it became evident that we had gleaned about all it
would yield. So, Bob began hopping back up to the cabin area whenever
the weather permitted.

We had long nursed a pet theory about this wreck, on which we had
found the first gold, the K'ang Hsi china and so many silver coins. It was
our contention that this region represented only part of the total wreck.
There were cannon there, yes, but there was no ballast stone, nor any
signs of heavy ship's timbers. This led us to believe the ship had broken
up in deeper waters and part of it had been thrown or washed in between
the first and second reefs. In using our crude means of searching in the
early days—towing divers underwater, the ill-fated aluminum sled, and
the airplane hops—we had been unsuccessful in ever pinpointing the
other half of the wreck, if, in fact, there was another half.

But with Fay Field's magnetometer, we felt we would have a good
chance to locate it now, and we talked Fay and Rupe Gates into joining in
the search. At worst it would be a break from the salvaging routine—if
picking gold and silver coins off the ocean floor can ever be classed as
routine.

Bob, Rupe, Fay and our young divers methodically began searching the
area in which in all likelihood the wreck remains would be. We had calculated that, since the 1715 hurricane had swept upon the fleet from the
east-northeast, this wreckage should lie northeast of the cabin area we had
worked. We first located some cannon, but they were actually southeast
of the other site—about 900 feet east by south to be exact. As we were to
discover, Fay and Rupe had mapped out a near-perfect picture of this
wreck. Without their dogged detective work we might never have found
this new part of the site.

Two days after this the *Derelict* anchored over the deeper point, and
within nine minutes the divers brought up three pie-shaped wedges of silver, just like the ones Harry had found back in 1960. Before the day was
over, nine more wedges were found, along with three clumps of silver
coins, several hundred loose pieces of eight and 10 big round discs, about
18 inches in diameter, weighing from 44 to 105 pounds each.

Poor Bob almost broke his back that day. He had Rex, Mike and Bob
Conkey working the bottom and securing lines around these discs, and he
had to haul them up by himself, hand over hand. The discs were partly
silver, but had a bastard assortment of metals in them, including, I think,

gold, platinum and copper among others. They had been found under about three or four feet of sand.

They also uncovered that day one of the strangest artifacts yet—a round "onion-shaped" bottle with its original liquid still sealed inside. Just what it is we're not sure, but if it is wine, it would be a safe guess to say it had reached full maturity. We are reasonably certain it's either wine or perfume.

Exactly how hot a spot the boys had found that day no one realized right away, even after these remarkable finds. We went the whole 1960 and 1961 seasons and recovered less than they had brought up in one day. We proved it was no fluke by recovering several thousand loose silver coins the next afternoon, and on June 24 we had another record day, of sorts. The take included 665 *pounds* of silver coins. Figuring 15 to a pound, that's nearly 10,000! Also hoisted aboard were a dozen more silver wedges, eight more of the strange metal discs, two biscuit-shaped chunks of silver, and one clump of coins.

From here on out it got damn near ridiculous. To read Bob Johnson's logbook, one would fall asleep from the almost monotonous entries:

—"June 25, several hundred loose coins; three wedges; one clump; three discs. June 26, several hundred coins, etc."

In about a week's time we had brought up nearly a ton of silver coins alone—a ton of pieces of eight! I can remember how I cherished that first silver coin I had found on the beach so many years ago, and now finding them was commonplace. It even got to the point—and this must surely be another historic first in treasure-hunting operations—where Bob told the boys to skip the scattered loose coins and concentrate on finding bars, discs, wedges and other larger items of more value. Skip the loose coins! Remarkable!

To make sure we covered every inch of the highly productive site, we employed a grid system, using as one base line or axis, a line running east and west and drawn between the cascabels of two of the wreck's scattered cannon. The second axis was drawn at right angles to the first, through the cascabel of the shoreward cannon in an approximate north-south direction. This system was developed by Mel's team.

To establish these two lines physically, we used lengths of ⅜-inch chain. As we moved along the bottom, working the area, additional lengths of chain, lying parallel to the base lines at 25-foot intervals, were stretched outward. Each significant find was recorded in relation to the nearest chains on graph paper as soon as possible after recovery. The lines running in one direction had grid points designated in letters; those in the other direction, in numbers. Thus, exact locations of each discovery could be identified.

Admittedly, this isn't the most scientific control system, but in these waters and on these sites, one simply has to improvise and come up with the most workable design he can, however crude. If we had unlimited visibility and calm waters, we could use the classic methods, but here this is not the case.

To reference our grid lines on the bottom, Lou drew up detailed charts, showing exactly the areas we had worked, where every major find had been made, where each clump of coral was, etc. Ideally, it would be better to have a photograph taken from the surface of the water looking down, but with our visibility limitations, this is imposssble, and scale maps are the next best thing. Lou has done an exceptional job on them.

Our finds at the new site were so fabulous and so steady we called Mel's divers up from Fort Pierce to share the action. Bob moved the *Derelict* to the fringes of the hot spot so Treasure Salvors could get a morale boost. As the days drifted into July, our decks continued to become laden with silver.

Bob Johnson had long hoped to find something on the site that would definitely identify the wreck. On July 7 we thought we might have a clue—with the recovery of the first real ship's timbers. They were probably part of the keel; the metal fasteners were still in place. Four days later we came up with a 125-pound clump of coins, 2 silver plates, 60 pounds of loose coins and an old apothecary mortar—but no more leads to the true identity of the ship. We're now almost certain this is Ubilla's *capitana*, on the basis of new evidence I shall explain later.

We were sure now that the ocean held no more surprises for us—that we had seen it all—necklaces, doubloons, rings, pieces of eight, pendants, chains, silverware, coin clumps, wedges, gold discs, fine china, bottles with the liquid still corked in—what more could be out there? On July 24 we got the answer—and it was an unexpected one that shocked the hell out of us. It was my nephew who made the first sighting. He quickly surfaced.

"Mr. Johnson," Rex exclaimed. "There's a chest of silver down there."

"Sure, Rex, sure," Bob returned, going along with the suspected hoax. "You just go back down and bring it up."

"I'm serious, Mr. Johnson," Rex pleaded. "There really is a chest down there, and it's full of silver."

Only in books do you find treasure chests, for off Florida, under the ocean, as I said earlier, the voracious teredo worms make short work of the cedar and other wooden fibers that encased gold and silver coins centuries ago. To find a box intact was too much to hope for, and we had given up this particular dream years before. Such an item just couldn't exist.

"Okay, fun is fun, but get back to work down there," Bob ordered, in a fatherly manner. Then Rex appealed to Del Long who was out with them that day, and finally Del consented to go down and have a look. But if this were some sort of joke, he warned Rex, he'd have some explaining to do. Two minutes later Del surfaced.

"That boy is 100 percent right, Bob. There sure enough is a treasure chest lying down there just as pretty as you please," he announced.

Then Bob suited up, and everybody had a good look at it. Incredibly, it was exactly as Rex had described it: a blackish-colored wooden container about three feet long, a foot or so wide, and about a foot deep. One end and the top were missing, but the rest of this remarkable chest was intact. Bob then surfaced to draw up a recovery plan. This was such a rare find—to our knowledge it's the only such chest in the world—that he didn't want to take any chances on damaging it.

He estimated the chest weighed about 200 pounds, and that created a lift problem, so Bob designed a scaffold-like platform using a chunk of plywood he had aboard the *Derelict* as the base. They would place the chest on this, secure it with lines, and then bring it up. But first they must carefully work the chest loose from the sands that had held it prisoner for so many years, and in so doing had preserved it from the teredos. It took four hours of painstaking work to free it. Then the divers slid the plywood platform under it and Del, Lou, Rex, Bob Conkey and Mike manned the four corners as Bob slowly hauled it up. They got it aboard unharmed, and immediately immersed it in a big tub of water. Had they not done this, the sun would have quickly dried out the water-logged wood, shrunk it and warped it out of shape, or rotted it altogether. We figure the lead-lined chest is cedar, and our guess is that there are about 3,000 pieces of eight inside. We may never know the precise number, for like the clumps, the coins are solidly fused together, making an exact counting impossible.

On the way into port Bob called me on the ship-to-shore radio and told me to round up all the Real Eight members, that he was bringing in something everyone should see. Somehow the news of a major strike had gotten out in the local area, as it inevitably does, and when we met him at the dock at three in the afternoon, there must have been 200 people gathered around to see what it was that would excite such hard-bitten hunters as us. They got their money's worth. It seems almost insignificant to add that the boys also found over 1,500 loose silver coins that day.

We have the chest submerged in fresh water in a glass case at our museum today, and it's one of our number-one attractions. But aside from the sheer glamour, we hope this unique find will fill in some gaps of history, such as verifying the size and construction of chests, how many coins they held, what type of woods and fasteners they were made of, and a dozen other points.

Of course, we've found nothing since that could match the chest. In fact, shortly after its discovery, we closed out another diving season. On August 1 we made one of our biggest hauls of silver coins—over 4,000, and a week later we found the first brass breechblock out of a cannon. It was an eight-inch-long hunk of metal, nine and a half inches around, with a handle and locking screw. It was used to ignite the powder in the cannon, and was in near-perfect shape. We also brought up four more of those peculiar onion bottles full of liquid, and a batch of pewter plates.

By September 7 we had to secure operations when fickle Hurricane Betsy went up past the Bahamas, turned around, and plowed south over Miami and then out into the Gulf of Mexico, eventually drenching Louisiana. It kicked up the sand and the seas enough to halt our work. The *Derelict* needed repairs anyway, so Bob Johnson shut his logbook, and we reflected on the most successful single season in the recorded annals of treasure salvaging.

We had thousands of gold coins, tens of thousands of pieces of eight, 40-odd discs of precious metals, a dozen or so silver wedges, scads of other valuables, and our chest. Not even Sir William Phips could top this! We found more in 1965 than in all our previous years combined. Better yet, our hot spot at the deeper cabin site was still highly productive when we quit for the year, so we're assured of continued success for some time to come.

It was a full five months before we got around to divvying up the spoils of 1965 with the state. Everything was locked tight in bank vaults from the summer until the first week of February, 1966. We didn't mind the wait too much, but Mel and his boys were hurting. They had sold most of their gains from 1964 and needed some capital for living expenses.

This time we spent more than a week behind closed doors, and the division was made—as equitably as possible—in essentially the same manner as before. This session took longer because there was more treasure and a greater number of artifacts to divide. These were primarily of historical value, and state officials were concerned about getting a well-rounded representation in their 25 percent.

As usual we made the front pages once again. The state insured their fourth for $460,000, and this, to headline writers, made the total allotment worth $1,840,000—or nearly a quarter million dollars more than the previous haul. Just how these figures were arrived at—particularly considering the large number of artifacts the precise value of which was hard to assess—I don't know, but who were we to argue?

Anyway, after Real Eight and Treasure Salvors halved what was left, everyone seemed happy. Mel had spending money to finance operations; the state had a hoard of treasure to add to its historical displays; and we had enough to beef up our own museum, or to sell—if and when the right price was offered.

14   Spin-off Benefits

Since 1964, when we first hit it big with the gold finds, my entire life has been changed. My thoughts, of course, have been concentrated on treasure for quite a few years now, but until the big gold strike in May, 1964, and the resulting publicity from it, my private affairs remained rather quiet and uncomplicated. That's the way I like it—a sip or two of brandy after dinner, a good book or a little television, and then bed by 9 P.M.

Since finding treasure, however, it's become increasingly more difficult to keep my homelife simple. There is literally not a night that goes by without someone calling at the house or the phone ringing from long distances all over the world. I live off the beaten path a little north of Sebastian. There's only a narrow dirt road there by the highway, and a blink of the eyes at night and you're past it. But I swear I think half the people in the country know exactly where my house is. When I open the front door these days, it might be my next-door neighbor, or a *Life* Magazine photographer; a cousin or an English lord; the local grocer, or Teddy Tucker, the fabled treasure hunter from Bermuda.

We have met all sorts of VIP's, from astronauts to Congressmen to generals. In September, 1962, when the late President John F. Kennedy came to Cape Canaveral for a look at the rocket base, Colonel Dan Thompson gave him one of the briefings. Then he presented Kennedy with a silver piece of eight and gave him another, mounted on a bracelet, for Jackie, and told him briefly of our operations. The gifts delighted the youthful Chief Executive.

In the past couple of years, every Real Eight member has literally been

(Courtesy of Del Long)

Treasure chest with fused silver coins, brought up during the 1965 summer diving season.

Mysterious "onion" bottles that were found off the cabin wreck site in 1965, one of them with original liquid still sealed within. Contents probably wine or perfume. Cannon breechblock in foreground.

(Courtesy of Del Long)

On the steps of a cabin facing the inscrutable Atlantic, Kip Wagner dreams of future discoveries and plans coming operations.

besieged with requests for interviews, demands for speeches, offers for promotions and countless other deals ranging from two-bit actions to legitimate propositions involving up to a million dollars and more. We get letters from all over the globe. In a way, I suppose, we've become some sort of heroes to all the world's underdogs, the losers and the dreamers. We're idolized because we made good. Thousands of people look for sunken ships laden with riches—we found them. And so, it appears we are destined to carry this reputation everywhere we go from now on.

I can't help recalling with a chuckle the letter a young lad wrote us. "I know you have lots of treasure," he said, "and I'd like to have nine doubloons—one for my father, one for my mother, one for my brother and six for myself. PS, if you can't send nine, send six!"

Other letters funnel in asking for everything from advice to our autographs; *our autographs,* mind you! We're not celebrities in the sense that we have to hide behind dark glasses on the streets. No one recognizes us in public outside of the Sebastian–Fort Pierce area, but nevertheless our time is not our own anymore.

The first real barrage of international publicity hit us at the end of 1964. The *National Geographic* had released some prepublication material in September, and we were big in Florida after the state exhibited its fourth of our treasure at the same time. But it wasn't until the *Saturday Evening Post* issue of December 12, 1964, hit the stands that we were caught in the full glare of public exposure, with all its intricate sidelights.

The *Geographic,* of course, had Real Eight sewed up under its contract for exclusive rights to our story, and, finally, it settled on a January, 1965, publication date. But once our gold discoveries had made the newspapers, reporters, writers, photographers, editors and publishers—representing every form of mass media—beat a steady path to our doors. To one and all we had to say no. We were committed until one month after *National Geographic* published. This fact didn't seem to deter some of the news-hawks. We were pressured, offered bribes, cajoled, sweet-talked, wined, dined and even threatened. But I can say in all honesty, despite the tempting offers, Real Eight stuck to its agreement. Even so, the *Geographic* got scooped on breaking the story not once, but twice.

Post was first. They sent writer Jim Atwater down, and he saw what the state had, researched the history of the 1715 fleet and then made a deal with Mel Fisher and Treasure Salvors for the rest of their story. *Argosy* was on the nation's newsstands a couple of weeks later with Bruce Ward's version of the action, as previously mentioned. Both articles, however, told only a small part of the story. How could they possibly tell it all without talking to any Real Eight member?

We have also negotiated with television and movie people over rights to recount our treasure finds. Jules Bergman, science editor for the American Broadcasting Company, filmed some footage on our operations in December, 1964, and aired it over his network sometime later. I even made an appearance on the popular TV show "To Tell The Truth," and got a heck of a kick out of it, though I wasn't able to hoodwink the panel.

We've had all sorts of requests from private concerns and free-lancers to film the Real Eight story. One company wanted to make a 30-minute documentary and proposed to split all profits 50-50. We weren't too interested. We've also had feelers from major studios in Hollywood and have exchanged preliminary correspondence with some of them. Probably someday our story will be immortalized in a motion picture. It certainly has everything—frustration, intrigue, excitement—everything except sex, that is, and I'm sure when the day comes, Hollywood will be able to gin up something on that angle.

We've also had all sorts of propositions to sell everything from a single coin to our entire holdings, and from lone shares of stock to 51 percent of Real Eight's interest. Our position has always been to listen attentively to any presentation and pursue it to the point where a bona fide offer is made. Then we fall back and examine it from all sides.

Most of the deals fall through before we ever get to this point. A lot of people are out to make the fast buck. Some of them must think we're real rubes. Well, we worked long and hard for our treasure, and we're not about to squander it on some swift and shady transaction. One Dallas promoter was interested in buying all our gold coins for an average of $600 per. He wanted the entire source, then he would market it at his leisure, doling out a few doubloons at a time. Dan, Mel and Frank Allen even flew out to Dallas to discuss the sale, but 15 minutes in the man's office convinced them he never had any intention of paying $600 a coin.

Another man, this one a professional coin dealer, came down and examined Real Eight's share of the 1964 season—more than 1,100 gold coins. After some lengthy rounds of verbal fencing, Dan told him we wouldn't take half a million dollars for the lot, and another deal collapsed on the launching pad. We think he had been prepared to offer $300,000.

Mel Fisher took a beautiful set of five dated doubloons to New York once, including one imperial, and showed them to a prominent dealer. When $3,000 was offered for the set, Mel agreed, on the condition that we could buy them back, since he hadn't checked with us. The man wrote a check on the spot, but when Frank Allen heard about it, he immediately demanded, and got, the coins back for the original price. They were worth a minimum of $10,000.

We've had major coin dealers from all over the country and the world appraise and offer to buy our gold, and when we get the right price we're ready to sell, but not before.

I guess one of our biggest "near-transactions" concerned a well-known Texas millionaire who is president of a large oil company, a real treasure bug. He was interested in gaining 51 percent of Real Eight's stock, and although we never got an official figure, the sum of $510,000—$1,000 a share—was bandied about. He even came down one day in the summer of 1965 and watched us unload a rich haul of silver from the *Derelict*. He seemed quite impressed. It was my understanding that if he had gained control of the company, he would have left the running of it to us, but would have exploited our findings in his own way. We never did get the concrete offer. It would have been interesting to see how we would have reacted to it.

I also had a lucrative offer from a South American concern. They wanted to buy my stock out for $475 a share, but I decided not to sell.

In the past several months we've had some rather bizarre and imaginative propositions presented to us by leading American businesses and industries. The Peter Pan Peanut Butter Company came up with the idea of running a nationwide, $50,000 "dive for gold" contest. They proposed to have the winners of the contest come down and dive off our boat to scoop up golden doubloons. It would have been a real corker, and the Madison Avenue advertising boys could have had a field day promoting it, but again, in the final analysis, it didn't—pardon the pun—pan out.

One offer that did, however, was from the Parker Pen Company. They put out a line called the Parker 75—a solid sterling silver pen, "personally tailored to write your own way." It sells for $25. One of their brighter young public relations people came up with the idea of a special allotment of these pens molded from our 1715 fleet silver. They made us a handsome offer for 4,000 ounces of silver, to be melted down from worn pieces of eight, and we accepted. They made up 4,000 pens from this with special inscriptions saying they came from Spanish galleons, and put them on the market for $75 each. I understand they made a big hit with executives and with men who have everything else. We certainly realized considerably more out of melting down these silver pieces than I did years ago when I gave away so many trinkets I had fashioned from melted cobs.

I might add that the consummation of the Parker Pen deal couldn't have come at a more opportune time. With the hiring of Bob Johnson and the divers to put us on a full-time salvaging basis during the 1965 season, our operating expenses spiraled. They averaged, for salaries and boat expenses and repairs, from $500 to $800 per week and hit a peak $8,000 one month. We needed some ready money badly to keep things going, and the Parker deal proved to be a real windfall.

We also sifted through scores of other proposals, and are continuing to do so. We are, in fact, swamped with offers each time another major find of ours is announced. You may see us promoted in almost any manner sometime in the future—if, of course, the proposition is legitimate and the price is right.

Being an adventurer at heart, the most interesting requests we get, to my mind, are from other treasure hunters or expedition financiers from practically everywhere around the world. They all have some sort of treasure to exploit—either they've found a sunken wreck, or they've discovered a lost mine. Mostly, they want our knowledge and skills. They want us to direct the recovery operations. Why argue with success? they reason. If we found a fortune off Florida, why couldn't we help them?

And I must admit some of these offers are really attractive. Even if we never found a coin on some of the sites I've read of, it would be a real thrill just to search. Take the "Emerald Lake" in Colombia, for example. Bob Johnson, Rex and I got tied up on this one. A party had discovered what it believed to be an ancient Indian sacrificial lake 10,000 feet up in the Andes Mountains in western Colombia. According to legends, several times a year the Indians, to appease their gods, sacrificed young men and maidens by tossing them into the cold, bottomless lake waters. Those sacrificed were bedecked with gold breastplates, gold earrings, necklaces and headdresses, and other ornamental pieces of jewelry. Then the Indians would circle the lake and heave in perfect, fist-sized emeralds.

The region surrounding this lake is known to be in the heart of emerald country, and Bob and I were shown one the size of a goose egg. To get to the lake—and we were invited down to look things over, all expenses paid—one has to climb high in the Andes and then penetrate miles of dense jungle. Surrounding the lake is a 300-foot-high ridge of granite-like rock. We know there is more than mere legend to go on, for in 1914 a British expedition cut through this rock and found a number of artifacts indicating that this was, in fact, the sacrificial lake. Bob braved the 45-degree waters and found that the lake was not bottomless after all. He hit mud at a depth of 74 feet. To find gold and the fabulous emeralds, we must set up an airlift operation. If we find any concrete evidence to prove our well-researched theory that this is the emerald lake, I may have to start commuting between Sebastian and Colombia. As I say, it's an intriguing affair even if we don't score big.

Other reports of finds—from the Florida Keys to the island of Ceylon —have come to us, and in most cases we are offered our own terms—expenses, straight salary or a percentage of the take, if there is any. Real Eight's operation off the Florida coast remains, of course, our principal interest, but in the winter months when we can't dive there, we may well go into some of these other sites—but it will be on an individual basis and not as a corporate effort.

To coincide with the January, 1965, release of our story, the *National Geographic* planned a full-scale exhibit at Explorers' Hall in their magnificent new quarters in Washington. It was to feature all our key treasure finds to date, including Rex's necklace, the gold and silver coins, gold discs, silver wedges, K'ang Hsi china and other artifacts.

The exhibit opened to an enthusiastic first-day crowd in mid-December, 1964, and for the next two months it broke one attendance record after another. With armed guards keeping an eye on our pride and joy, tens of thousands of Washingtonians filed through the exhibit. Sometimes, I was told, the lines of people waiting outside to get in stretched for two blocks and longer.

There is a magic about recovered treasure that fascinates people. It must be that they relate themselves to it—that they believe, if they went out on Sunday afternoons and strolled the beaches and paddled out in the water, they could have found it themselves. Whatever this phenomenon is, you could see it in the intense faces of the people as they peered at our finds. Some, in fact, came back again and again during the exhibit.

The exhibit next moved, intact, to the Florida State Museum in Gainesville, and again it shattered crowd records.

I think Harry first came up with the idea. It was in the fall of 1964, as our coins and wedges and china and jewelry were getting ready for the formal showing at Explorers' Hall in Washington.

"We ought to have our own permanent exhibit," he said one night at a board meeting. "No, it ought to be even more than that. What we need is a museum. We could charge admission, sell coins and at the same time dispense some 'live' history to those who came to see it."

For once, one of us had come up with an idea that found no challengers. We were unanimous in our agreement, and began mapping out plans almost immediately. The exhibit would remain in Washington until the end of February, and then the Florida State Museum had it until April 28. We thus shot for an opening date of May 1. This gave us a few months, yet there was so much to be done. A suitable place had to be found to house the collection; display cases and partitions had to be built, exhibit boards drawn up, slide presentations put together, tape recordings made, and a publicity campaign organized.

Harry is a director at the First National Bank of Satellite Beach, about 35 miles north of Sebastian on highway A1A, and he obtained a lease for us on some rooms attached to the bank. It seemed perfect for our purpose. The architecture is colonial and in fine taste, and by setting up shop next door to the bank, we felt we would obtain an added measure of protection.

Now we needed a curator, and the boys had a good one in mind—a friend of theirs who had been in service with them at Patrick Air Force Base and Cape Kennedy. Joe Salvo retired from the Air Force with the rank of lieutenant colonel after a distinguished career spanning more than two decades. He had worked closely with America's astronauts as chief of Bioastronautic Operational Support. It was during this tour of duty that he met Dan and Harry. We got a real bonus in Joe, for he is a conscientious curator who takes his work seriously.

There was one hell of a lot of last-minute scurrying to get things in shape. With the Florida State exhibit closing on the 28th, we had only about a day and a half to get everything in order for a preview VIP opening of the museum April 30. Somehow we made it, and it was a proud night for us when the mayors, city councilmen, and a host of other dignitaries from miles around passed through the doors to view the objects we had worked so hard to bring up from the ocean floor. One look at their faces seemed to make all our labors and frustrations worthwhile. They were simply overwhelmed by our display.

Joe arranged a county-wide press conference for our formal opening the next morning, and after being splashed across the papers, we drew record crowds—as many as 400 a day, which made things pretty crowded at times. In the first half year we were open, more than 25,000 people from every state in the nation and many foreign countries, including Scotland, Spain, Brazil, Japan and the Philippines, visited the museum. Some came back several times. One of the most memorable visits was that of a lady from Scotland. She was totally blind, yet when we allowed her to feel a heavy gold disc, valued at more than $20,000, her face lit up the entire gallery. It was, Joe told us, a very moving experience.

In all modesty and honesty, I must admit there is nothing quite like our museum anywhere else. Perhaps the number-one attraction is that $50,000 gold dragon chain that my nephew Rex found on the beach at Sebastian. It makes an exquisite showpiece, set off by a background of red velvet. The treasure chest we brought up in 1965 is another crowd pleaser. We have it submerged in water, just as we found it.

In one display case we have a large cluster of several hundred pieces of eight fused together; a mint-condition imperial doubloon valued at $10,000; and a solid-gold ingot that weighs seven pounds. In another case is the K'ang Hsi china. Other items we have scattered about include knife blades; hinges; brass nails; lead sounding weights; pieces of silver; jar rings; tin plates; finely designed, paper-thin gold earrings; gold crucifixes; that flask still filled with the liquid it contained more than 250 years ago; an apothecary jar and mixer; bar shot; musket balls; cannonballs; a ship's anchor; a copper pot handle; wooden ship's sheaves; a gold hairpin seven inches long with an ornate top; part of an incense burner, base metal plated; assorted buckles; navigators' dividers; pottery from Guadalajara, Mexico; a salt shaker; the half and one reals in a clump that had been carried in a pouch, which I found in 1958; the silver moth stopper Del Long found; copper coins; silver pieces of eight; golden doubloons; a silver cup and a silver figurine, winged and cloven-footed, probably a pot lid finial; a nest of scale weights; an ax, with wooden handle intact; a sea-horse latch for scale weights; a 20-pound sounding lead dated 1712; huge earthenware containers; silver forks; pewter and silver plates; gold wedding bands; silver wedges and ingots; an ivory knife handle; and a silver piece of eight with a piece of burlap sack still attached to it. This list, impressive as it is, is by no means conclusive. There are dozens of other items, and we add more to the collection each time we bring something up from the ocean.

Total value? It would be near impossible to assess, but by conservative estimate, the figure would easily top half a million dollars for the museum collection alone. The bulk of our recoveries, however, is locked safely in bank vaults.

With such a treasure we have of necessity become extremely security-minded. Lest anyone forget, it was just a couple of hundred miles south of our museum, in Miami, that jewel thieves plotted the Star of India and DeLong Ruby robbery. And, with our coins and jewelry, there would be no such disposal problems with fences, as Murph the Surf and his crew ran into. Gold and silver have international value, and thieves would merely have to get it out of the country—as near as the Bahamas—to cash in on the worldwide market.

Thus, we have made elaborate preparations to discourage any such notions. We have armed guards stationed in the gallery at all times, and a number of other security safeguards that must remain secret. I can say only this: we're not burglar proof, yet neither are the crown jewels of England. But we feel our treasure would be just about as hard to steal, and that we have a more-than-adequate security system. It is something we cannot take for granted, and we don't.

Visitors to the Real Eight Gallery invariably ask questions—dozens of questions. We've prepared tapes to help answer them, and Joe is familiar with all phases of our history and operations. The most frequently asked questions are: "What is the most expensive piece on display?" (The gold chain—appraised at $50,000); "Where are the sunken ships?" (About 35 miles due south of the museum); and, "If we went there and found anything on the beach could we keep it?" (Yes).

Schoolchildren are not so easily satisfied. They can really throw some hookers at us, and demand detailed explanations of the equipment we use, our metal restoration processes and a number of other complicated points. When poor Joe does get stumped, which doesn't happen often, he tells them the information is classified. Sounds like some politicians I know.

We are particularly proud of the reception we have been given by schools in the state. We invite the students free, for we feel our museum adds a special sense of life to their studies. This is especially true of the fifth- and sixth-graders who are studying Florida history and the Spanish influence. It is one thing to read about history in a textbook, but it's something else again actually to see a part of it.

At the gallery we sell a few coins, mostly silver pieces of eight, but now and then a golden doubloon, too, and some other items.

It is ironic that this collection, linking us more closely to the past, is housed in an area where modern-day history is also being made. In fact, Joe points out in his lectures that the newest, most powerful rockets and spaceships, launched from Cape Kennedy, program out over the Atlantic close to where the 1715 armada went down.

As this book went to press, we were wrapped up in plans to build an enlarged, permanent museum of Spanish treasure, to be located probably somewhere near Cape Kennedy. We honestly feel that what we have is of such genuine historical significance that it should be shared openly with the public.

15 Millions To Go

Despite all we have found off Sebastian in the years we have been diving, we have barely scratched the surface. We have brought up abundant amounts of gold and silver and found priceless jewels and artifacts. We have undoubtedly uncovered more treasure than any salvage team in history. Yet, in a very real sense, we are only beginning.

What more is out there? We may unlock some of the answers soon, for in September, 1965, I fulfilled another of my longtime dreams by traveling to Spain with Alice. I went under a grant from the *National Geographic* to continue our research into the history of the 1715 Plate Fleet.

In Seville, at the Archives of the Indies, I was literally overwhelmed by the mountainous stacks of records, documents and volumes. I could have spent months there. My only disappointment was in not seeing Dr. Peña, the curator. I had corresponded with him for seven years and looked forward to meeting him in person, but he had fallen ill and an interview was impossible. His secretary, however, was most cordial. She brought out my file of correspondence, and I was amazed at the size of it. It must have been a couple of inches thick.

After spending hour after hour in the musty confines of the archives, I realized I would never be able to ferret out all the information I sought without professional help. So I hired two researchers and outlined to them the general areas of data I was seeking. I'm convinced, from the cursory examination I made while there, that we will eventually come up with more detailed manifests listing precisely what was on each ship in the 1715 fleet, what went down in the hurricane and what was recovered by Hoyo Solórzano and others.

I also spent several days in Barcelona, and these were without question the most pleasant of my trip. Señor Xavier Calico, the man who had bought so many of our coins at the 1964 auction, and a prominent numismatist in his country, was our host. He showed us this fine old city in all its splendor. Alice and I did things, saw sights and ate meals I'd never imagined.

Of course, I had some work to do in Barcelona, too. The Spanish Maritime Museum is located there, and it has one of the finest libraries on Spanish history on the seas in the world. After more digging, I marked the areas I wanted investigated in detail and hired another researcher.

In Paris I put on two more people—I was beginning to feel as if I were personally bolstering the economy of the Continent. I wanted them to delve into the French archives. We're particularly curious as to what happened to Don Antonio Daré, who captained *El Grifón*, the sole surviving ship of the 1715 disaster. We want to learn for sure exactly what treasure Daré carried home.

Our last stop was in London, where I sought specific facts on ships and ship construction for the period around the beginning of the eighteenth century. Two additional researchers were hired here to aid in the quest for information. I also visited the Victoria and Albert Museum in Kensington, which houses one of the finest collections of K'ang Hsi china in the world. I was surprised to find it had no pieces quite like the cups and bowls we found in 1963 at our cabin wreck.

Just how much benefit all this researching will mean to us in terms of material value, I'm not sure. But historically, I know we'll be able to fit in a lot of the loose puzzle pieces when all the data is extracted, assembled and translated. One thing for sure, if the big-time quiz programs, like the "$64,000 Question," are ever revived, I'd feel confident of going all the way up the plateaus if there was a category on the 1715 Spanish Plate Fleet.

Specifically, treasure-wise, we know King Philip's jewels are still out there somewhere, and there's quite a story in that. Doc Kelso dug it up on one of his literary excavations. Seems Philip's wife died in late 1714, and he soon after became interested in the seductive Elizabetta Farnese, the Duchess of Parma. He wanted to marry her and he was getting anxious.

The duchess, as Doc tells it, played it a little more coolly. She agreed to go through the official wedding ceremony with Philip, but refused to share the bedroom with him until he enwrapped her with a rich assortment of jewelry. Philip apparently agreed to the terms and ordered craftsmen as far away as China and Manila to assemble jewelry from gold, silver and precious stones, the likes of which no queen had ever seen before. When the Plate Fleet sailed from Havana in July, 1715, carefully stashed in locked chests aboard General Ubilla's flagship were these rare gems—the keys to a rejuvenated sex life for the King of Spain.

Thus, when the fleet sank off the Florida coast a few days later, and Philip heard about it, he was furious—not so much at the loss of millions in gold and silver that ruined so many of his country's merchants, but because the jewels for Elizabetta Farnese were wasting away on the bottom of the Atlantic Ocean while he continued to lust for his new wife.

He dispatched orders to find the crown jewels at all costs, but poor Hoyo Solórzano had no luck recovering them. There is, in fact, no record that any of them were ever found. The *capitana*, according to a parade of witnesses, was thoroughly searched and nothing was uncovered. According to Spanish accounts, the gems were not found in boxes or chests of clothes. How this affected Philip's frustrated sex life, and whether the duchess ever did grant him boudoir privileges, I don't know.

We did learn that Hoyo Solórzano was called on the carpet in Spain on two separate occasions to explain why he couldn't find the jewels. Spanish officials strongly suspected that he had, in fact, recovered at least a portion of them and kept them for himself, an allegation he vehemently denied. We are, naturally, hopeful that he was an honest man and thus told the truth. In either case, whether or not he pocketed anything, we are sure there is still a fortune in gems hiding under the sands a short distance from shore.

We know, from our researches, of a few specific jewels in the collection. One, for instance, is a magnificent, pinecone-shaped piece bedecked with a perfect set of 128 matched pearls, brought up by native divers who risked, and often lost, their lives to the giant octopi in deep Pacific waters. Eyewitness accounts at inquiries following the fleet's sinking listed a few other individual pieces of jewelry that were to have been worn by Elizabetta Farnese. Among them were:

—A three-ounce pair of beaded cords of gold with 38 pearls on each one.

—A rosary of coral that looks like chick peas with "Our Father" engraved in gold.

—Three small medallions and a little rose that decorates a cross.

—Two pearls in the form of an almond, one of which has a black spot exactly on top and the other perfectly clear and "very beautiful." Between the two, they weigh 28 carats, and other grains of pearls are applied all around the side with one white spotted pearl that weighs eight carats.

—Three gold rings, one with an emerald.

—A gold piece with the image of Santa Clara, and adorned with 21 pearls.

It will take a master stroke of luck for us ever to know beyond a doubt what ships in the fleet went down where. We have eight of the 10 wreck sites fixed, and hold leases on eight of them, but unless we're fortunate enough to come up with the actual name of a vessel somewhere, we'll never have proof positive.

We do have opinions, some supported strongly by documented research. We draw our conclusions from three primary sources of information: the Spanish archives in Seville; the eyewitness accounts of survivors; and recently acquired data from Havana archives.

Here I must acknowledge the tremendous amount of help lent us by Carl J. ("Tony") Clausen, the state's able young archeologist, who has worked closely with us the past couple of years. Tony ploughed through reams of Cuban red tape and finally obtained important documents from Havana files pertaining to the 1715 fleet that led us to revise much of the earlier information we had previously gathered. With the aid of a friendly Cuban professor who has followed our treasure story with great interest, Clausen has acquired papers, ship manifests and significant salvage reports.

Tony and Lou Ullian have also worked feverishly over additional material sent to us by Dr. Peña from Seville, and they have exhaustingly pursued a more thorough translation of the eyewitness accounts. Much of their work involves a painstakingly detailed cross checking of the new data against old sources and references, and believe me, sometimes things have gotten pretty confusing.

For instance, for a long time we felt the wedge wreck off the Fort Pierce Inlet, which we salvaged so extensively in 1960 during the trial run period, was Ubilla's *urca*, the *Nuestra Señora de la Regla*. We based this assumption on salvage reports that this ship did not smash to pieces on the reefs, but was fairly well preserved. Eye witnesses said a long boat and supplies for survivors were salvaged from the ship.

Yet we now have reason to doubt the identity of this wreck. *Urca* is

Spanish for hooker (sloop grade or two-masted vessel), and there is a notation on Bernard Romans' early map that lists a Dutch hooker as having sunk off Fort Pierce. Thus we now wonder whether this wreck could actually have been the Dutch nao that sailed with the fleet rather than being the *Nuestra Señora de la Regla*.

Conversely, if this is true the gold wreck south of Fort Pierce, which we had at first believed to be the Dutch one, must be another ship altogether. What it is, however, we don't know for sure. Lou and Tony believe it's possibly the *Nuestra Señora del Rosario y San Francisco Xavier*, De Echeverz' *almiranta*. They reason that the amount of gold recovered here, plus the number of cannon at the site, indicate that it was one of the fleet's more important vessels.

The more we learn of this master puzzle, it seems, the less we know!

Our opinions on what the cabin wreck may be have also changed recently, and we're now in nearly unanimous agreement. For years we felt this was Ubilla's *almiranta*, but the latest research information now strongly suggests that it is his *capitana* instead, the flagship of the fleet.

Our early beliefs were based on the large cannon, the china, and the jewelry found on the site, including fine gold chains, intricately made earrings with delicate, filigree gold, and other gems. These items, we felt, were destined to adorn Elizabetta Farnese's throat and ears. Research pointed out that Ubilla's *almiranta* sank within a stone's throw of shore, so since the shallow cabin wreck, which we worked for several years, was pretty close in, we thought we knew what ship was down below. We had, however, noted, curiously, that there were no ballast stones or heavy timbers in with the 20 large guns.

What really set off our thoughts that this wreck might possibly be the *capitana* occurred after we had located the deeper part of the site in 1965 and found some brass breechblocks. The only ships to carry these were men-of-war, *capitanas* and *almirantas*.

But Clausen's probings into the Spanish eyewitness accounts brought out additional data concerning the sinking of Ubilla's *capitana*. The reports told how the flagship hit a huge reef in five fathoms of water, ripping its bottom out and spilling cargo and ballast on the ocean floor. The lightened ship was then carried over the reef, shoreward, where it smashed into a second barrier of rocks. The upper works and deck broke loose from the hull in the battering and washed in closer to land.

Also, early salvage reports state that work on the *capitana* was carried on at two different depths—two and a half and five fathoms. These are the exact depths of our shallow and deep cabin sites! We are thus relatively certain this is Ubilla's *capitana*.

I've discussed earlier our feeling that the Sandy Point wreck near Vero Beach is quite possibly De Echeverz' *capitana, Nuestra Señora del Carmen y San Antonio.*

We may never know for sure if our convictions are correct. Our main hope along this line is the fact that Spanish merchants marked certain items of their cargo with brands. We know this from the manifest lists, and we know what merchants' goods were on what ships. So if we are ever able to recover an item with one of these brands on it, we may well verify the name of the ship. But, luck will have to be riding with us all the way. We've brought up a vast amount of goods to date without finding any names or markings. Still, we have not given up hope.

What are our specific salvage plans for the future? Not even we are sure at this point. However, to cover our lucrative, deep-water cabin site scientifically, we figure a minimum of three or four more prime diving seasons are needed. We still have about a million square feet of unexplored ocean floor to search. Our records indicate there is more gold on this wreck than at Fort Pierce, and we haven't scratched the first chestful yet. The silver hot spots we mined during the summer of 1965 are still productive, so it is likely this will be the area we will concentrate our efforts on for some time to come.

Manifest lists have shown there were 2,290 *cajones* (chests, most likely filled with silver) on Ubilla's *capitana* and *almiranta*. Of the 1,300 on the *capitana*, which we believe to be our cabin wreck, 940 were recovered by the Spanish. Of the *almiranta*'s 990 chests only 136 were officially salvaged. These listings, plus the fact this was just the *registered* number of chests (there were probably hundreds more of bootleg variety) make us all the more anxious to continue the hunt.

We know that no salvage team, no matter how successful, can ever expect to bring up 100 percent of the treasure that went down on a specific ship. It is scattered over too broad an area and buried too deep. If we can manage to recover between 50 and 75 percent at any one site we will consider ourselves extremely fortunate.

One day in the near future, we hope to get back to the part of the cabin wreck in the shallow waters between the reefs where we found our first coin clumps. We know that lying down there under a few feet of sand awaiting recovery is a rich storehouse of K'ang Hsi china. And we know it is probably in perfect, undamaged condition, carefully preserved in its original packing.

When the waters are too rough and clouded to dive off Sebastian, we'll move 30 miles south to the gold wreck off Fort Pierce and seek out another chestful of doubloons. There is much left unrecovered here also. The site a little farther north, where we found our first piece of treasure, a silver wedge, back in 1960, and the wreck at Sandy Point, have both been pretty well worked over.

Our pine wreck, a little north of the cabin site, is difficult to pinpoint. I first found a pile of ballast rock there years ago while fishing for grouper with Libe Futch. It is in relatively deep waters, and for the present will have to remain one of our long-range goals—as will one other wreck site south of the cabin. Both of these are totally unexplored, and we feel we cannot justify spending any appreciable amounts of time on these points while other areas are still yielding a steady supply of treasure.

When we do run dry at our present locations, the next most attractive site is one that we call our green cabin wreck, off Wabasso Beach. We have made exploratory dives here, and things appear very promising. There are some fine-looking cannon on the bottom. But it will require a lot of concentrated time and effort before we hit pay dirt again.

So, considering the brevity of our good diving weather each season, and the tremendous amount of searching still ahead of us, I think it would be a safe bet to say we'll be diving on these 1715 wreck sites as far into the future as we can see—and right now that runs until 1975, when our leases expire. Some of us, I'm sure, will be treasure hunting for the rest of our lives.

How much do we stand to gain on what has already been recovered from this Spanish Plate Fleet? This is a question we hear every day, and our answer is always the same. We honestly don't know. Only a small fraction of our coins have been sold, so we really have nothing to go on as far as evaluating the entire collection is concerned. If we used as a yardstick the $400,000 for which, after our gold finds in 1964, and the subsequent division with the state, Florida insured its fourth of the treasure, our portion up to then would have been worth in the neighborhood of $1.2 million. And we've found far more since 1964. It is quite possible we now have $2 to $3 million or more in gold, silver, jewelry and artifacts. But who can say for sure?

How much more can be expected? That's another unanswerable question. For one thing, no one knows for sure how much treasure went down out there. Jacobo de Pezuela, in 1868, published a set of books on the history of the island of Cuba. In the second volume he referred to the plate fleets, and specifically to the 1715 fleet. He verified the fact that 10 ships went down carrying $14 million in registered cargo. But what hit us between the eyes was his statement that the total worth of the treasure— registered and unregistered—was $65 million!

We hope, of course, he's right, but we are pretty certain he far exaggerated the figure. It is likely that several million more than was included on the official manifests did, in fact, go down with the fleet. It is even possible that this bootleg gold, silver and jewelry exceeded in total value that which was registered. But $65 million is a little way out. So just how much actually did spill on the bottom of the Atlantic we shall never know for sure, other than that the total was probably far greater than the listed $14 million. We could thus eventually recover further large amounts in sunken treasure before we're through. Keep in mind, however, that the state gets one-fourth of everything; that there are 10 Real Eight members and several more crew men in Treasure Salvors. So what we find will be well divided—*after* the Federal income tax bite has been taken.

I'm sincere when I say, however, that we are more concerned about the historical significance of our finds than how many dollars they will bring on the open market. None of us in Real Eight is anywhere close to being in dire financial straits, though none of us is rich either. But as a group we are hopeful our work over the years will help others to understand better the events and significance of the Spanish Colonial period around the turn of the eighteenth century.

We feel that through our discoveries more will be learned of the plate fleets, the ships, ship construction, their cargoes. New light will be thrown on the New World mints, and on the quality and quantity of coins turned out by them. Such data, if correctly parlayed, could have a far-reaching bearing on our knowledge of the cultures, communications and economics of that long-ago era.

We would like, if we can possibly find some way to do it, to keep our treasure intact. If we had to sell it we would want to do it to one concern, with the idea it in turn would donate it to a museum like the Smithsonian and then write it off as one monumental tax deduction. But such a public-spirited collector is about as rare as a pure gold bar on the bottom of the ocean. We've yet to find either one. Perhaps, if no organization can afford to buy it, we can maintain it in our own museum. We don't know now whether we can do this or not, but to a man we would regret seeing everything split into separate parcels, no matter how enticing the sales price.

I know I personally get a greater thrill out of watching a school kid's eyes light up as he fingers one of our cannon or anchors, than I do from selling a shiny golden doubloon. Through our treasure, history becomes a tangible, living thing—and this is one of the original goals Doc Kelso and I set out to accomplish so many years ago.

Has it all been worth it, and would we do it again? These are questions we *can* answer—with a unanimous, resounding YES! True, there have been periods of frustration, of depression and despair. There have been times when we were ready to throw in the towel altogether and write off our search as a fool's folly. I have said I'd never do it again, but I know damn well I would.

In sticking together as a team, we have accomplished something no one else in modern times has done. We have scientifically, systematically and with premeditation discovered and brought up from the ocean a fortune in sunken treasure—perhaps the greatest such fortune in history. Ours was the long shot that paid off. Thousands of people chase the pot of gold at the end of the rainbow—some as a hobby, others as a profession. Few ever find anything. We have found everything.

I cannot give enough credit to my close friends and partners in Real Eight, for without everyone's individual contributions, bonded together through an intense mission of purpose, our goals could never have been realized. To Doc Kelso, Lou Ullian, Del Long, Dan Thompson, Harry Cannon, Bob Johnson, John Jones and Rex Stocker—the active team members—and to Mel Fisher and his hard-working crew, Rupert Gates, Dick Williams, Walt Holzworth, Fay Field and Moe Molinar, I can only say that what successes we have reaped have been well earned. It has been a true team effort all the way.

I remember years ago standing on a desolate stretch of wind-whipped beach front near the Sebastian Inlet and looking longingly at the pounding surf. I knew treasure was out there then, and I dreamed of the day I would find it.

All my dreams have been fulfilled.

APPENDIX *Major Finds of*
Treasure and Artifacts
Made at the Wreck Sites

1. The silver wedge wreck off the Fort Pierce Inlet is believed to be either the treasure fleet's (General Ubilla's) store ship, the *Nuestra Señora de la Regla*, or the Dutch nao that sailed with the fleet. (Some historical accounts refer to the store ship as the *Urca de Lima*, but this was probably only a nickname. She was well salvaged by the Spanish after the hurricane, many of the survivors' supplies coming from her.)

   Salvaged items include the following:

   15 silver wedges, averaging slightly under 4 pounds each.

   3 clay animals, probably made for children of Spanish nobility.

   Numerous cannonballs.

   Countless shards of K'ang Hsi china and Mexican pottery.

2. The Sandy Point wreck, just south of Vero Beach, was quite possibly De Echeverz' *capitana* or flagship—the *Nuestra Señora del Carmen y San Antonio*. Documents from the Spanish archives in Seville and survivors' eyewitness accounts of the 1715 disaster state that the *Carmen* was wrecked on a point of land. The only such landmark in the entire wreck area is Sandy Point, which shows as a small cape on early charts. The size and number of cannon at this site indicate a smaller ship than one of Ubilla's ships of the line, but larger than a merchant nao.

   Salvaged items include the following:

211

2,000 silver pieces of eight, badly worn by sand washing.

3 gold coins, 2-escudo denomination, Bogotá mint.

Part of a silver plate. A clay pipe.

A ship's bell, brass, in good condition. It was at first hoped this would have the ship's name on it making wreck identification positive, but it carried no name.

Miscellaneous shards of Mexican pottery and dozens of cannonballs.

3. The cabin wreck, south of the Sebastian Inlet, is believed to be Ubilla's *capitana*, the general's flagship, a 40- to 50-gun frigate. Wreckage layout and size and number of guns all correlate with descriptions of the *capitana* and with eyewitness accounts. Also, Bernard Roman's original chart shows the "Admiral's" ship went down here. The English did not understand the Spanish use of generals to command a fleet and often mistakenly called them admirals.

Salvaged items include the following:

Hundreds of pounds of loose silver pieces of eight, most in excellent condition, from the Mexico City, Lima and Potosí mints.

20 clumps of silver pieces of eight, one weighing 77 pounds, and many others weighing more than 50 pounds and containing hundreds of coins. The pieces in the center of the clumps, when exposed, are mint-fresh in appearance, showing no signs of corrosion from the sea such as mark the outside coins.

Wooden, lead-lined chest, approximately 3 feet long, 2 feet wide, 1 foot deep, containing approximately 3,000 (estimated) pieces of eight fused together by action of sea. Top and one end of chest missing.

36 gold coins of 8-, 4-, 2- and 1-escudo denominations, minted in Mexico City in 1714. One coin is dated 1702.

Golden dragon and chain (found on beach opposite wreck site). The chain contains 2,176 individual handmade links, each shaped like a flower rosette. The dragon pendant has a gold toothpick in its back and an ear-cleaning spoon for its tail. The mouth forms a whistle. This spectacular piece of jewelry, the single most valuable find made by Real Eight, has been appraised at $50,000.

Gold chain and parts of several others, without pendants.

2 gold rings: one with a 2½-carat diamond and 6 chips; the other with beautifully carved flowers and a separate gold rope to hold it together.

Gold-plated sea horse probably used as a latch on a box.

Gold cross.

Portion of a gold-plated jewel box. The base metal is lead or another low-value metal, and it is possible the Spanish were going to pass this off as a solid-gold box.

Gold pendant and chain. The single plain gold chain is about 9 feet long. The pendant has a small eroded oil painting of a woman on one side and what appears to be Christ on the other side. Both are covered with ovals of glass.

Silver cross. A beautiful religious artifact with the carved figure of Christ on the cross held by tiny silver nails through His hands and feet.

2 sets of nested weights used for precious metals. One set fits into a covered container with a sea horse latch, the other set is cemented together.

Silver brooch, hinged, with oil pictures. One is of a woman in royal robes wearing a crown.

5 complete silver plates and parts of others.

40 to 50 pewter plates.

15 to 20 silver forks. All have the King's purity mark, the eagle, and the New World silversmith wrought his forks with the name "Gorlez."

1 complete silver spoon.

Silver statue of the Greek god Pan, blowing his horn. The base of this piece, like the candlesticks, has screwheads cut into it for attachment to an urn lid or similar device.

Silver moth on bottle lid.

Parts of silver containers and handles of silver knives.

Silver cup and 6 silver candlestick holders.

28 pieces of K'ang Hsi china, intact. There are three distinct styles: blue on white designs; pure white, with only a faint tracing visible where a decorative border once circled the rim; and bowls covered with black enamel with traces of gold decoration. The decorative trim was probably a gilded border of flowers, foliages, fish and shrimp.

10 pieces of Mexican pottery, intact.

3 sets of bronze apothecary bowls and pestles.

4 muskets.

1 pewter inkwell with a religious carving on it.

Hundreds of musket and pistol balls of varying sizes, including some split ones (to inflict more damage).

42 large discs, about 18 inches in diameter, and weighing from 44 to 105 pounds each. These are made partly of silver, but also contain, it is believed, percentages of gold, platinum and copper.

20 silver wedges weighing about 6 pounds each.

3 cannon; ship's fittings, including all of the iron straps used to secure the rudder to the stern of the ship.

Numerous cannonballs in three sizes, 4-, 8- and 12-pounders. Some have the Roman numeral VIII stamped on them.

Onion-shaped bottles with original fluid still inside. It is probably wine or perfume.

Cannon breechblock, brass, 8 inches long, with handle and locking screw.

At a point some distance from the cabin site a ship's anchor was found and recovered. It is 11 feet long and weighs nearly one ton.

4. Based on the number of gold coins recovered at the gold wreck, south of Fort Pierce, it is thought that this ship was one of the more important ones in the fleet. It was not, however, one of Ubilla's warships, because the cannon are too small. It may well be De Echeverz' *almiranta*.

Salvaged items include the following:

2,500 silver pieces of eight in fairly good condition.

Large numbers (a few thousand) of gold coins of 8-, 4-, 2-, and 1-escudo denominations from mints at Mexico City, Lima, Bogotá and Cuzco. Included in these are a few, very rare coins called "imperials" or "royals," specially struck and in perfect condition. One such coin sold at an auction for $3,600 and was reportedly later resold for over $10,000.

4 gold chains and 16 gold rings.

3 large gold discs with an average weight of 7½ pounds. Each one has a lot mark on it in Roman numerals: XIV, IX and XII. And each has assayer's marks.

1 small marked gold disc and parts of two others. This small disc has mint marks and other Spanish markings on it and sold for $17,000.

2 small silver discs, average weight 27 pounds. One dated 1695.

6 small silver discs and many indescribable silver pieces.

1 silver bar, weighing 36 pounds.

3 plugs of silver.

2 silver plates and parts of pewter plates.

3 silver candlestick holders and 6 broken silver forks.

4 pair of brass dividers.

Dozens of cannonballs and pistol and musket balls.

1 lead sounding weight (20 pounds) dated 1712, and 2 undated lead sounding weights.

INDEX

Note, E. Stands for English. F for French D. for Dutch and Da. for Danes

P. OF NOR TH NEW FRANCE

AMERICA.

LOUISIANA

Mississipi R.

Ouabach R.
Sault R.
Waterus R.
Anne

Mount Lat. 36.
Fort Prud. home French
Cusanes I. French I.
Cus. R.
Charalleys
Georg.

Chickesans
Casaws
Chatta hues
Westras

Ca do aquios
Cenis Fort
R. de Cenis
Natchitoches
ochfaskes
O. F. Louis
F. Mob le
Pensacola a Span. Fort
Apalata

Colorado R.
R. le Cenis

NEW
Presidi del Norta Fort
F. Louis De mol.
Bay St Louis
I. de Aste sion
St. Ios. B. A Spanish Fort
Missisipi R.
Balay Bay

FLORIDA
C. Florida
S. Fallas
Tortugas S.

MEXICO
Bocca de Leon
R. de las Nassas
Panuco
GULF of **MEXICO**

y Flota from Vera Cruz to y Havana occasionally by y Trade winds

Panuco R.
C. Roxo
Panuco
Tamonte
MeXICO
Mexico

MEXICO
Xigu Sacan
Catalula
Acapulco
la Vera Cruz
V. Rica

Yucan Dulus Cpt.
P. de bit Sordo
The Tract of y only Passage
Negrillos
Bermeja
Areas
C. Condusedo
Tryangles
S. Martins Pt.
Bay of Camp.
Alerana
Sisal
Merida
Campechy
Yucatan
L. de Bacalal
Cozumel
Campeche
Havana
Havana
B. Honda
C. Antonio
I. Or. I. Pinos

NEW SPAIN
Guatimala
Soconusco
Trinidad
S. Sant
Tabasco
Chiapas
Port Royal
Lagu. Stal
S. Iago
C. of Gua. ios
C. of Gua.
Truxillo
Honduras
Comajagua
G. of Honduras
I. Guayana
Camaron
S. Millan
Serranilha
St. Georges
Hondo B.
Vare R.

The GREAT
SOUTH SEA
Realejo
Amapal
Leon
Nicara g ua
Nicaragua Lake
Costarica
S. Lucar
C. Blanco
Catalina
S. An
Nicaragua I.
Conce pcion
Veragua
Publear
Chagre
Panama
Burica P.
Kygusta I.
P. Mala
Bay
Grahos I.
Pearl
Mosquitos

Note These Rivers almost meet, both of them are Navigable, and all the Cannon and Stores for Acapulco are Carryed from the North to the South Sea by them.

20 40 60 80 100   200
English Leagues 20 to one Degree